I0616274

BESSIE AND COMPANY

SEA MONSTER ADVENTURES

NADINE NADER

with
PATRICK TALMADGE

HANGAR 1 PUBLISHING

To my beloved grandchildren, Joseph, Guiliana, and Esme.

CONTENTS

CHARACTER LIST

Bessie, a child of Nessie the Loch Ness Monster, lives in Lake Erie. She was befriended by Sash, a sasquatch who keeps her safe. Bessie lives in a series of caves, one of which is attached to Sash's. She and Sash have a close relationship. Bessie was once a dragon—until her wings were cut. She and her siblings had to become sea creatures to survive.

Esme is a TV reporter for a local station and a friend of Janet Smith. While trying to report on the strange happenings at Lake Erie, Esme becomes fast friends of Bessie and Sash.

Commander Guiliana Burke is a Navy operative who conducts secret missions studying the antics of cryptids. She befriends Janet and Sadie and is instrumental in helping them when the cryptids are seen by humans.

Janet Smith, mother of Sadie and widow of Joseph, is a reporter for a local paper. She has worked from home since her husband's passing. This allows her to take care of Sadie. She is concerned about Sadie's vivid imagination when it comes to Bessie.

Sadie Smith, daughter of Janet and Joseph, is a curious child who believes her grandmother's stories about Bessie. A trusting girl, Sadie enjoys her adventures with Bessie and Sash.

Sash is a sasquatch who lives in a cave in Lake Erie that is connected to Bessie's caves. A complex cave system lies underneath Lake Erie where Bessie and Sash can hide if they are seen by humans. Sash has authority over many sasquatches in the US Midwest.

Veronica is Janet's mom and Sadie's grandmother who was friends with Bessie when she was a child. When she passed away, Sadie found her grandmother's drawings of Bessie.

BESSIE

PROLOGUE

"And now that we have been found, we are vulnerable," said Nessie. "No longer can we live here together. Go forth and find fresh water sources. Once you have ascertained it is a safe place, send me a message. I will beam the list of where we all live once I have heard from all of you."

Bessie clung to her mother. "Please, Mom, I can stay with you, right?" Bessie curled her tail around her mother's. Nessie sighed. Bessie was her favorite daughter. To be hugged by her was a balm for her soul.

"It is not safe here now that I've been seen. A fatal error. Forgive me."

Bessie clung to Nessie. None of the sea dragons had ever left the continents of Asia and Europe. Gently, Nessie said, "There is a place on a different continent that has five large bodies of fresh water, the best the world has to offer. Go there and choose one. I'll be sure that no one claims the bodies until you have scouted them all. Send me messages about them. I want to place the best of us in each body."

1

—————

"**M**om, who's Bessie?"

I jumped at the mention of the name. I splashed soap suds on my face. As I reached for a towel to dry off, I asked, "Bessie?" My seven-year-old daughter had surprised me with their question.

"Yeah, I mean, yes," she replied, her brow wrinkled in curiosity. "I found these drawings of her."

I wondered where she had wandered into those old drawings that my mom made in her childhood, ones of an imaginary friend my mother said she had when I was seven. My mom, a fanciful thinker, could say strange things after a couple of glasses of wine. My brother and I laughed it off. So why is my heart pounding when my daughter, Sadie, asks about them?

"Yeah, Mommy. She looks friendly. Like the friend I told you about when we were at the beach last week." Sadie brushed her brown feathered bangs away from her forehead.

I dropped the sponge into the sink, dried my hands, and took the drawings from her. I lathered hand cream on my wrinkly fingers. I sat at the kitchen table, and Sadie scrambled on my lap. She was getting too big for it, but I savored that she still wanted the closeness.

Bessie. How long ago was it that my mom told me about her,

believed in her, and thought she was my mom's best friend? Thiry years ago, or more. Mom was an only child with no friends. She said that she created Bessie so she wouldn't be lonely. My mom wanted me to see Bessie, too. I never saw a thing.

I hadn't realized that Mom had given me her drawings. Maybe they were in the basement with the other stuff from mom's house that I took when she died a few months back. I looked at the crude green crayoned lines showing the outline of Bessie in the lake. Mom took me to the lake often when I was young. She'd pack a picnic lunch of peanut butter with marshmallow fluff and banana sandwiches, carrot sticks, and oranges. As soon as the air in spring was warm enough, off we'd go to our favorite spot. I'd take off my t-shirt and shorts and run as fast as I could into the cold waters of Lake Erie. Mom couldn't get me out until my lips were blue and I was shivering.

"Janet," Mom would call. "It's time for sandwiches."

"Aww, Mom," I'd cry, but my tummy was usually growling by then.

Mom would wrap me in the special fluffy, green blanket she saved to warm me after my cold frolicking. I'd chew my sandwich slowly. Usually, the sun, blanket, and full tummy would make me sleepy. Mom would tell me to rest and that Bessie would come. She never did.

"Tell me about Bessie, Mom," Sadie pleaded.

Sadie was getting heavy on my lap. I led her into the living room, and we scrambled into our favorite spot on the couch. I pulled the fluffy blanket, the same one Mom would wrap me in, onto both of us. Sadie rubbed her face into the soft velvet side of the blanket.

2

I saw Sadie's eyes droop as soon as I wrapped us in the blanket. I told Sadie the story of Bessie could wait until after her nap. Sadie protested but fell asleep immediately. I left her sleeping on the couch.

I settled at the kitchen table with my herbal tea. I would have time to think about Bessie—alone. I would have time to tell her what I thought she should know. I remembered the story my mom told me:

I remember being woken by the water dripping on my head. "Mom, stop it," I said groggily.

I heard a laugh—at least, I thought it was a laugh, but it wasn't Mom's. Slowly, I opened my eyes. I saw her. She was huge.

"What are you?"

"I'm Bessie, silly. I'm not a what. I'm a who," the strange iridescent creature said. Green, blue, pink, and yellow sparks shot off her skin. She was the most magical creature I had ever seen.

I should have been scared, but something about Bessie was calming. She was shining in the sun. Plopping down beside me, she went on, "I live in the lake. My momma had me stay here for safe keeping. I am still waiting for her to ask me to come back." Bessie rolled onto her back and looked up into the sun.

"When was that?" I asked.

"I don't know. Yesterday, maybe, or ten years ago." If Bessie had shoulders, she would have shrugged.

"Do you miss her?"

"Yes. But sometimes I see someone that reminds me of her. Then we play together."

I nodded. I wondered what it would be like to be dropped in a lake and left alone. I couldn't imagine my mom doing that to me. I decided to change the subject, because the conversation seemed to make Bessie sad. I'd never had a friend before, but it didn't seem right to make her sad.

I handed Bessie what was left of my sandwich. "You hungry?"

Bessie laughed again. She motioned to the lake. "I eat fish."

I nodded.

Bessie stood up. She must have been ten feet tall. I had to shade my eyes from the colors radiating off her skin.

"Gotta go," said Bessie, and she lumbered into the lake. "See you again?"

I nodded eagerly.

The first spring I saw Bessie was rainy. Mom and I didn't go to the lake often. I was anxious to return. Afterall, I told Bessie I would come back. One morning, the sun was bright, and I begged Mom to go.

"It's sunny now," Mom said, "but it's going to rain. You'll be disappointed if we must leave early." I was alarmed. All this time, I'd thought the rain was keeping me from Bessie, but she was out there in the rain. Did she get cold? Had her mom come back? Were there enough fish to eat?

"We have to go, Mom. We just have to."

"Why?"

I didn't know how to tell Mom about Bessie. "I made a friend there."

Mom looked perplexed. "A friend?"

"Yes, Bessie."

"Okay, Bessie can come here. I'll call her mom."

I didn't know what to say. Bessie didn't have a mom. And, did animals like her have a telephone? "Bessie doesn't have a mom," I said.

Mom nodded. "Who does she live with?"

"I don't know. Near the lake. We meet at the lake."

Mom sighed the sigh that I knew meant I had won. Off to Lake Erie we would go.

I figured that part of the story would be safe to tell Sadie. I would tell her that Bessie and her grandma played that summer, but in the fall, she was too busy with kindergarten to visit. I needn't tell her her grandma saw her the next summer and the horrors that happened.

After I told Sadie the story, she begged me to go to Lake Erie. "It's too late in the day, Sadie. I promise we will have a picnic there tomorrow." She seemed appeased.

3

"Bessie, Bessie, I'm here. I knew Veronica," Sadie yelled as I settled our chairs, blankets, and picnic baskets on the sand.

"Sadie, hush. I don't think that is how your grandma found her. Go play in the lake. I'll join you in a minute." Sadie squealed in delight when she plunged into the water. It was early June, and the water was still chilly.

"How does Bessie stand the cold water, Mom?" Sadie called.

"She's used to it."

I followed Sadie into the water. It was cold. I went in the lake to my knees, but Sadie was fully submerged. We played Marco Polo, and then both of us floated a while on our backs. We played in the water for nearly an hour before I noticed Sadie's lips were blue. "You're cold. Let's warm up."

Anticipating that Sadie wouldn't wait to jump in the water, I had packed a thermos of hot chocolate and the big furry green blanket. Sadie's teeth chattered as she sipped the warm liquid. I suggested a game of Uno before she jumped back into the lake.

"You always win, Sadie," I said. "How do you do that?"

Sadie smiled and shrugged. I saw her glancing at the lake for Bessie during the game. I knew she would be disappointed. Bessie was something my mom imagined. I was worried about how disappointed Sadie would be when Bessie didn't appear.

When I couldn't hold Sadie back any longer, I let her play in the lake. She opted to make houses in the sand near the water. "I want to show Bessie how we live," Sadie said.

I smiled. Why do adults lose their imagination as they age? I wish I could believe in Bessie as much as Sadie did. I kept a careful eye on Sadie as she created a mound of sand and then destroyed it, wanting to get the house just right. I noticed her eyes starting to droop.

"Sadie, nap time," I said.

I was surprised Sadie didn't protest. She wrapped herself in the blanket and fell straight asleep. I settled in with my laptop to work on some articles that were due for my boss. I loved that he let me work from home so I could spend more time with Sadie since Joseph died. His loss devastated us both. I'll never forget him saying to me just before he passed away from injuries in the auto accident that he saw something unbelievable just before he died. In fact, he said whatever it was tried to help him to safety but was scared away by the ambulance sirens. He said the thing told him he would look out for Sadie and me. I had wanted a goodbye or a take-care-of-Sadie message, but he was incoherent.

I had brought some of the news articles my boss sent me for editing. I'm not sure how long I'd been working when I heard Sadie call, "Look, Mom, look! Did you see her in the water?"

I scanned the shoreline. I didn't see anything but the clear blue water and small waves.

"See what, honey?" I asked.

"Bessie!"

Sadie hurried over to tell me her tale.

"I was asleep, and just like what happened to Gramma happened to me. I felt water dripping on my head. I told you to quit it. I thought it was you, Mom. But when I opened my eyes, there she was, just like Gramma drew. She was so tall that the sun blinded me, so I didn't get a good look at her face.

"Bessie said, 'Veronica! You're back.'" She picked me up and hugged me so tight. I thought she was an overgrown boa constrictor like we saw at the zoo. I screamed. She let me go and held me up to her face. She looked at me closely and said, 'You aren't Veronica, but you look just like her." I was still trying to catch my breath from being squeezed, but I was able to tell her that Veronica was my gramma. Bessie cried real tears when I told her that Gramma was gone. She asked me to come back and tell her stories about Gramma. Bessie really loved her, Mom. I can't believe you didn't hear me scream. I can't believe you didn't see her."

I didn't know what to say to Sadie. Her imagination was as vivid as my mom's was when she was drunk and told me Bessie stories.

"I think you've had enough sun and excitement today," I said as I started to pack our things.

"Oh, Mom, no!"

"No arguments, or we don't come back."

Sadie picked up her sand toys and brushed the sand from her bathing suit. She knew I kept my word. When we got home, Sadie began drawing a picture of Bessie. She didn't draw Bessie as brightly as my mom had. I wondered why but didn't want to indulge in the fantasy.

4

Sadie was disappointed that the rest of the week was rainy and windy. She fretted about Bessie getting too cold.

"She might be in her cave she told me about, but I don't know if it has heat," Sadie said.

I nodded. I was still working on the same article as at the lake. "Sadie, I have a deadline," I scolded.

"Sorry, Mom." Sadie looked crestfallen. I hated when I had to shoo her away.

"Can I paint today?" she asked shyly.

Feeling guilty for having talked to her harshly, I helped her settle with watercolors. I knew it would keep her busy for at least an hour and that I should be done with my work by then.

About an hour later, I looked up. Sadie was still hard at work on her painting. I left the room to fix lunch. When I returned with the ham sandwiches and chips, Sadie was cocking her head from side to side examining her work.

"May I see it?" I asked.

"Not yet," she said as she threw herself over the painting. "I'm not done."

We ate on the covered backyard patio, though the rain had

stopped. The air smelled so clean after a rain shower. I glanced up, and there it was. A full double rainbow. "Look, Sadie!"

Sadie stood up in awe. "Take a picture! I want to show Bessie."

Sadie said, "I wonder if Bessie saw it? She might have gone into her cave."

I took out my phone and clicked a few pictures. I ignored her comment about Bessie. No need to indulge her.

The next day was sunny and clear. I knew when I arose that Sadie would beg me to go to the lake. Since my deadlines had been met and no assignments had come in, I decided we would go. I would stay with her during her nap and assure her the Bessie she saw was one she dreamed.

Sadie played hard at the lake. She built two houses in the sand, one she said we lived in and one for Bessie. She wanted Bessie to move in next door.

"The neighbors have a swimming pool. She could stay there," Sadie said.

I laughed. "If Bessie is as big as you said, she wouldn't fit."

Sadie looked horrified. "You're right." She thought for a minute. "We could move here," she exclaimed.

I laughed. "Where would we live?"

"Bessie has a cave. Maybe we could move in with her?"

"I don't think that would be a good idea. It's underwater, isn't it? How would we get in? Sadie thought for a moment then scurried back to the lake. I could see her scanning the water looking for Bessie. I worried about how attached she had become to the imaginary beast. I knew Sadie was a lot like my mom. They were almost identical in looks. Me, I looked more like my father. But Sadie could be my mom's identical twin. I didn't realize Sadie had Mom's imagination. I wasn't quite sure how to manage it. What if in the fall she told her tales to her classmates? She might be teased for her stories.

I could see Sadie winding down and urged her to eat her sandwich and to nap. I pulled my beach chair next to where she was sleeping. I wanted to assure myself that her dreams were full of Bessie and that the water didn't contain a mythical animal. The sun was making me sleepy. I struggled to stay awake. I must have dozed off, because cold water sprinkled on my head woke me. I tried to grab my towel to wipe it off, but someone—something—was using it to dry me off. I looked up, and there she was. She had the towel in her mouth and was gently wiping me off. Her colors were blinding, yet I couldn't look away. Her look mesmerized me. Bessie—just as Sadie described her. I gasped. I didn't hear anything but knew Bessie was talking to me.

"I learned from Sadie that humans don't like to have drops of water on them. She told me how to wipe them off. Is Sadie your child?" Bessie asked. I nodded. "Don't be afraid," she continued. "I used to play with your mother. We were best friends."

"Mom told me," I said.

"She did," Bessie communicated. She seemed genuinely moved.

"Was my mom correct in saying there were problems when she saw you? I don't want that happening to Sadie." I was wary of her intentions. I still wasn't sure I wasn't dreaming.

I swear, I heard Bessie sigh. Her colors dimmed. "I won't let that happen again. I promise," Bessie assured me. "Being confined changed me. I have not approached humans for years. But I was drawn to Sadie. She looked like Veronica, who I dearly loved. Sadie said Veronica has passed on. I do remember feeling diminished a few months ago, like a boulder was on my chest. When I saw Sadie, it lifted. My colors paled."

"How do you know you won't be found again?" I asked.

I felt big drops fall on me. It wasn't the water falling from Bessie. I could see she was dry now. Were those tears coming from Bessie's eyes?

"I know better now that I can't interfere with humans. I don't leave the lake. I only appear when I know Sadie is here. I have a group of friends who take care of me and my siblings now. My friends rescued me when the humans came with nets to capture me."

Mom's story came back to me:

I loved visiting Bessie. One day, I decided since she could be out of the water for long that I would take her home with me. If she became faint, I could use our hose to wet her down. Bessie was eager to see where I lived. No sooner than I reached my street, I heard sirens. They seemed to magically appear and surround us.

A loudspeaker blared, "Get on the ground."

I immediately hit the ground.

The loudspeaker said, "Not you! That beast."

"She's not a beast," I cried.

"Move away from the beast, little girl."

"I'm not leaving her alone." I was crying. My mom by then had heard the commotion and was running toward me.

"Veronica!" She cried. "Come here. Come here, right now!"

"Mom, the police want to arrest me friend."

My mom came toward me. Bessie stepped away from me so Mom could take me.

I collapsed, sobbing in Mom's arms. "Don't let them hurt her."

Mom and I stood by while the police slung a rope net around Bessie and began dragging Bessie away. "Where are you taking her?"

"To the zoo."

"She will be safe there," my mom reassured. But I knew that wasn't true. How could she be safe away from her lake and cave?

The newspaper was full of Bessie stories the next day. The reporter didn't call her by name. He described the "Lake Erie Beast" as a large eel-like creature with the power to strangle people just as a cobra would. The article said Bessie was in a locked tank. She kept trying to break her way out. I knew Bessie wouldn't communicate with the police. She only chose special people to talk to. She had told me that when she spots something unique in a person, she makes friends. I was unique, she had said. I wasn't sure then what unique meant, but I was flattered to be chosen.

I was so depressed the next few days. I begged my mom to take me to the zoo to visit Bessie. She refused. She finally let me walk to the lake. It was only two blocks away.

I sat by the lake, crying. I had brought some of the pictures I had drawn of Bessie. I had to be careful not to let my tears drop on them. They were all I had left of her.

The day had been hot and sunny, but now, a big cloud covered the sun —I thought. Yet I could still see the sun, even though I was in the shade.

Then I heard, "Veronica, don't be afraid. Don't turn around."

My entire body shook.

"I am Bessie's friend. My name is Sash. I live in a cave that's connected underground to Bessie's. I have seen you play with her. You must be special. She doesn't make friends easily. Tell me what happened to her. She hasn't returned. I'm concerned. I might be able to help."

I turned to see who was communicating with me.

"No, don't. I don't want you frightened," the invisible voice said.

I turned anyway, saying, "I'm not afraid of Bessie. Why should you scare me?" I was bluffing. I was terrified.

There stood before me the largest creature I had ever seen. I gasped in horror.

"What are you?" I whispered.

"My species is known as sasquatch. We live all over. Our goal in life is to be a protector of the misfortunate. If you tell me where Bessie is, I will rescue her."

I nodded. But I was worried. Sash was nearly ten feet tall and covered with matted brown and black hair. When he smiled, I could see huge teeth.

"I'm not sure it would work. They will capture you like they did Bessie." I wasn't sure I should trust him, but I didn't want to get another creature jailed.

I could have sworn I heard Sash laugh. "I will bring friends. They can't get all of us," Sash said. "Now, scurry home. I need to gather my friends."

5

Sadie started to wake up, knocking me out of my memories.

"Bessie!" Sadie exclaimed. "You're here." Sadie glanced in my direction. "See, Mom, she's real." I nodded.

I was in shock. This beautifully colored animal was standing in front of me. I guess she was standing. She looked like an eel with teeny-tiny feet. The feet moved all at once when she moved, giving the impression she was gliding over the sand. I couldn't see how long she was. More than half of her body was still in the water, and I could see about ten feet of her. As I observed Bessie, I felt a sense of calm come over me. Was I being hypnotized?

"No, Janet," Bessie said to me. "I don't hypnotize humans. I just felt you needed some comforting."

Oh, no. She could read thoughts. I kept thinking that this wasn't happening. That I'd wake up, and it would all be a dream.

"It's not a dream," Bessie told me. "Let me tell you about my people. You and Sadie, sit and listen."

I told Sadie to get her chair and set it next to mine. She did and brought the snack box too. "Too bad we don't have popcorn," Sadie joked. I laughed, and so did Bessie.

I came from the Himalayan Mountains, where I was born along with my brothers and sisters. We lived in caves high in the mountains, flew like dragons, and breathed fire. There was only my mom, Nessie, and my siblings. Daddy had been captured and killed by some type of animals carrying torches. Now, they were coming for her. They climbed the mountains and followed my mom to the cave. One animal in the group said he knew how to get to the cave from an opening on dry land. Nessie heard them plotting to capture her and called all her children over to her.

"I called you here to say that we are not safe. When I went looking for your father, I was seen. I can confirm your father is dead. I saw his body hung from the top of the mountain, hanging from a tall tree for all to see. Unfortunately, those animals saw me. We cannot stay here. I want you to disperse around the country as our ancestors, the dragons, did. Find a body of freshwater near underground caves. Then, telepathically signal to me where you are. I will keep communicating with you through our network. Make haste. I know the same animals are plotting, but I haven't sensed when they will strike. Go! With my love, I will always be with you."

I began to weep. Mom came to me, and I felt a soothing calm come over me. Her love was like a layer of softness that melted my soul. "You must go, too, my favorite one."

I knew she was right. But leaving my mother was something I had never thought would happen. We were a clan of close-knit animals. Our ancestors, who descended from dinosaurs, were dragons who lost their wings and fire after a confrontation with the animals who sought our meat. In an epic battle between us and the animals, they were able to sneak into our ancestors' caves in the Great Mountain and clip our wings. My ancestors were in pain. Some bled out. We lost half of our colony. Those who survived cried so hard, they lost their flame from the deluge of tears. No longer having our wings or fire to protect us, we went to our leader, who decreed that we must now adapt to water. About a third of us did. We were warned to never show our faces to the animals who killed us. The water would be our refuge.

Mom relented and let me stay with her. I hoped it would not make my siblings jealous. I knew I was the favored one.

My ancestors left our mountain lofts and searched all around the world for freshwater lakes with caves. Some of us couldn't adapt to the water. They drowned. For years, we mourned the loss. We kept to ourselves. Generations of us lived happily in the water until a species known as homo sapiens emerged. We quickly learned to hide.

Mom was the only one who ventured out. She scouted the waters where the best schools of fish were gathered and reported back to us so we could join her. Food was sparse. Often, only some of us were able to eat the fish. Many times, the fish were gone by the time the weak or elderly came to eat. Again, we lost members of our clan.

We were a sad group. Mom, the eldest left from the time of dragons, became our leader. She ruled with fairness and instilled in us compassion for each other. Later, she told us to feel for other species. Our feelings could spare us someday.

At that time, we had no way to communicate, but Mom worked with us to develop our telepathic methods. In time, we all learned to send our messages far and wide. We spent many years communicating to our clan to find out if any of our ancestors were left. I was fortunate enough to discover a group of dragons who lived high in the Himalayan Mountains. When I explained what happened to us, they voluntarily left their mountain and found freshwater. There, they cut off each other's wings. And again, the tears extinguished their flames. Once they were healed, they traveled to us. We rejoiced to find those who were like us. I became the revered daughter of Nessie who helped save our species. I lived in luxury. I did not have to compete for fish. They were brought to me. In time, my colors became brighter than the others. I was distinguished among my species.

Eons later, when we thought it was safe, we all met at the loch and celebrated our transformations. Our revelry was too loud. Our dancing and singing alerted humans to our caves. Once again, the humans tracked us with our sounds. Mom urged all of us to disperse. We were all too scared, but most of us managed to spread out through the loch. I refused to leave my mother.

Somehow, the humans found the opening to our underwater caves from the land cave near the shore. We had thought the foliage was a good cover. Also, we did not inhabit the caves closest to shore.

I waited with Mom as we sensed the humans emerging. Mom said she felt a presence like none before. She said it was hostile to the humans, yet it seemed sympathetic to us. Then we heard human screams and cries. Mom and I cuddled together and drew strength from each other.

The human cries subsided. We didn't dare move. We could not understand what had happened. Why did the human cries end? What was the kind presence my mom felt?

Mom sent a message to my siblings that the danger seemed to have passed. She urged them to stay where they were until we could ascertain why the humans had stopped their pursuit. Mom and I did not venture far from the cave to eat. Fish in our area became sparse. Mom was concerned we would starve.

One day when we woke, a large cache of fish was at the back entrance to our cave, the one we didn't use because it opened to land. I sniffed the fish. They appeared fresh and were of a species we had not seen for a long time. We wanted to eat greedily but had to be cautious since we were not sure when we'd get such a bounty again. I sensed that if we ate all the fish, there would be more. I told my mom. She warily agreed, and we feasted for days.

A few days later, more fish appeared. From then on, every few days, fish were delivered. I decided to sleep by the cave opening near the land and see who was providing our meals. Mom was worried about my plan.

"What if the humans are luring us out?" she said.

"I don't believe it's humans," I said. "There is a friendly aura around the fish. I do not believe the humans are capable of seeding fish with feelings."

Mom reluctantly let me sleep near the entrance. She slept in her usual nest. I was scared sleeping alone. I was used to cuddling with Mom at night. I hid behind a stone abutment so whoever was leaving the food would not see me. I struggled to stay awake. My effort paid off.

I could not believe what I saw. It looked like a tall, tall humanoid, but not like the humans, who are hairless. Covered in brown and black fur, the humanoid opened a sack and spilled out what would be our next meal. I was afraid to confront it, but I knew I had to. Our lives depended on its kindness.

"Who are you?" I boldly sent my message to the humanoid.

"Sash. I'm Sash."

"What are you, Sash?"

"A protector."

Before I could ask what that meant, he was gone.

I couldn't sleep the rest of the night. I didn't want to wake Mom before I stopped shaking and could explain what happened. Mom told me to stay away from Sash, but I was drawn to his peaceful nature.

More eons passed. Regularly, Sash left fish for us. Occasionally, I slept near the rear exit of the cave and tried to talk to Sash. I felt he was more afraid of me than I was of him. Sash explained that he didn't want to become close to me. He feared the humans might find us.

Sash and I had brief exchanges when he came with the fish. I found out he too had many siblings. He was cagey about where they lived but shared that they were charged with taking care of lost, abandoned, and lonely species. I told him that I hoped we could be friends. He seemed to smile, but I could tell he was still wary.

Mom began to get signals from my scattered siblings that a benevolent soul was leaving them fish too. "I don't think it's just Sash, Bessie," Mom said. "I think there is a network of his species that are aiding them. Why? I don't know."

"I think Sash is keeping all of us alive," I said.

Mom looked thoughtful. "We can't depend on Sash forever. He is risking his species being found out. I think it's time to call all your siblings together. I have a plan."

Over the next few weeks, my siblings began to arrive home. We wanted to celebrate being together as a family but were wary of our revelry attracting attention. Our network of caves grew crowded. Some of my siblings had children while they were away. I loved playing with the babies, but the overcrowding was testing our familial love.

When all of us had gathered, Mom announced we were to find bodies of freshwater all over the world, not just in the Himalayas. She suggested a place for each of her children. Only five of us were left. Four were dearest siblings. I begged mom to let me stay with her, but she announced there were five great lakes that had recently formed. She gave me the first choice, and I was to report back on the suitability of the other four bodies.

We had two predators: the animals who killed us long ago, and now the humans.

6

Sadie and I were mesmerized by Bessie's story. But the sun was going down. I insisted that we had to go home. Bessie, I could tell, was tired too. We agreed to meet the next day, weather permitting.

Sadie insisted on watching the local news at dinner to see the weather report. The next day would be cloudy with a slight chance of rain. I was wary of visiting a sea monster on such a day, but I knew the weather wouldn't be bad enough to deter my brave little girl.

I had to file some stories in the morning. Sadie had wanted an early start to the lake and was not happy with me. I put her in charge of gathering what we would need. I washed the blankets and towels; she was to take them from the dryer, fold them, and then put them in my tote. I had made lunch the night before.

It was almost noon before we reached the lake. The weather looked a bit ominous when we arrived. The weather was often fine a few streets from the lake where we lived but different at the beach. Sadie started to call for Bessie.

"Honey," I said. "Remember that Bessie hears thoughts. Just think what you want to say. We don't want to draw any attention."

Sadie nodded. She closed her eyes tightly. While she was

summoned Bessie, I was spreading out the blankets when I felt a presence behind me. I heard someone say, "Don't turn around."

The voice was deep. I started to shake with fear, but then a feeling of safety floated over me. "Who's there?" I said.

"I am Bessie's friend, Sash. Bessie is worried about you. She wants me to take you to my cave. The entrance is on land, and then it joins Bessie's cave underwater. She will be waiting there for you."

"How will I know where to go if I can't see you?" I asked.

"You will know. I'll be behind you and Sadie and guide you with my thoughts."

"Why can't I see you?"

"You would be scared of my appearance."

I laughed. "I've seen Bessie. I'm up for anything."

The voice seemed to stop. Maybe he was thinking.

"All right. Turn slowly. Do not scream."

I slowly turned around. I stifled a scream by putting my hand over my mouth. He was at least ten feet tall and covered with brown and black unkempt fur. I thought his mom hadn't done a good job combing his hair. As I was debating whether Sadie and I should leave, Sadie came running.

"Hi," she greeted the large wooly man—or monster or whatever. "You must be Bessie's friend, Sash." She ran up to him and they embraced.

"Sadie, no!" I shouted. It was too late. They were embracing and communicating silently. Sash, as Sadie called him, was gentle with her. I could see he had a tear in his eye. What was this thing?

Sash heard my thoughts. "I'm a sasquatch. There are many of my kind throughout the world. We have been the protectors of Bessie and her family for eons. Come with me and Bessie, and I will explain."

Sadie started to follow Sash. I had no choice but to follow too. He led us through the wooded area by the lake, a place I had never been. I was shocked that the foliage was so overgrown. At times, Sash lifted logs and moved branches to ease our way. His strength was beyond anything I had seen. We must have traveled about a mile when Sash stopped and began to roll a huge rock. When he stopped, I could see the opening of a cave. Sadie ran right in.

"Sadie," I said, "stop!"

"It's okay, Janet. I cleaned it to human standards. Bessie is waiting inside."

When I entered the cave after Sadie, I was amazed at the size of the cave. The ceiling was at least fourteen feet high; the floors were paved with stones in an intricate pattern. There was a place for a fire. Over the fire, spun a spit roast. The cave had a fishy smell.

Sadie ran right to Bessie. They were hugging. The smell was coming from Bessie. Now Sadie had her scent.

"Hello, Janet," Bessie said. "The weather will be nasty. I asked Sash if we could meet here." I nodded.

"Do you have more stories to tell?" Sadie asked.

Bessie nodded. "But I needed Sash here. He's part of our history."

Sash had two chairs set by a table. I was confused. Did he entertain humans regularly?

"I raided the dump. I know humans prefer these things to sit on. I prefer the floor."

"Donuts," exclaimed Sadie.

"Ah, no, Sadie. We have our lunch." I wasn't sure I wanted her to eat something Sash had touched.

"Easy, Mom," said Sash. "They're fine."

Sadie grabbed one and gulped it down. I heard Bessie and Sash laughing. "I told you humans liked those things," Sash said.

"Well, I'll be," said Bessie.

"Mom," Sadie whispered to me, "you need to take one to be polite." I smiled and took one. I had never tasted anything like it. I sat politely in one of the chairs that Sash had scavenged. It was surprisingly comfortable. Sadie took her place in the other chair.

After the donuts and milk, of all things, Bessie and Sash settled in to tell us their story. Sash sat first, and then Bessie leaned against him. I could tell they had genuine affection for each other. Bessie continued her story.

25

"This part of our history is painful. Sash and his clan pay a huge part in it." Sash hung his head. "It's okay, Sash," Bessie said. "Your clan grew in understanding. Some species never do.

"Remember I told you about the animals that cut our wings? You do. Okay. When I tell you about it, don't blame Sash. He is blameless."

"Stop. I don't think this is appropriate for Sadie. She's only seven," I interrupted Sash.

"I can understand you being hesitant. I think Sadie can handle it. She knows how we lost our wings. I'm only revealing who did it."

I still wasn't sure. I looked at Sadie's face. I could tell she was disappointed in me. I so wished her father was here. But would Joseph have allowed the friendship to go this far?

Reluctantly, I let Bessie continue.

"All of us lived in the great mountains in what you now call Asia. The sights were spectacular. You know that eons ago, the air and water were purer, the colors brighter. We had huge wings bigger than our bodies. When we weren't flying, we groomed each other's wings. While flying, we pick up bugs and debris. Leaving it on our wings would make us sick. Flying from mountain top to mountain top to see friends and relatives was common. We shared our hunting kills and fishing catches with each other. Feasts were regular occasions. Since we were so high in the mountains, we didn't worry about being seen. We didn't know that Sash's ancestors could blend into the terrain and spy on us.

"The attack was a total surprise. All were gathered at the Cave of Festival. I helped with the decorations. We had talented fire-breathers, who could take a tree or a leaf and carve it into a gorgeous centerpiece. We could heat stones to cook our prey. My mom was the best cook. She could control her flame so the meat and fish were cooked and not charred. Not every female dragon had Mom's talent. They tended to overcook. Most of the other females made what you humans call salads from seaweed and other aquatic plants.

"My father had found some fermented fruit, and many of the males were eating them. Mom wasn't happy. She knew the feast could get out of hand. Yet, our yearly feast was a special occasion. A few of the men started the fire-breathing contests. You know—who could blow the biggest flame, hottest flame, bluest flame, reddest flame. You get the idea. Of course, my father always won the biggest flame contest. It was so big that year that it burst out of the cave.

The main feast had started. Mom called the males to the feast early because they were getting a bit rambunctious. We all overate, which meant none of us could breathe fire or fly after one of these events. We were at our most vulnerable. Mom started organizing where we all would sleep, when we heard ungodly yelling. Since most of our communication was telepathic, our ears began to bleed from the sound. When you don't use them, skin grows over them. I put my wings over my ears, as did most of us, but it didn't help.

"All we could see was black and tan fur coming at us. The animals had big metal pieces that when wielded cut our skin. Forgetting we couldn't fly in our current state, we furled our wings. We tried to shoot fire but couldn't. Howls of pain filled our cave. The wings were an easy target. The animals took our wings and left us bleeding and in pain. Many of us died that night, mostly those from other clans.

"The pain was unbearable. We never knew we could weep. The weeping continued as we discovered deceased relatives and friends. By morning, none of us could breathe fire.

"My father was undeterred. Once he could stand, he led the elder males out of the cave. They followed the tracks and smell of the animals. Sadly, the men were used to flying. We rarely walked. They needed frequent breaks. Many times, they had to hunt for water. The crying had dehydrated them. It took them days to track the animals to their home.

"Father reached the animals' home first. He crawled into the hovel and saw the animals roasting and eating our wings. With all his might, he threw himself at the biggest of the animals. The animals were quick. They took their pieces and metal and stabbed my father. There was blood everywhere. Mom rushed to help Dad, and my siblings held me back. The animals that attacked us were picking up our father and taking him away.

"Mom was inconsolable. Not one of us had ever died until now. Many bled to death from their wings being removed. Mom had spent her time consoling friends and family, but with seeing Father being carried away by monsters, she seemed to fade. Her beautiful colors of green, purple, red, and yellow faded. She tore at the scabs forming where her wings had been. She wanted to bleed. She wanted to die without my father.

"I spent many years consoling Mom. Other ex-dragons had left our lair. Soon, it was just my mom, my siblings, and me. When Mom realized she had neglected to fill my father's shoes, she rose from her nest and decreed, "We must leave this lair and see where our friends have gone."

"Mom sent me and my closest siblings out to scour the world to see if we could find our friends and encourage them to come back into our fold. We searched for years and found nothing. Searching the land was tedious. We, who were so used to flying, now had to walk. We weren't built for that. I noticed that on my closest sister's back, strange slits had formed. I examined the three; each had the same slits. My siblings confirmed that I had them too.

"The slits didn't hurt. They seemed to open and close. When they opened, we had an extra burst of energy. When they shut, we felt like we had no breath. Our walks were short bursts that we did when the slits were open. We rested when they closed.

"Once, we were walking on an island. We took long drinks while walking along a great body of water. My two siblings, who sometimes had differences, began to fight. I stepped in to break them up and scold them.

"We must continue the journey. No more!" I bellowed.

My one sibling pushed me, and I fell into the water with quite a splash.

"You've killed her," cried my sister.

"Although I was deep in the water, I still could hear them. I must have still been alive. I pushed my head high and found I could move easily in the water. The slits were gills that let me breathe underwater.

"I couldn't wait to get to the surface and show my siblings my new skill, but I'd get sidetracked moving my body this way and that. It felt so good. When I emerged, my siblings were on the shore crying and trying to figure out a story to tell our mother about how her favorite daughter had been killed.

"I emerged from the water and slithered onto the shore. My siblings heard me and were awestruck I was still alive.

"'Our slits let us breathe underwater, I shouted. 'The water lets us move gracefully. We swim and breath like fish now.'

"One at a time, my siblings jumped in to see if they too had these powers. We played in the water until we were almost too exhausted to surface. Then my brother found a cave. The water went only a few feet into the cave; the rest was dry. We scurried into the underground cave and slept better than we had in eons. The next morning, we decided to swim to our home. Our discovery would alleviate the melancholy that had plagued us for eons.

"Along the way home, we discovered other lands and large bodies of water. Some of the water was salty. The salt made us sneeze. We tried to avoid those areas, but we knew we would have to swim through one to return home. We would surface every now and then looking for our friends.

"One day, we were on the shore resting and stumbled across a field of bones. When I touched one, I felt an electric shock and then heard a voice. 'This is what is left of us. Go home and be safe. It's dangerous.'

"I told my siblings to touch a bone and listen. They heard the same message. We knew what we had to do: swim home."

Sadie interrupted Bessie's story. "Where were you, Sash, when this was happening to Bessie's family?"

"Shh," I said. "Let them talk."

"I guess this is as a good time as any to explain the despicable history of my kind," Sash said with a sigh.

"I was there as a teenager when my kind killed the dragons. I know we were afraid of their fire. The Council of the Elderly convened. We revered our elders and put all our faith in their decisions. After several days, they emerged from their deliberations and declared that the dragons were a danger to us. They appointed five of us to study the dragons and find where they were most vulnerable.

"After months of study, the group of five reported to all of us that they had found the perfect solution: *cut their wings off.*

"Now, we had never been bloodthirsty. We tried to stay away from other species so as not to be found.

"Many of us had questions. Why their wings? The Group of Five said that taking the wings would ground them. They wouldn't be able to shoot at us from the sky, even though they never had.

"Someone countered that the dragons lived on a high mountain and could still hit us with fire from there. Others worried cutting the wings off would kill them. What if the dragons retaliated and burned our forests?

"Then, our eldest elder stopped the discussion. 'We have never killed. We will not kill.'

"The others on the council murmured to each other. One on the council had been trying to dethrone the eldest elder. He bellowed, 'Now is not the time to kowtow to the eldest elder. We must take our land back from these fiery creatures that terrorize us.'

"The crowd roared in approval. 'Take their wings. Take their wings.' The chant grew louder and more raucous.

"My father and mother were appalled that my grandfather had been the one to call for the wings. My father said, 'Stop. Stop this. We are not violent. We are peaceful. We need to send a coalition to reach an agreement with the dragons.'

"'What folly,' screamed my grandfather. 'They will toast the coalition, and we will be worse off than now.'

"I found courage to speak even though I had no authority. 'Dear

Grandfather, what have the dragons done to us? They fly. I like to see them light up the night sky. Their colors are beautiful. If they aren't bothering us, why start trouble?'

"I saw some heads nodding in agreement.

"'Ha!' said my grandfather. 'Don't listen to the young. They have not seen what the elders have seen.'

"Although he was asked to tell us what they had seen, he refused. 'It's not for everyone's ears.'

"Our cohesive species had splintered into two factions—those that wanted to take the wings of the dragon and those who wanted to leave them alone.

"My father became the head of the peaceful coalition. We organized a commission to study the dragons' actions and understand their rules. My father added me to the commission as its leader.

"You see, I had been studying dragons for some time. I had been fascinated by their power. Each young sasquatch had to have a project and present it to the council of elders to be given a place in our society. I had chosen dragons for study. What I had not disclosed to my father, or anyone, was that I was communicating with a young dragon. We had met. In fact, when we first made contact, I thought I was talking to a sasquatch from another region. I knew my species was all over the world. Our telepathic communication allowed us to keep different groups in touch. The one I was talking to was about my age. I thought I had met the love of my life and was trying to attract her. I thought she was a sasquatch."

Bessie and Sash started to laugh. Sadie and I were confused. The story wasn't funny, but the two laughed until Bessie was rolling on the floor. Sash had doubled over from his belly laughs.

"What's so funny?" I asked.

Sadie chimed in, "Stop laughing. I want to hear the story."

Bessie caught her breath. "Sash was talking to me." I swore I saw Sash smile. Then I got it. The two of them were in love many years ago. No wonder Sash was a staunch protector of Bessie.

"You are a hero to the sea monsters, aren't you?" I said.

"Yes, he is," Bessie said.

"No, it wasn't just me. Let me tell you the rest of the story." Sash began again.

"When I realized that Bessie was a dragon, I realized how harmless the dragons were. I did not disclose my feelings for Bessie. I told my father they used their fire to cook food and to celebrate. Their main mode of transportation was their wings. They loved to celebrate with each other. The fires from their mouths were most potent when they were giving each other kudos. They could walk short distances but preferred to view the world from the air. I envied their ability to see the world from a different point of view, something I would never do. They were no danger to us. We were being led by elderly sasquatches who were afraid of everything different. When the dragons had decided to stay in our area, they panicked.

"I wasn't sure how to proceed. I decided to tell my father I was communicating with a dragon and that they were a peaceful species. My father listened carefully. He said he would talk to his father, the eldest elder.

"My grandfather would not listen to my father. He was hellbent on maiming the dragons. My father led the peaceful coalition to defy the elders, but the elders held more sway with the average sasquatch. Even when my father appealed to our peaceful ways, there were some who had bloodlust in their souls.

"My father gathered the coalition and told them to create a plan that could curtail the damage that would be inflicted. We had one, but it was too late to stop the carnage.

"I woke one morning when I felt drops of something wet landing on me. It was red. I knew it was the blood of the dragons. I charged out of the family cave and heard screaming from the dragons. Blood flowed in rivers down the mountain. The peaceful sasquatches were caught unawares and couldn't escape the deluge of blood. They were not able to mount any defense for the dragons.

"Remember, I was young and very much in love. I urged all of us to at least try to save the dragons. Some of us younger sasquatches were able to douse ourselves in the lake that surrounded the mountains and charge up the mountain to the battle. We came at them with torches, knowing the invading coalition was afraid of fire. We were too but overcame our fears.

"When we arrived, we found it hadn't been a battle, but a massacre. We could intuit the pain of the dragons. At first, we were stunned, but I was finally able to give orders.

"'Grab a dragon and use the torches to stem the bleeding.'

"Instinctively, I knew which one was Bessie. She was bleeding profusely. I went to her.

"'No, help my mother,' she cried. She refused help until I had her mother stabilized. I then worked on her bleeding.

"I wanted to stay with her to be sure she'd be all right, but she wanted me to save as many of her relatives as I could.

"We saved most of Bessie's clan. Some dragons, friends of Bessie's group, were terrified of us. They ran away. I found out later they all had bled out."

Sadie was crying. I was near tears. "I think that's enough for today," I said.

Sash nodded. Bessie urged Sash to cook some of the fish she had gathered that morning so we could have a meal. I told them we had a picnic lunch, but they insisted. We all feasted on the fish and our picnic items.

7

Sadie had nightmares. We slept together in my bed so I could soothe her. I know my sleep was restless too. I rose before Sadie and tried to make her favorite breakfast. I noticed I was shaking as I broke the eggs for the French toast batter. I needed Joseph there to guide me. Just as I was about to give up on breakfast and take Sadie out for food, I felt an unusual peace flow through me.

How could I be calm after hearing those horrific stories? I leaned against the counter and tried to force back tears.

"Mom," said Sadie. "Are you okay?"

Sadie had entered the kitchen and was hugging my leg. Of course, that was the feeling of peace, not some weird signal from this strange species we had encountered. I looked at Sadie's face to see she looked serene—not the scared little girl I had tucked into bed.

As I gathered her into my arms, I found that her peace was entering me.

"Mom," Sadie said, "don't be mad at me, but Daddy visited last night."

"He was in your dream, Sadie."

"I know. But it was so real."

I hugged Sadie tightly. I too had dreamed of Joseph. I felt so rudderless after the stories we had heard yesterday; I figured it was my subconscious' way of soothing me.

"Pleasant dreams are soothing after what we heard yesterday," I told Sadie.

"When can we go back and hear more?" Sadie asked.

"Let's give it a few days. Okay, sweetie?" I said.

She nodded. I was surprised she hadn't put up a fight, but I guessed she was as emotionally whipped as I was.

I set up Sadie's painting station and settled in with the new assignments that had come from my boss. Sadie was content to paint all morning. I was restless and couldn't concentrate on the first story my boss had assigned me. I turned to the second.

I couldn't believe what I was reading. My boss indicated that there had been a sighting of a strange creature near Lake Erie. I was to investigate and interview those who had witnessed it. I had the names and phone number of a commander in the Navy. I was shaking. Had Sash and Bessie been seen when we were there? How much danger were they in?

I left the dining room table where Sadie and I worked and called the number of the commander from my upstairs office. I didn't want Sadie to hear the conversation.

"Hello," the woman answered.

I introduced myself as a writer for the local paper and asked if she would talk to me about what she saw.

I needed to find someone to take care of Sadie. I did not want her there when I interviewed the woman. I called my boss, who said he'd send his assistant over to care for her. I was fortunate to have a boss who accommodated me when I needed a sitter. He had stepped up when Joseph died.

I was explaining to Sadie that I had an assignment, and that Sheri was coming to stay with her. She squealed in delight. I realized I hadn't fed Sadie lunch, but when Sheri arrived, she had stopped at Sadie's favorite fast-food place. The food smelled wonderful to me, even though I never ate it. I had forgotten to eat. Luckily, Sheri figured as much. She knows that when I work, I shut out bodily needs. She had a salad for me. What a gem!

After I wolfed down my food, I left for the woman's home. It was just a few blocks from where I lived. If I had known, I could have walked, but I had taken the SUV. I parked on the street, made my way to the door, and knocked.

A woman in a nautical uniform answered.

"Hi, I'm Janet Smith from the *Lake Erie Examiner*. I was told you found some interesting things while exploring the infestation of zebra mussels in the lake."

The woman opened the door wider and urged me to come inside. I was shocked to see the living room full of computers, sonar, and other equipment I couldn't identify. At each station, someone was working feverously.

"I'm Commander Burke from the US Navy. I was called in when the scientists reported to me what they found."

"What can you tell me?"

The captain motioned me to the kitchen. "Would you like some tea?"

"No," I said. "I'm good.

"I hope you don't mind if I make myself some."

When Commander Burke finished making her tea, she sat across from me at the table. "I barely know where to begin. I'm usually not at a loss for words."

"Commander, maybe first you could tell me something about your mission here," I said.

"Call me, Guiliana," she said. "The scientists were here studying the invasion of zebra mussels causing trouble in the lake. I was called in when the national scientists found some unusual caves." She continued:

While doing underwater research for the invasive zebra mussels that have been infesting Lake Erie, the scientists found a previously unknown underwater cave. Due to the new cave's proximity, they suspected that it connected to Crystal Cave in Put-in-Bay on Lake Erie just off the shores of Ohio.

Within a week of the groundbreaking discovery, the researchers anchored three additional ships off Put-in-Bay that contained all the underwater surveying equipment they needed to begin mapping the area.

The first ship was going to circle the island while using LiDAR—light detection and ranging, a remote sensing technology that uses lasers to measure distances and create a 3D map.

The second ship carried four underwater robotic rovers, or ROVs. A ROV is a remotely operated vehicle, tethered to the ship by a cable and controlled by a pilot on the ship.

The third ship carried three AUVs, or autonomous underwater vehicles. The AUVs were not tethered and instead were controlled by an autonomous computer. Untethered, AUVs could go further into caves.

While the first ship continued mapping around the island, the scientists would use one of the ROVs to inspect the new cave. They were excited to begin the search since it is rare to have a cave on an island like Crystal Cave, and it would be a scientific goldmine they could gain important knowledge from. The city council of Put-in-Bay was even more excited about the find because it would mean a windfall for the town.

The personnel aboard the ships would bring much-needed money into the town's coffers, since they would be spending money in stores and restaurants. More importantly, the new cave would attract tourism revenue for years. The city council was already making press announcements about the discovery in hopes that tourists would like to come to watch the ships exploring. Even if the new cave was not connected to Crystal Cave, it would still be a money-making attraction, especially for underwater explorers and divers.

While they were preparing the first ROV to explore the new underwater entrance to the new cave, the ship doing the LiDAR scanning discovered four additional previously unknown underwater caves that the scientists suspected were connected to the famous Crystal Cave due to their proximity.

Once they announced the discovery of the four new caves, the crew aboard the ROV went into double time preparing the first rover for explo-

ration, knowing they now had four more caves to work on. They also had to fly in six more pilots to operate the other ROVs. The crew normally only used one or two ROVs at a time and two pilots, but with five caves to explore, they needed more pilots so they could operate twenty-four hours a day.

A day later, they dropped the first ROV into the water and sent it into the new cave. The cave entrance was forty feet under the surface of the water and surprisingly large for an underwater cave. The measurements showed that it was thirty feet in diameter. Once inside, the cave went up at a shallow angle for about 250 feet until it came out into a large natural grotto. The pool in the grotto was 200 feet in diameter, and there was a soft sandy shoreline that wrapped completely around the water. The dry area in the grotto extended 300 to 400 feet in all directions but one. In that direction, there appeared to be a long tunnel that disappeared around a corner about 600 feet from the shoreline.

When the ROV crew shared the grotto's dimensions, the AUV crew quickly prepared one of their crafts to be dropped into the water to explore the tunnel. The AUV was designed to explore wet or dry caves, and the mysterious tunnel was perfect for its design.

While waiting for the AUV to arrive, the first ROV began exploring the shoreline. Inside the first new cave, they found what could only be drag marks and footprints from a huge creature going in and out of the water.

The ROV ship's captain heard of the drag marks and footprints and called me in. I was to supervise his work. The scientists feared they might have found a dangerous that may have been planted by the enemies of the United States. After I boarded the ROV, the captain instructed one of his dive teams to hit the water immediately and head into the cave to explore the shoreline for further signs of a creature. Twenty minutes later, a dive team of eight was in the water heading for the cave below.

Once the divers came out of the water, they used their equipment to check the air quality. Their readouts showed normal oxygen levels with no traces of harmful gases. Once given the green light, the divers took off their masks and tanks and prepared to explore. Each diver had shoulder-mounted lights to explore in the dark. The divers' first order of business was to set up thermal imaging and inferred lights, plus they installed remote *monitoring cameras. The thermal imaging and inferred lights would be invisible to any creatures or animals that might enter the cave, but the crew manning the ships monitoring equipment could see the whole cave using their special equipment.*

Once the lights and cameras were set up, the dive crew broke into four groups of two. The rule was that when diving or exploring, they always stayed together as a pair. Two of the pairs took pictures and measured the footprints and drag marks while the other two pairs began walking in opposite directions around the shoreline. They were going to survey the shoreline first then move further away from the water, recording their findings.

As they searched the shoreline, they discovered what they suspected was some sort of nest. In all, they recorded over two dozen of these beds or nests. The smallest was fifteen feet across, the largest thirty. From the size of the footprints and drag marks, they suspected the aquatic creatures to be anywhere from fifteen to sixty feet long. The nests were simple rock circles, about two feet high with various fish bones and sea grasses scattered around them. One pair of divers collected samples from the nests for further examination to determine what exactly was using them.

The scientists aboard the ships begged the captain to allow them to dive down and inspect the nests themselves, but the captain told them it was too dangerous until they knew what was using the caves. The captain knew they had no idea what these creatures were, and until they did, he wouldn't allow the civilian scientists to go down. For now, the scientists had no other recourse other than to sit and watch the cameras.

Once the nests around the shoreline had been inspected and mapped, three dive pairs began mapping further from the water and found more nest-like rock circles. While the three pairs of divers mapped the nests around the shoreline, the fourth headed towards the tunnel that disappeared 600 feet around a corner.

At that point, I stopped Commander Burke and asked if I could record her findings. I was having problems keeping up with the details. She agreed and began again:

The pair of divers were pulling a wagon loaded with survey equipment. The first thing the pair reported was that the tunnel was an ancient lava tube, and that the floor appeared to be well worn. Not only that, they could also tell that some of the debris on the tunnel floor had been dropped recently. The leaves weren't so old that they were dry, and the sticks still felt soft and pliable. When they reported their findings to the captain, he cautioned them to stay vigilant and not to take any chances. Each member of the dive team carried a 9mm handgun and a speargun for protection.

I gasped. "Guns?"

The commander nodded. "We could not take any chances with our top scientists risking their lives."

"But what if the species you have discovered are sentient and kind?" I asked. I was worried about Bessie and Sash. Had they been seen? What danger were they in?

"Why would you ever think they would be aware and kind? Kind? These are gigantic animals. Nothing that big could be kind. Their sheer size means they are dangerous."

Now I was worried. I needed to end this interview and warn them. But I needed to know more about the operation. Commander Burke began again. "Where was I? Oh, yes. The guns."

When they realized the tunnels had recently been occupied, the divers pulled their 9mm handguns out and kept them locked and loaded. They and the captain thought it might be bears or a big cat that had been using the lava tube, so they decided stayed ready. Each time the pair rounded a corner, they placed a pair of remote monitoring cameras so that one pointed from where they came from and the other up the lava tube they were headed. That way, they could watch whatever was coming and going.

It took about twenty minutes to find the exit of the lava tube, where it came out onto the island. Much to their surprise, the entrance was almost completely covered with brush. Oddly, there was a large bush that easily moved aside so one could go in and out with plenty of clearance. When the bush was put back in place, the entrance was invisible to anyone even ten feet away. Whoever or whatever had done this did not want the entrance to be found.

The divers contacted the captain about the discovery of a purposely hidden entrance, and he suggested they quickly finish. When they were done inspecting the area around the lava tube entrance, the pair placed remote cameras on trees pointing at the hidden entrance. The captain wanted them back as soon as possible in case whoever or whatever had hidden at the entrance showed up. By this time, the two divers were scared enough they were ready to head back. They had placed cameras all along the lava tube and outside the entrance, so if whatever was using the lava tube came back, they would have pictures.

Fifteen minutes later, the pair reached the grotto. The three surveying pairs had finished their task and were ready to leave when the fourth arrived.

The six divers that had stayed to survey the grotto had also found smaller nests further from the water that were unlike the nests by the water. These new nests were smaller and lined with moss, soft ferns, and leaves. Apparently, whatever used the nests by the water were large aquatic creatures of various sizes. The nests that were further from the water appeared to be for land-dwelling creatures. The divers had gathered samples from nests by the water and the smaller ones near the outer edges of the grotto. Their goal was to run DNA analysis of the samples to determine what creatures were using the caves.

When all their surveying had been completed, the eight divers gladly left the grotto and headed back to their ship.

Commander Burke said, "We plan to go back to the new caves in the next several days."

"I've got to go," I said. I stood up quickly and banged into the table, spilling the commander's tea. I realized I had to leave and warn Bessie and Sash that they had been discovered.

"Mamam, will you come back?"

"Yes, yes. Call me when you have more."

I jumped into my car and raced to the beach. I could see the equipment stationed at Put-in-Bay that Commander Burke had told me about. I took that as a good sign. I scurried to Sash's cave, figuring I would find him there.

The cave was empty. And totally clear of the furniture and nests. Sash already knew. I tried to reach Bessie's cave, but I could hear the water rushing into it. I knew I wouldn't be able to access it. Since I could hear what Bessie and Sash were saying to me even when I wasn't with them, I stood in Sash's cave and sent them this message, even though my ability to send messages telepathically was inferior to Sadie's:

Bessie Sash, you are about to be found out. The US Navy found your caves while researching zebra mussels. Leave immediately. Let me and Sadie know where you are. Don't go to Put-in-Bay.

I stayed in the cave, hoping for a return message. But there was none. I sent the message again and began to drive home, wondering how much I should say to Sadie, if anything.

Sadie and Sheri were fixing dinner when I arrived.

"Sorry, I'm so late," I said. "The interview went longer than expected."

"Mom, why are you wet?" Sadie asked.

"Am I? I'll change. Sheri, can you supervise dinner until I'm done?"

Sheri nodded.

When I had dried off and changed, I wanted to pay Sheri, but she said that would be double-dipping since my boss was paying her. I laughed. My boss took good care of his employees.

"Oh, I almost forgot. The boss wants that story tonight for tomorrow's edition," Sheri said.

I must have looked horrified, because Sheri cocked her head at me. "Okay, I'll get it done," I assured her.

The dinner was done when I entered the kitchen. Sadie had set the table. I only had to serve.

"Mom, did you go looking for Sash and Bessie?" Sadie asked as I sat down to eat.

"Why do you ask?"

"Bessie told me what was going on at the lake. Her caves on the island were ransacked. She went to warn Sash. They plan to visit Bessie's sister in Lake Ontario. Right now, they're hiding in another cave in Canada."

I hugged Sadie. I knew she was worried for her friends—our friends. At least they were safe and had a plan.

"What are we supposed to do?" I asked.

"Nothing until we hear from them again."

"The woman I interviewed today told me what was going on at the lake. I left her and went looking for them."

Sadie nodded. "I knew you did when you came home all wet."

I smiled. The rest of the dinner passed in silence. Sadie didn't have much appetite, and neither did I. She said she was tired and would tuck herself into bed. I was relieved. I could write the story without interruption.

The story was hard to write. I found myself wanting to editorialize, but I kept to the facts. I had it sent to my boss a bit before the midnight deadline. I must have fallen asleep the minute I got into bed. My dreams were strange that night. Sadie and I were riding on Bessie's back through the lake. I was cold and wet. Sadie loved it. I was wary of the ride. Then I heard Sash say, "You'll be safe with us if something happens." I didn't know what the dream meant. How could Sadie and I be in danger?

The next morning, I turned on the TV to see if any other news source had picked up the story. What I saw was unbelievable. Put-in-Bay, an island that catered to tourists, was on the screen. Naval ships were bringing the residents and tourists to shore. The small park that Sadie and I frequented was full of people being put on buses. Area hotels were offering them rooms for free until the monsters were caught. I must have cried out, because Sadie raced into the TV room.

"What's wrong, Mom?" Sadie asked.

I pointed to the TV. She could see what was happening and burst into tears. I hugged her, and we hugged each other until the report ended. I don't know how long we would have stayed that way; I finally let her go to answer my work phone.

"Janet! How could you write such a benign piece?" my boss screamed into my ear.

"Benign? I reported the facts that Commander Burke gave me."

"You didn't emphasize the danger. We were caught flatfooted and outreported by a TV station."

My boss constantly worried that the paper, even though it had an online presence, would go bankrupt because of TV.

"But what if there is no danger? Maybe the animals are friendly." I was near tears.

"Friendly? What are you saying? Friendly monsters. You know how big they are? The reports say that they estimate one of them to be nearly fifty feet long. The one with feet could be fifteen feet tall."

I didn't know what to say.

"You still there, Janet?" my boss asked.

"Yes. What do you want me to do?"

"Get your butt down to the lake and file a new piece with descriptions of these monsters." I heard the phone call end.

I realized that Sadie had overheard the conversation. "I'm going with you. You know we aren't in danger."

What could I say? I had no sitter, and I needed to get to the lake quickly. Leaving the half-made breakfast, we grabbed our water bottles and granola bars and took off.

I had to park over a mile from the park. Those from the island were filling the small parking lot there. TV trucks and radio towers clogged the parking lot. Sadie was a real trooper and didn't complain about the walk.

"Have you heard anything from Sash or Bessie?" I asked as we hurried toward the chaotic scene.

Sadie, tears in her eyes, nodded no.

I asked a couple with children if Sadie could stay with them. I explained I had no sitter and had to report the story. They nodded. I left the granola bars with them. They hadn't eaten in a while.

I spotted Commander Burke and raced to her side. "Commander, do you remember me from yesterday?"

"Yes, yes. I was pleased you wrote a piece that didn't increase the fear."

"Thanks, but my boss is none too happy. What more do you know?"

Commander Burke said flatly, "There was a sighting of a long, colorful snakelike creature loping through the water. We snapped a few pictures, but even with high-end cameras, they are blurry."

I looked carefully at the picture. Bessie! I wondered if she was traveling so fast that she blurred the picture.

"Commander, maybe she was traveling at a high rate of speed," I said.

"She?"

"Uh, the creature." I had slipped.

"I hadn't thought of that. If it was, it must have gone farther than we calculated. I must go and tell the scientists to recalculate. Please excuse me." The commander ran off.

I saw that a TV reporter was giving a live report. Darn! I had been scooped. What would my boss say? I hurried over to the staging area and listened. The reporter, Esme, a good friend of mine, was in the middle of his report:

After the divers returned to the ship, it was decided to immediately begin searching the other four caves. Since the first cave appeared to have been empty for at least a few days or a week, the scientists thought that the creatures might be out in the lake feeding, which meant it might be safe to explore.

The ships' captains sent out ROVs and AUVs to explore the other caves before they sent in diving teams. That is when tourists on Put-in-Bay saw and photographed a colorful, snakelike creature slithering through the lake.

The reporter held up the pictures of Bessie. I gasped, but not for the same reasons the crowd was gasping. It was our Bessie. What kind of trouble was she in? The reporter continued:

*After further exploration, the scientists found that each cave had a sepa-
rate, well-hidden entrance up to the surface of Put-in-Bay Island. What
astounded the researchers was that the trail into each cave entrance was
well-worn and recently used. The researchers could find no record of these
trails or the new caves. There was no folklore of the caves, no survey map
records. After asking the residents, they could find no one who knew
anything about these trails, let alone the caves.*

*When it came time for the scientists to explore the caves, the first thing
they determined was that the nests for the land-dwelling creatures were
like the nests great apes built, but much bigger. The nests were rock rings,
about three feet high and fifteen feet across, filled with dried grass, moss,
and a soft top layer of eastern hophornbeam tree leaves.*

*DNA was found in the nests and floor. The scientists are rushing the
results. That's all I have for now. Esme Benavides for TV3, WKYC,
Cleveland.*

I was stunned. I found a space at a picnic table near Sadie and the
family I left her with to begin writing my report. Sadie ran to me in
tears. She had bloody knees, and her hands were cut by rocks.

"Those kids are playing kill the monster. I told them Bessie wasn't
a monster but my friend. They pushed me down."

I was thunderstruck. I hadn't told Sadie not to say anything about
Bessie.

"Oh, honey, sh... Don't say any more. We could be in danger if you
tell."

Sadie started crying harder. "I didn't think. I didn't think."

I looked up from her tearful face and found a crowd had gathered
around us. Word had spread.

"What does your child know about the monsters?" asked Esme. "I
heard rumors she has seen and played with them."

"Esme, you are my friend. Kill this story. Sadie has a wild imagination."

Esme looked at me closely. For a minute, I thought she would be
on my side. Then she said, "Janet, Sadie knew details about the

monster that the Navy hasn't released to anyone. Commander Burke is looking for both of you. And I can't ignore this story."

I grabbed Sadie's hand, and we fled. We looked back, and Navy officers were on our tail. Our car was so far away. I didn't think we'd make it.

Just as the Navy officers closed in on us, large, furry hands grabbed us both. We screamed. Then Sadie said, "It's Sash."

The Navy officers drew their weapons, but not in time; Sash had taken us into a cave, one we didn't know about. Bessie was there too.

"Bessie," exclaimed Sadie. She ran and hugged her.

"No time now, Sadie," Bessie communicated. "How long can you hold your breath?"

We shrugged.

"Okay, you will have to for a while. Get on my back. I will take you to my sister in Lake Ontario. Don't be alarmed. She is still a dragon, but she put out her own fire after she was sighted many eons ago. You will be safe with her."

"Where will you go?" Sadie asked.

"For now, back to my mother in Scotland. Sash and friends will be nearby in case you need him. He has your credit cards and the money you have stashed at your home. He will bring it to you so you can start a new life in Buffalo, New York."

I didn't have time to think. We simply allowed Sash to put us on a seat he had built for us to ride Bessie. Before we could protest, we were underwater. After what seemed like an eternity, we were out of the water. Sadie and I gasped for air, but we were okay. We held Bessie tightly and awaited our new life in New York.

EPILOGUE
A REPORT FILED BY ESME

When the scientists ran DNA analysis of the nest floors, they found a previously unknown reptile. The problem was that there weren't any modern reptiles large enough to make those footprints or that needed nests as big as they found.

Underwater sonar found a huge pair of underwater creatures. The scientists, with the help of the Navy, set up cameras in the new underwater entrance. The scientists entered the new caves through the four new lava tubes and found that the new lava tube entrances onto the island were camouflaged like the first one they found. The scientists were accompanied by a fully armed crew from the ship. Each group of scientists came to the same conclusion when they saw the land-based creature's nests. The scientists believed that the land-based creatures were building nests like the ones great apes build. With this realization, the scientists were anxious to get the results of the DNA sampling. After they finished surveying the new underwater caves and lava tubes, the ship with LiDAR got hits that looked like a huge pair of underwater creatures. The largest was about sixty feet long, the smaller about twenty feet.

The scientists extracted DNA from these nests. It seemed the creatures were distant—very distant—decedents of a fossilized creature related to apes. The scientists began researching local lore about a creature called yeti or sasquatch. In their search, they found that people all over the world reported sightings of this creature.

It was obvious that the cave nests had been occupied within the last few weeks, since the leaves appeared to be recently placed in the nests. The researchers hid dozens more remote monitoring cameras, as they had done in the first cave and lava tubes, in hopes of glimpsing whatever was using the caves.

Two days after they picked up the creatures using LiDAR, the alarms went off outside one of the lava tubes.

When the first sounds began coming from just inside the cave entrance, the researchers were confused. It was a series of loud clicks from multiple individuals. It wasn't until they saw the creatures that they figured out the noise. Each creature was walking along while making clicking sounds with its tongue. The hairy creatures were using the clicks as echolocation to walk in the dark caves, like what bats and blind humans do. The scientists were amazed that the sasquatch had developed echolocation and hypothesized that early man had also utilized this method of exploring deep caves, since they never found evidence of soot in any of the caves where early humans lived and drew cave paintings.

A young child, Sadie Smith, who disappeared with her mother, Janet, called the sea creature Bessie. She said Bessie, and the sasquatch she called Sash, had used all the caves. Anthropologists, who were called in by the Navy, using radiocarbon dating, found that both creatures had been continuously using the caves by for over 200,000 years.

The researchers were confused how that many sasquatches could be on Put-in-Bay Island, since it is only 3.7 miles long by 1.5 miles wide. The island itself is three miles off the coast of Ohio. They were sure the sasquatch couldn't swim, so they began searching for other ways to the island. It took twenty searchers three weeks using ground penetrating radar to find how the sasquatch traveled to the island. The new caves on the island were nothing compared to the surprising way the sasquatch traveled from the mainland to the island. They found a huge lava tube that started two miles inland from the shores of Lake Erie in Ohio to the island five miles away. The lave tube was no small deal. It was over thirty feet tall and twenty feet wide most of the way. Surprisingly, the it had been cleared of lose rocks, most of which were used in the sasquatch beds inside the cave or to build short walls to separate the sasquatch nests from the Bessie nests. There was no indication that the two species had any issues with each other, and it appeared that they lived in harmony.

Apparently, the sasquatch were omnivores like humans, and Bessie ate fish, so there was no competition between them. Conversely, it appeared that the Bessie shared their fish with the sasquatch, and the sasquatch brought Bessie small game like birds and rabbits, which were plentiful on Put-in-Bay Island.

The researchers found that 2 million years ago, there had been an underground volcanic eruption that created half a dozen lava tubes on the mainland, extending out into Lake Erie. The largest tube went all the way to the island, and the geologists found that the eruption had created Put-in-Bay. At some point 200,000 years ago, the sasquatch found the lava tubes and subsequently found Put-in-Bay Island.

As the Navy releases more information, I will duly report it. Esme Benavides for TV3.

WHERE'S SASH?

PROLOGUE

Sadie seemed agitated. "What is it, honey?" I asked.

Sadie whispered, "Bessie and her sister are arguing about us."

I nodded. Bessie's sister, Spitzy, had welcomed us into her home. I thought she was getting tired of us staying. We had been in Bessie's sister's cave for a few weeks now. After riding aways on Bessie's back, she took us to a series of underground tunnels that connected her cave to her sister's. We were unable to use the caves to travel the entire way because some had water too high for us. We walked for days. Bessie guided us at great risk to herself. She could only withstand being out of the water for a short time.

"Bessie, you've been out of the water for seven days now. Are you okay?" I asked.

"What's a day?" Bessie looked confused.

"You know—twenty-four hours. Daylight and night."

Bessie was still befuddled. "I can stay out of the water for a century. That's what I meant by a short time." Sadie and I doubled over in laughter. A century? The human sense of time is different from sea creatures.

Bessie had told her we'd be here for a century, tops. Bessie had delayed her trip to Scotland to hide with her mother. Sadie and I had traveled many miles on Bessie's back, escaping the hostile environment near our home, when it was discovered that we were friends with Bessie and Sash. Sash had told us he would meet us there with money and credit cards so we could establish a new life. He was a no-show. Sadie, Bessie, and I were beside ourselves. We knew Sash started out going through the series of underground tunnels that Bessie and Sash used to visit relatives. Sash's siblings were scattered throughout the Great Lakes region. It was too dangerous to travel by land most of the time. Groups of people had formed who said they had seen Bigfoot. Sasquatches were insulted by the name. *Everything* about them was big.

What had become of Sash?

Bessie sent telepathic messages to Sadie as we sat in the cave waiting to hear what she and her sister had decided. She was trying to reassure us all would be well. I could not believe that it would be. Aside from not having a home or a job, we were very worried about Sash's whereabouts.

After what seemed like forever, Bessie slithered into our part of cave. "Spitzy is not upset you are still here. You've been here just a few minutes. We were arguing about who should go look for Sash. Spitzy's sasquatch, Chichi, is willing to join her on the journey. I wanted to go, but Spitzy forbade it. Sisters," Bessie said indignantly.

Sadie communicated back, "Sisters. I wish I had some." She looked glum.

"I didn't mean it, Sadie," Bessie said. "I love all my siblings. But we do squabble."

"What are you saying?" I asked Sadie. Bessie could send messages to Sadie and block them from me. At times, I could receive her messages, but not all the time. I was a bit jealous of the relationship between Sadie and Bessie.

Sadie quickly explained the plan. Spitzy and Chichi would begin the search for Sash. Chichi was incredibly worried about her brother. Bessie would gather her relatives as she searched. Chichi would stay to take care of us. Neither needed to prep for their quest, since they could catch their food as they traveled. We would need Chichi to feed us.

Early the next morning, Spitzy left. She hugged Sadie and me before she left. Her hug gave me a serene feeling. I hope the feeling will last.

1

I can't keep running like this for much longer. I think my captors are far enough away that I can climb into a tree after I grab some food.

I keep thinking of the last message Bessie received from Sash nearly a week ago. Sadie and Bessie have not heard a word since.

Bessie thought it would take much less than a century for Sash to reach us. He hasn't arrived. Spitzy has been a wonderful hostess. Her sasquatch, Chichi, has been finding meat and vegetables for us. She is risking her own safety for us, two refugees she hardly knows. Spitzy had extinguished her flame to mourn the loss of the dragons' wings and fire. At much physical risk, she relit her fire to cook the food for us. I am amazed at the generous nature of these sea creatures. When Spitzy told us her story, Sadie and I wept. She told us about her life when we first arrived:

DXERT. Oh, sorry. I forgot you don't speak sea creature. When my family and friends were attacked, I was traveling. Mom, Nessie, used to become enraged when I went on a long journey far in the mountains in Asia. But there was so much of the world to see. On the other side of the world, there was a huge land mass with glorious mountains. They stretched from the top of the mass to the bottom. High in the mountains, it was cold—a *delightful cold—with gorgeous scenery. I loved winter. I would make snow creatures in the snow to keep me company. I made one to look like Bessie and one to look like Mom. I cried when they melted. I was lucky my flame didn't go out.*

I was staying there when my family was changed forever. I knew I should finish the exploration of this wonderful world and head home, but I was just too enamored with the new place. I wanted someone in my family to move here with me. There was no reason for all of us to live in Asia. I thought it would be good for us to expand our species' environment.

I had sent Mom messages telling her of this magnificent new world, but she refused to let any of my siblings or friends join me. I was quite angry with her and stayed longer in my new home. Bessie and my other siblings begged me to come home. I guess Mom was hard to live with when she was angry. I was the child who tested her. Bessie was the obedient daughter. Mom loved her best. None of my siblings minded. We all adored Bessie. She was good at mediating fights, warning us of danger, and finding the best morsels of food.

I loved the lair in Asia. There were thousands of us. The best times were when Mom and Dad sent all of us on a hunt for food. Our friends would stay behind and prepare part of our area for a festival. At festivals, we would play all kinds of games.

My favorite, because I always won, was to see how far we could send our fire into the air. Those that entered the contest flew into a circular arrangement and hovered above the mountaintops. One at a time, we would send fire into the middle of the circle. I lost my first match, but in the later years, I had practiced my skills. One of my friends decided to challenge me at the last festival. I barely won. I was ashamed of my performance and took off to see the world against my mother's and father's advice. I refused to return until I could breathe fire farther than any of us could imagine.

I had been in the mountains in the new world for nearly an eon, much to Mom's shame. Other families were gossiping about how she couldn't control her children. One day, I was knocked from the air in terrible pain. I kept hearing screams from family. Every nerve in my body was on fire. I couldn't move my wings or feet. I landed on my side on the top of a moun-

tain that was not near my liar. One of my wings was broken. I was in agony, but I received a faint message from Bessie. She told me not to come home. It was unsafe. I now know what I felt was the maiming of my family and friends.

I don't know how long I was trapped on the unfamiliar mountaintop. For centuries, I couldn't move, and I was slowly starving. I tried crawling down the mountain to look for food, but the pain was too severe. None of us had ever died, that we could remember. I didn't know all our friends died from the maiming and my family was barely hanging on. I knew I'd be the first in my family to die. I tried to send Mom and Dad a message to come help me. They didn't respond. Had I angered them so much that they had abandoned me? I feel bad now that I know they were suffering too.

On what I thought was my last day, I was awakened by the smell of food. I figured I was hallucinating. I opened my eyes to a feast. I stopped myself from gorging on it because I knew my stomach would rebel; having a large amount would make me vomit. I also noticed my wing had been tampered with. I couldn't move it at all. I was terrified at first; then a calm came over me that explained it was a splint to keep it in place so it could heal properly. I would have less pain this way.

I stayed on the mountaintop for several centuries as the wing healed. I kept receiving rations of food. I had no idea who my benefactor was. One day I woke, and the splint was no longer on my wing. I moved it gingerly. It moved in the correct way but was stiff. I had no range of motion. Again, I felt a presence that told me to exercise the wing daily, but to do it on the mountaintop. The presence said not to fly until the wing was stronger. I obeyed the presence. It seemed to have my best interests at heart.

Another century passed before I could fly, and only short distances. It took many years to gain back my strength. Although I was being taken care of by the presence, I knew I needed to go home. I was realizing that the horrible pain that caused me to crash was a signal that my family was in great danger.

One day, I had the courage to begin my journey. I didn't get far the first few days, not wanting to tax my repaired wing. I knew I would need super-dragon strength to fly over the large body of water that separated the land mass I was on to get to the land mass where my family was. I didn't know *there was an underground cave system I could have used. As a dragon, I hated to walk, but I could have flown, rested, walked, and then flown again. We all use this system to hide when we have been spotted.*

Sadie interrupted, "Spitzy, does that mean Sash is hidden in that system?"

Spitzy nodded. "We can hope."

I could tell Spitzy wasn't sure. She had confided in me that she had stopped hearing from Sash. Spitzy was baffled that Sash's communication method had been stifled. She worried the authorities were experimenting on him.

"Sadie," I said, "let Spitzy continue."

Where was I? Oh, yes. Luckily, the wind was with me when I left my adopted land mass. I knew I would never see it again and felt terrible about it. The land and the presence had been good to me.

When I arrived home, I didn't hear the usual buzz of my species. All I saw were decaying wings and blood. How had the wings been severed? The bigger question was why.

I rushed to my parent's lair. Mom was lying on her side. Where her wings had once been was bandaged. My father was nowhere to be found. When I approached Mom, her eyes were swollen shut.

"Momma," I cried. "What happened?"

"I'm glad you have returned, my dear daughter," Mom said.

She never called me dear. I tried to question her further, but she fell back asleep. Mom must have summoned me when she was hurt. It was best to let her sleep. Where were my siblings and friends? I went to other lairs looking for my siblings. I could not figure out why my species was not out and about. Why were my siblings, especially Bessie, not ministering to my mother?

I went to Bessie's lair first. I had to step over the severed wings. I decided to hover over them to make better time and not get blood on my feet. I was tired from my long trip, so I used my last bit of strength to find out what happened.

As I approached Bessie's lair, I picked up her signal. She was crying for me to come home and help, yet when I entered the cave, she wasn't there. Where could she be?

I did not know where to go. Going up and down the mountain would tax me. I decided to go to my lair and rest. It didn't look like I would find anyone today.

I have no idea how long I slept. At least a century, I suppose. I was hungry when I woke. Beside my nest was a meal. Who had delivered it? I ate as much as I could. Then I set out to find my kind.

Sadie and I wept. Even though Bessie had told us the story, we hadn't known these details. I suppose Bessie tried to spare us the pain of knowing. Spitzy was much more direct in her storytelling.

While Spitzy was relaying her thoughts, Bessie had been sending signals to Sash. She ran into the part of the cave we were in.

"Sadie... Janet..." Bessie was communicating with both of us. "I heard from Chichi that a signal has been sent to the sasquatch in the area to gather. She doesn't know why. She will send more news as she gets it."

There was tension in the cave that night. None of us slept well.

2

More time passed. It was hard for me to keep track of the days. I had a paper calendar in my purse when we left our home, but it had been damaged by the water. I crossed off each day. I felt it necessary to stay on human time even though, to the sea creatures, time was measured in centuries with a century being a day in their minds. Another two weeks passed.

I knew Bessie and Spitzy were squabbling; Sadie could not get a read on what about. I was concerned we had overstayed our welcome. I had no idea where we would go. I only had a few dollars in the purse I brought with me. We had no time to go to the bank or gather important documents. Sash was going to do that for us. He also planned to sell our house, so we'd have a nest egg. I was upset that the house had to be sold. It was the dream home that Joseph and I built, my last tie to my dear husband.

Sadie eventually found out we were still safe with Spitzy. I was relieved we still had a place to stay. I was still concerned about Sash. We didn't hear for a while why Chichi had called a meeting, until one day when she appeared in our cave.

Sadie ran to hug her. They embraced for a long time. Then Chichi came to me and laid her huge hand on my heart. I had this overwhelming feeling that Joseph was nearby. How could that be? He was gone. But the thought comforted me more than anything I had ever felt from a sasquatch. Chichi also let me know that the sasquatches were gathering to look for Sash. Chichi would stay to protect us and give us food. The others would find Sash. She assured me that they would find them. When I communicated to her that I didn't understand how she knew that, she gave me a knowing smile. I believe that sasquatches had different intelligences than us humans. Some of those were superior to our way of knowing. Maybe large creatures aren't something to be afraid of.

Bessie left to join the sasquatches on their journey to find Sash. I was surprised how much I missed her presence. She must have known, because her signal came to me as clearly as it always had to Sadie. All we could do was wait.

One day, I asked Chichi, "Does every sea creature have a sasquatch?"

Chichi nodded. "We felt so bad for maiming innocent creatures that we made a pact with them to each choose a sea creature, or sometimes more to protect. The sea creatures have been most forgiving, even helping us when sasquatches are in distress, that we come together as sasquatches to find our lost brother or sister.

Chichi was so good with Sadie. I think she could have a stand-up comedy act, except no one would go. She played endless games of Uno with Sadie. Sadie expressed to Chichi that she wished she could jump rope. Chichi said she had some rope. I cut a piece so Sadie could jump. Chichi wanted to try it too. She cut a long piece for herself. When she started to jump, the entire caves swayed and churned.

"Stop, Chichi," I screamed over the loud roar coming from the earth. But Chichi was having so much fun, she kept jumping.

Sadie kept sending Chichi signals to stop. It wasn't working. I was afraid the entire cave would collapse. Then I saw Sadie's face light up like it did when she had an idea. I could tell she was contacting Bessie. Within seconds, Chichi stopped. Sadie and I collapsed in each other's arms.

Chichi looked at us and at the cave and saw cracks in the walls. Items from the shelves were all over the floor. My nest was shattered; Sadie's too.

Chichi looked shocked and embarrassed. "It felt so good. I could think of nothing else. Thank goodness you had Bessie send me an emergency signal. I'm so sorry." I wanted to strangle Chichi. I was beyond words. Didn't she know her massive size almost killed us?

Before I could admonish Chichi, Sadie said, "We know it was an accident. But don't do it again!"

I almost laughed. Sadie sounded like I do when I correct her. I stifled the laugh and began to tidy the cave.

"No, no," said Chichi. "It's my fault. I'll clean."

I wanted to let her for the trouble she caused, but Sadie has a bigger heart than mine.

"We all live here. We all clean up," said Sadie.

Sadie was right. She must have received her kind heart from her father. We all pitched in to repair the damage. It still took a week in human years. At night, while Sadie and I slept, Chichi left the cave to scavenge for supplies for the repairs. The system worked well. We were rested when the supplies arrived and could start right away. I know that Chichi worked on the damage to Spitzy's cave. The pounding affected areas far and wide. In fact, Bessie messaged us and said an earthquake had been reported under Lake Ontario. Scientists were baffled because there was not a fault there.

I wrote most days, even as I helped repair the cave. I was trying to capture the entire experience. Would it be a bestseller? I was hoping. If it were, I would be able to support Sadie and send her to college. The writing was therapeutic. It calmed me. At times, I felt like Bessie was guiding my writing. Words just flowed onto the page.

To help my writing, I asked Chichi one day how she came to be Spitzy's protector.

"You didn't figure it out?" Spitzy asked.

Sadie and I shook our heads.

Chichi let out a belly laugh, something she had learned from us. When she stopped laughing, she said, "I was the one who found

Spitzy on the mountains on the other land mass. I took care of her. After I heard that the sasquatch were who cut off the dragons' wings, I urged sasquatches to make amends to the dragons. The dragons were mostly sea creatures by then. But the complex tunnel system that goes all over this world and our telepathic communication allowed me to find the source of Spitzy's accident. I roamed to Scotland and found that my blood relatives were the ones who killed many dragons. I ministered to the ones left, which happened to be Spitzy's and Bessie's family. Then I lead the coup."

"Coup?" I asked

"Yes, a few of the younger sasquatches were upset by the carnage. We were able to overthrow the old leadership. Our first act was to round up the leaders of the carnage. They were banished. They now live far atop the world in a land of snow and ice."

Such a long, rich history. I was even more compelled to chronicle it.

While we waited for word, we all wore on each other's nerves. One night, Chichi was agitated. She had snapped at Sadie. I knew she had been in touch with Bessie. I was afraid to ask what she had heard. Chichi was blocking the news from me.

Where was Sash?

3

"Esme Benavides reporting for TV3 News in Cleveland. Scientists who are still searching the lava tubes and caves around Lake Erie have reported seismic activity in the caves. They were able to trace the waves that rocked our city to underground activity in Lake Ontario. Some scientists are speculating that the sea creature associated with the hairy creature that the Navy has in custody in Buffalo, New York, is in some way related to the earthquake. The team is rushing to Buffalo, where they captured the hairy monster.

"Commander Burke says Navy Seals have been called in to explore the underground caves connected by lava tubes. The area that was explored was to the east. The Seals found footprints of a large creature walking eastward. The trail ended in Buffalo, but the commander could not share any more details. They were classified.

"The scientists have been called in to explore the trail. I am traveling with the scientists as the lead reporter. Look forward to my reports in the next several days from Buffalo."

4

Janet, I'm trying to break through the ties that bind me. The humans found me in my Buffalo cave just as I was closing in on Spitzy's cave. I was so close. I have hidden what you need in a lava tube that is hidden. It hasn't been found. Yet. I was so close to you when I was hit with several electrical shocks that incapacitated me. I must have been unconscious for days. I'm not hurt, but I am tied down by large bands of metal. Hug Sadie for me, but please don't tell her that I have been captured. Can you send help?

5

I was awakened by a message from Sash. I wondered if I could send it to Bessie so she would know he was captured. I tried. I am not sure it went through. But if he could contact me, he could contact Bessie, right? Those two should be the same species. They love each other so. They are soulmates, just as I was with Jospeh.

Joseph had been on my mind. We met under the most unusual circumstances. I was reporting my first story for the Erie paper. He was the photographer on the story. Usually, I have little to say to photographers. They were visual and artsy, even if this one was super handsome. They are also women chasers. I dated one for a while. What a mistake. I was verbal and dealt with facts. Usually, visual people and I clash. I was avoiding him. I didn't want a kerfuffle on company time. I left the scene and hurried home.

That evening, I had just settled in with tea and the dating site I was on when my doorbell rang. I had no idea who could be ringing so late. I had talked to my mom earlier, so she knew I was beat. I urged her to stay home, to not bring soup. I was in sweatpants and a ponytail. It couldn't possibly be my ex-boyfriend, Fred. I had warned him that the next time he came over, I would file for a restraining order. I sure could pick losers.

The photographer, Joseph, was at the door. He was soaked through from the rainstorm that had plagued me when I was covering the story. I knew I had to be polite and let him in—against my best instincts. I guess the two of us would have that fight.

"What do you want?" I glared at him.

He laughed. "You don't even know me; why are you so hostile?"

The rain was coming down. He looked like a drowned rat. "I know your type."

He laughed. I opened the door for him to come in. He dripped water in the foyer. I ran to get him a towel.

"I knew you were kind," he said as he dried off.

"I just didn't want water on my wood floor." He looked ashamed. The soft side of me asked, "Do you want some tea?"

"Sure." He didn't step off the tile floor in the foyer until he was dried enough to not drip. At least, he had manners.

I motioned to the chair across from my couch. Before I sat down, I put another log on the fire. He was shivering. I told him to take the throw on the back of the chair and wrap himself in it. Why was I being so kind? I knew how the evening would end. Fight!

It ended, but not the way I thought. We talked until dawn. He crashed on my couch.

When I woke in the morning, he was still sleeping. He had the goofiest smile on his face in his sleep. I couldn't help but smile.

We were together from that night on. We married six months later. Mom was furious. She said we didn't know each other well enough. Joseph had been kind to my mom during while she was hostile to him. After our five-year anniversary, when I was pregnant with Sadie, she relented.

In Spitzy and Chichi's cave, for some reason, Joseph seemed nearer to me than ever.

The next day, I woke to Chichi's face. I was startled.

"I didn't mean to startle you," she communicated.

"I was dreaming of my husband," I said.

"Keep dreaming. Dreams come true." Chichi left my nest with a smile.

I decided to get up and rose from the nest. I had to check myself for bugs. Bessie had been careful to keep the nests clean, but since Bessie left, Chichi wasn't as vigilant. Sadie already had her breakfast. Chichi was so good to her. My breakfast was there for me to eat.

I was exceptionally calm that day. Chichi was still upset but had tempered her mood so as not to upset Sadie. I worked all day on my book. I would have to publish it as fiction, right?

6

I received a message from Sash early the next morning:

I feel my brothers and sisters are nearby. They are risking their lives for me. I worry about Bessie. She is with them. She's my soulmate. Why did she risk her life to save me? I only want her safe, even if I perish.

Before I could answer Sash, I received a message from Bessie that they had located Sash, but he was in trouble. She didn't give details. She and I had found out that Sadie's ability to receive messages telepathically was growing. Sadie would sometimes intercept messages meant for my ears only. I hastily transmitted Sash's message to Bessie along with pleading with her to stay safe for Sash.

Sadie and Chichi were not in the cave when I arose. I was a bit concerned, but I knew Chichi would guard Sadie for Bessie and me. I was still concerned. I spent the morning practicing my telepathic powers. Sadie had given me some lessons.

"Where did you learn these tricks?" I had asked her.

"Bessie has been giving me lessons. She told me it's your turn to learn."

I was doubting my sanity. I'm sitting in an underground cave that is part of a worldwide system of caves and lava tubes outside Lake Ontario with creatures I used to read about in storybooks. That was bad enough, but now I was taking instructions on how to hone my mind to be telepathic?

I worked on the lessons that Sadie had conveyed to me for over two hours. I had completely forgotten I had not seen Sadie that day. My mind was hearing so many voices. I had found an entire new world of creatures who used their minds. Sadie told me that, at first, I'd have trouble tuning out the voices I didn't want to hear. She was right. I heard foreign languages—French, Italian, Portuguese, Spanish, German... I was sidetracked by two Arabic-speaking lovers separated by miles. I was crying at their plight. Their story was tragic like mine was with Joseph. I finally shook my head like Sadie showed me to clear the voices, but one remained. It sounded familiar.

Sweet, Jay-Joe. I still love you. I miss Sadie. Trust the sasquatches.

Jay-Joe! I nearly fainted. Jay-Joe was what Joseph and I called each other. I could have sworn it was Joseph's voice. I knew it couldn't be. I was tired, confused, and worried. I knew I was hallucinating Joseph's voice because I had lost Sadie. The last thing Joseph said to me before he died was to take care of Sadie. I had let him down.

Where was Sadie? I began to call for her telepathically as I walked through the chain of caves. Spitzy and Chichi had a grouping of caves underground. Some had water. Some were dry. Chichi and Sash, on one of his visits, had created a water-purifying system. He said it was a precaution in case they needed to house humans. Sash always believed that they may have to jail humans who were their enemies. The hope was that they could show the humans they meant no harm. The water system wasn't needed until we arrived. I enjoyed the fresh water it provided. Sash had even put in a human shower on a subsequent trip. He had spent centuries, along with his fellow sasquatches, studying humans. He knew we liked to be clean. I had noticed a shower in Sash's cave. When I asked him about it, he looked ashamed.

"What's wrong?" I asked him

The message came to me in a whisper. "I found I liked a clean body, too. When I visit my kin, I must throw dirt on me and roll in the mud before I see them." I chuckled and assured him his secret was safe with me. I had already been sworn to secrecy by Chichi, who I caught in the shower one day.

Chichi told me that most sasquatches were wary of humans. But not Sash. He thought they were amazing creatures. His study of us was eons long, since we were Australopithecus. He and Chichi had been fascinated by how much they looked like us. We tried to communicate telepathically, but their brains weren't developed enough. We kept an eye on them. A branch of Australopithecus developed into other hominoids. It was when homo sapiens sapiens developed that we found a brain developed enough to communicate with. Most humans ignored our messages, but we found that children were more apt to believe we were real.

It made sense, I thought. My mother was a child when she talked to Bessie. So was Sadie. I realized, it wasn't until the sea creatures and the sasquatches had chosen me to be the first adult.

As I searched madly through the caves for Sadie, I kept hearing voices I thought I had turned off at the end of my lesson. The one that sounded like Joseph kept giving suggestions to her. Damnit, Joseph, let me know where she is. In an instant, I felt the word *safe* flow over me. Safe? But where? Where's Sadie? Where's Sash?

7

By the time night fell, I was exhausted. I had searched every cave. I knew she wasn't in the caves I knew of. I feared going into caves I had never seen. Who might lurk within? I also knew Chichi was not with her. Terrible fatigue overcame me. I just had to lie down and sleep. As I slept, something kept waking me. I would call for Chichi or Sadie, hoping that they returned, then doze off. I felt like I had been drugged.

8

"Esme Benavides reporting from Buffalo, New York, by the coast of Lake Ontario.

"Events have been fast paced since I arrived. The scientists quickly set up their equipment to see where the seismic activity had occurred. The equipment kept failing to read the waves. Scientists were baffled. The Navy sent some of its equipment. It too failed.

"I talked to Commander Guiliana Burke today. I'm sure my viewers remember her reports in Erie. Commander Burke said as soon as the divers arrive, there will be underwater exploration of the cave system. The same lava tube system is present.

"Esme Benavides reporting live for— Wait, I see a disturbance not far from me. Fred, can you move the camera over where the Navy officers and local police are gathered? ...What? Wait? I'm getting messages in my earpiece. Hold on....

"The Buffalo Police have apprehended Sadie Smith and a monster. Sadie has been taken to the local jail. Sadie, if you remember, was the girl who said that these unexplained creatures were her friends. She caused a local panic. Erie Police have been looking for her and her mother, Janet Smith, ever since that fateful day in near Lake Erie where the creatures emerged. Sadie is only seven years old and appears to be brainwashed by these creatures. I'm now walking over to the commander to see if she knows more.

"Commander Burke, do you have a minute to talk?"

"Not really, but I can answer a couple of questions."

"Is it true that Sadie Smith and another hairy monster have been captured?"

"Yes. The Navy Seals were instrumental in capturing them. They were hiding in a cave near land. The hairy creature is strapped in the same way the first one was. This one is quieter than the large male we apprehended three weeks ago. I believe this one is a female. It's hard to see the genitals because of the fur. This one will be shaved, as was the first. The girl is at the police station. She is in surprisingly good health. It amazes me. She is clean and well fed. She will not explain how she kept clean, who she was with, or the whereabouts of her mother. I need to go now, Ms. Benavides."

"Viewers, it is confirmed that there is yet another hairy creature in police captivity. Signing off for TV3, Esme Benavides."

9

I snapped out of my delirium. I realized that one of the sasquatches or sea creatures had drugged me until the worst was over. Now, I was hearing Chichi's cries. I couldn't understand her. It was a garble of English and sasquatch language. I kept trying to send calming signals to her. Eventually, Chichi calmed, and I deciphered her message.

Chichi said she and Sadie had been captured. It was part of her plan to free Sash. All the police around Sash had left to capture her. This would give Sash time to escape. He had told Bessie he thought he could break his chains. If not, his brothers were on their way. He'd be out in no time. She said Sadie was a real trooper and not giving any information to the police. Her biggest fear was that the scientists would shave her as they had Sash.

I was relieved. I didn't want her giving any more away. Then it hit me—my baby was in jail. I tried to contact her, but my mind was too garbled to send much of anything. The authorities were torturing Sash. Chichi would be next. I had to go to them. Chichi was sending me a frantic signal not to leave the cave system. I couldn't listen. I had to go to my child and friends.

Since I had become accustomed to the smell of Chichi, I thought I might be able to track her by scent. Once I exited the cave system, I was overwhelmed by the smell of the woods and the industrial areas around the lake. I gave the smell idea up. What made me think I could track like a sasquatch?

I figured Chichi and Sadie had taken off through the woods to hide as long as possible. I made my way through the forest, and it gave way to an industrial park. I could see in the distance what looked like TV cameras and lights in front of a large building. I wasn't sure what industries were around the lake. Were the factories spewing toxic waste? I wasn't sure if I should approach. I wanted to, but we couldn't all be in jail.

Suddenly, I was grabbed by both arms. Whoever it was put my hands behind my back. "Don't be afraid. Shh."

"Esme?" I whispered.

"Yes. Let's go back into the woods."

Once we thought were shielded from the press, we collapsed on a large stool that had been carved into a most comfortable seat. We looked at each other and said simultaneously, "Sasquatch!" I wonder how much Esme knew about them.

Esme had with her some bottled water and protein bars. I had left the cave with no provisions, so I wolfed down both.

"Have you seen Sadie?" I asked with a mouthful of protein bar.

"She's fine. She's a brave girl."

I was relieved that someone I trusted had seen her. I could relax a bit. "What do you know about the sasquatch and sea creatures?" I asked hesitantly.

"You tell me," Esme answered.

"No, what is your interest?"

"A Pulitzer Prize-winning story."

I gave Esme a harsh look. "Figures. My daughter is in danger, and you want a story."

Esme looked chagrined. "I'm sorry. That must sound cold-hearted to you."

"Tell me what you know about the sasquatch," I demanded.

"I grew up on the shore of Lake Huron. I knew Bessie and Spitzy's sibling, Mithilesh. He's called Meow." I must have looked puzzled, because Esme continued, "He's built like a cat."

"A cat?"

Esme nodded. "When the dragons took to the water, some turned into creatures who look like Bessie. Others stayed on the land and took on land animal characteristics. That's what happened to Meow. While on land, he was bit by a lynx. He didn't think he would live and was unconscious for a few centuries. When he woke, he moved differently. He went to the lake, not far from where I lived, and saw his reflection. It scared him so much he fell in and sunk all the way to the bottom. He found he could breathe underwater. As he explored the bottom of the lake, he discovered what looked like an ancient civilization. He explored the civilization for an eon. There had been an active city there, but he couldn't tell what kind of creatures built it."

"Whoa, Esme! My mind can't take any more monsters."

Indignantly, Esme said, "He's not a monster."

"I'm sorry, Esme," I said. "I didn't mean to call Meow a monster. It's been so overwhelming, and with Sadie missing..."

Esme interrupted. "I understand. Meow was my first love. I'm not sure I could ever love a human that way." Her eyes pooled with tears. Sadie isn't missing. I know where she is. She and Chichi are distracting the Navy and police from Sash. He should be able to escape."

"Yes, I know that. Chichi told me. I came to see if I could help."

Esme looked upset. "Janet, you are wanted, too." I nodded. "Chichi knew you would follow, so she left no message. How good are you at receiving the sasquatches' telepathic messages?"

"So-so, but I'm working on the training program that Sadie set up for me."

"Good. Now, you stay in the woods until you receive an all-clear signal from Bessie, Sash, Chichi, or me. I must get back to reporting. The commander will have missed me by now."

Esme rushed out of the forest. I had wanted to ask her more. I contemplated following her from a distance. But if I were captured... I stayed put as Esme had advised.

10

I kept pacing in the forest. My stomach growled. The protein bars hadn't lasted long. I was used to succulent meats and nicely roasted vegetables that Chichi prepared. She had studied humans thoroughly. I had finally paced so much that I was exhausted. I used the bench Esme and I sat on as a bed.

I must have dozed off. I was awakened by a message. I wasn't sure who from. The transmission was weak. I thought it said to go to the jail. I would be able to see Sadie there. I asked whoever it was to repeat the message. I heard *go to jail* this time. I ran out of the woods as quickly as possible, heading where I had seen Esme go. When I arrived, the TV cameras were gone. The area was deserted. I could see where the ground had been swept. Why would anyone sweep the dirt? What were they trying to hide? As I tried to plan my next move, I received another, clearer message. I thought it was Sadie. The message made no sense: *Mom, it's me, Sadie. Come help me.* But she didn't say where she was.

I made my way to what looked like the heart of the city. I asked a man who was walking briskly down the sidewalk in the downtown area where the jail was. He gave me directions. It wasn't far. I walked about three miles before I reached it. I was hot, sweaty, and scared.

Would I too be arrested? I couldn't think of that now; I had to find Sadie.

I slowly opened the door to the jail and was immediately wrestled to the ground. My heart was beating fast. I started hyperventilating. I tried to resist, but whoever tackled me was so strong—sasquatch strong. I gave up struggling. I knew couldn't outwrestle a sasquatch. As my heart slowed and breath returned to normal, I knew it was Sash who had me.

"Sash," I whispered telepathically.

"Yes," Sash said.

I turned and hugged the big galoot. "Nice," he told me. "We have no time. Chichi and Sadie are trapped. Bessie couldn't help them."

"What happened?" I asked.

Sash told me to follow him and then explained as much as he could since I had last seen him:

I was so close to getting to Chichi and Spitzy's cave system. It was so much more complex, with different passages that led nowhere. Chichi, Spitzy, Bessie, and I had designed the maze to have some dead ends so we could trap predators. Their entrance led to a metal gate being launched to keep them there. We have never had to use it. I was hopeful that Chichi and Spitzy would remember it in case their maze was invaded.

For a while, everything was a blur. I knew I'd been captured in a big net. I also knew the captors had incapacitated me. I have no idea how long I was unconscious. I was terrified when I woke and found myself tied down with metal bands from my feet to my head. I struggled to break them. I could tell I had weakened them, but whenever I did, an alarm alerted my captors. They would come into my cage, see I was still bolted down, and leave. They never checked if the bands had weakened. I kept working on the bands between the captors checking on me. I knew if I were to break free, the captors would be on me again and render me unconscious. That is when Bessie received my distress signal asking for a distraction to move the captors. She summoned Chichi and Sadie, who willingly came to cause it.

"You put my daughter in danger, Sash," I cried. "You were supposed to protect us."

"She's not in danger," Sash said. "The plan has more steps. Chichi and Sadie made themselves known to the captors and were willingly captured. Sadie is not chained. Chichi is. I sent Chichi a message about how to snap the bands. They are loose right now. She could easily escape."

"Why hasn't she?" I asked.

"Because you have to be the distraction this this time."

"How will that help?"

"You will surrender to the captors. While they are processing you and boasting to the press about her capture, Chichi will break free, grab Sadie, and all of you will escape together."

"I'll go into harm's way to free her?"

"You will not be in danger. Chichi has summoned several human adults she played with when they were children. She asked them to guard Janet when she was in custody. Once they receive a signal that Chichi and Sadie are safe, the human volunteers will grab Janet. My fellow sasquatches are waiting for the signal to escort the volunteers and you to safety."

"I am skeptical," I said. "But it doesn't matter as long as Sadie is free. You, Bessie, Chichi, and Spitzy will raise her. Ask Esme for help. She knows—"

"I know Esme well. Since she was a child on the coast of Lake Huron, I met with her many times when I visited Meow. He's such a fun fellow. When he's dry, I love to pet him and hear his purrs."

"Okay, okay."

Sash gave me directions to the part of the jail I would need to go to surrender. Then he left to help his brothers guide me out of the jail unharmed.

11

I started walking toward the place of surrender, when I was
apprehended by the people Sash had called captors. They were
Navy Seals and Coast Guard officers. Commander Burke was leading
the group. When she made eye contact with me, she said, "Janet
Smith, you are under arrest for treason."

"I want an attorney."

"You are a threat to national security. You are not entitled to one."

"I am. I am."

Then I noticed that Commander Burke made a slight head
motion from side to side. Was she trying to tell me something.

I put my hands out for the handcuffs. One officer came forward to
lock my hands, but before he could, Commander Burke said, "That's
not necessary. She doesn't have the strength of the monsters." She
said it with such distain for those I loved. Had I misinterpreted her
head movement.

"I'll take charge of the prisoner," said Commander Burke. "We
have a history."

Janet escorted me to a room she was using as an office.

"Sit there," the commander barked.

I did as I was told. The commander crossed the room and

slammed the door. Once back to her desk, she collapsed in her chair and sighed.

"I need a cup of coffee. You?" she asked.

I was confused. She had harshly led me to a room and shouted an order. Now she wanted to know if I wanted coffee. I figured she was employing a torture technique to throw me off. I refused to answer.

"Janet, it's me, Guiliana Burke," the commander said. "I'm on your side." I still refused to talk. I was not going to be tricked. "Janet, relax." She went to her coffee pot and brewed a single cup for me. I refused it.

"Okay. I guess I'll have to be the one to talk," the commander said. "I am part of an underground militia sanctioned by the Navy to explore sea creatures and their companions. For over twenty years, I have run missions to uncover just who the sea creatures are and their symbiotic relationship with the sasquatches. Yes, I had an encounter with a sea creature as a child, which made me join the Navy in hopes that I could protect these wonderful creatures. I had to rise through the ranks to be able to form a creature task force. Most of my soldiers are not aware of the true mission. They have been trained to eradicate the sea creatures and the sasquatches. A few were attracted to the unit because they too had encounters."

I gasped. "How many are there of us who know?"

Commander Burke said, "Under a thousand, that we know of. Some refuse to join our mission, afraid we are not going to be benevolent to the creatures. I'm proud to say we have saved more of them than harmed them. The harmed ones sustained their injuries from uncaring humans. We have been able to nurse some back to health. Some, we failed." I could see tears form in her eyes. She continued her story:

"My greatest loss was a sea creature I played with as a child. I can't share the story, as it is classified. Needless to say, I was devastated....

"Where was I? Yes, back to this operation. You will stay in my custody. I have a jail cell adjacent to my office where you will stay. Trusted men will bring you whatever you need. When the time is right, the mission to rescue you and the others will happen tomorrow.

"Sash told me you know part of the plan already. Now that you are in custody, Sash said he and the others will strike tomorrow."

"Janet," said the commander, "you look exhausted. Go rest. I'll lead you to your cell."

The commander was correct; it was a cell. I could see it had already been altered to have a blow-up mattress and a porta-potty. There was a table that held a platter of spaghetti and meatballs. I guess Sash or someone had told the commander that was my favorite meal. I wished I could share some with Sadie. Was she hungry? Cold?

I ate what I could and then fell into a dreamless sleep. The commander woke me up the next morning before light filtered into the cell. She said the operation was underway. I could hear commotion in other places in the jail. I heard several of the sasquatches screaming—the scream they used to terrorize humans. Before I could process all the sounds, Sash appeared at my cell and grabbed me out of it.

"Act scared!" he said.

I screamed and kicked. I could tell Sash was laughing at my attempts. "Make it sound authentic."

I doubled my effort.

I'm not sure what exit Sash was using to whisk me out of the jail. We went through an underground tunnel that I could tell had been hastily constructed by the sasquatches. No sooner than we were in the tunnel, I saw Chichi holding Sadie just ahead of us. I could relax. She was safe.

After an hour or so of walking, all of us made it to Spitzy's cave. She was already there preparing a meal. She even baked a cake. We all hugged and cried in relief. Then we had a feast and a long nap.

12

The next morning when we all woke, Sash called a meeting. I noticed something slinking in the dark corner of the cave. I didn't sense danger, but I could tell the thing, whatever it was, was wary of Sadie and me.

"We can't stay here," Sash said.

"Well, duh," said Sadie.

"Shh," I said to her. "Let Sash speak." Sadie turned to me and hugged me. She had been doing that once in a while since we returned to the cave. I noticed that Bessie was lying on Sash's lap. True love. I suddenly missed Joseph. I needed his arms to comfort me.

"It's okay, Janet," said Sash. "She's still running on adrenaline. Let her vent." I nodded.

"Let me introduce Meow," Chichi said.

Out of the shadow of the cave, crept a long red and black creature that looked like a lynx. I understood now why he was called Meow. He had a silky tail that was at least six feet long. His body was sleek like a cat's. He seemed to have fur not scales, but I was sure the fur was waterproof. His back legs were hunched up, and the paws seemed to have normal catlike claws. The front claws were six feet long. I heard a low, soft sound. He was purring. I had to resist the urge to pet him. I heard a voice.

"Please pet me. I like behind my ears."

So, Meow communicated like his siblings. I moved toward him, and he threw himself on his back and exposed his belly.

Chichi, Sash, Bessie, and Spitzy laughed. Chichi finally regained control of her laughter and said, "Once you pet Meow, he'll be a friend for life. He will follow you around asking for catnip."

"That's okay," I said. I loved cats, and Meow was a magnificent creature. I wasn't scared by his claws or teeth. Did I mention the teeth were at least three feet long and pointed?

"I can slink through the forest with Janet and Sadie on my back. I can run a thousand miles an hour. The two of you will be in my cave system in an hour," purred Meow.

"I will meet you at the cave," said Bessie. "I'm still in danger. So are Chichi and Spitzy. Chichi will go with Spitzy. Spitzy can still somewhat fly. She will keep her flame going to ward off any problems they may encounter."

I knew it would be a dangerous journey for all of us. Before we left, we had a huge feast courtesy of Chichi and Sash's hunting: chicken, duck, quail.

"We leave in the morning?" I asked. The creatures nodded. Then Sadie and I embraced the enormous and loving creatures. Sadie and I fell into a deep slumber, and I dreamt of the new places we would see in the morning on the back of a sea cat.

MEOW

PROLOGUE

Nearly a hundred years ago, in a small town on the Monongahela River near West Newton, Pennsylvania, a small town in the mountains near Pittsburgh...

"Alice," said Vera, "where did these muddy clothes come from?" Alice was hiding under her bed. She had gone to the river to play with Ogua again after her mother had strictly forbidden her to. She related to her mom and dad strange stories about a giant turtle over 500 pounds with a fifteen-foot tail. Spikes run down the middle of the creature's back. Ogua was a turtle-like creature. He seemed to be painted a fluorescent green; it could glow in the dark.

"I know you are under the bed," said Vera. Alice could see her mom on all fours peeking at her. Alice scurried farther under the bed. She ran out of space at the wall. Her mom reached under the bed, caught her arm, and pulled her out.

"That hurts, Mom," Alice cried.

"You don't know what hurt is yet," Vera said. "Wait until your father gets home."

Alice wasn't worried. Her daddy loved her stories about Ogua. She couldn't wait to tell her father all about how Ogua had made its way from the Himalayas, where it had lived as a dragon until its wings were cut off. He and his siblings were all maimed by sasquatches. His family recovered from the wounds, but most of the other dragons died. Accidentally, the maimed dragons found they could breathe underwater. Some of them morphed into long—very long—creatures who mostly lived in water. Some of them could live on land or sea. Ogua could live in both places. He loved to swim in the Monongahela River, especially now that he had found Alice.

"Daddy," Alice said while sitting on her daddy's lap. "Don't tell mom, but I got all muddy when I fell off Ogua's back."

"Honey, doesn't his back have spikes?" Daddy asked.

"Don't interrupt the story, Daddy. There's enough space between the spikes for me to sit. I hold on to the spike in front of me. Today, Ogua heard people coming and needed to hide. He forgot I was on his back and jumped into the river. I was knocked off and fell in the mud."

Daddy nodded thoughtfully. "Okay. But you better not go to the river again. Your mother is mad she had to wash your play clothes again."

After Alice went to bed, Vera confronted William. "William, you are indulging her fantasies. That can't be good for her."

"Let her have an imagination."

"What was her punishment?" Vera demanded.

"Not to go to the river ever again."

Vera seemed satisfied with the answer. Little did Vera realize that Ogua would become part of her family's lore.

1

_____

"Tell me more about Ogua," Sadie told Meow.

"Enough stories for tonight," I said. "Bedtime."

"Aw, Mom. I'm not tired."

"You used that line to get the last story. Enough. Bed." I playfully ruffled her hair. Both Sadie and I were in dire need of haircuts. I had lost track of the days since Meow whisked us to his tunnels and caves. I knew we had spent at least a month with Spitzy while hiding from the police. I had no idea how long I had been with Meow.

Bessie and Sash left us for their caves near Lake Erie, since the activity there had been declared a mass hallucination that seized the town for weeks. How Commander Burke, or Guiliana, as she wanted me to call her, concocted the story of a massive dose of foreign pollen infecting the entire town of Cleveland. I was still with Meow because Sadie and I were suspected of releasing the pollen. Spitzy and Chichi were with Sash and Bessie. Buffalo was still looking for them. Guiliana thought she had collected all the cameras and pictures that were taken of Spitzy. One was missed and was winging around world online. No one in Buffalo fell for the pollen story.

After Sadie settled for the night in a new nest that Meow insisted that she needed, Meow and I had our warm milk before bed. I found if I could get Meow to drink the milk, he wouldn't purr in his sleep. If you think snoring is bad, you have been spared the loudest snore-purr ever.

"How long do you think we will be here?" I asked Meow.

After taking a long slurp of milk, he answered. "Humans are so impatient."

"Yes, we are. We don't have centuries and eons to live."

Meow motioned for me to climb on his lap. His fur was soft and warm. Nearly every day I found myself on his lap when I woke up. "I forget that I won't have you forever," Meow murmured.

I snuggled in his fur. For some reason when I slept in Meow's lap, I had vivid dreams of Joseph. I'd wake thinking I was lying in Joseph's arms, not on Meow's lap. Morning came, and before I knew it, Sadie was calling, "I'm starving, Mom."

I reluctantly left Meow's lap. Sash had given me the money, identification, and credit cards I had asked him to bring to Spitzy's cave. I was able to go into the town nearest Meow's caves, Port Huron, to buy Sadie and I some clothes, set up a bank account, and bring back food. It sure was easier pouring her a box of Fruity Pebbles and milk. The problem with the milk is that I had to ration it, or Meow would drink 150 gallons a day. I needed to go into town again for supplies and a calendar. Mine had been ripped to shreds by the wind when Sadie and I were riding at a thousand miles an hour on Meow's back.

I was anxious to contact my boss in Erie and send him some of the stories I had been working on. My savings wouldn't last forever. I needed work. I consulted Sash telepathically, and he urged me not to. He felt it would be better to publish it as fiction. I also wanted to rent an apartment for Sadie and me. I loved Meow's cave, but it just wasn't natural to live with a thousand-pound cat. Meow had been making excuses as to why I couldn't live outside of the cave. I promised him that we would visit often. He did have one practical reason: My savings would last longer if I didn't rent a house. I dropped the conversation. A few days later, I mentioned it again. He sulked for days.

Again, I asked Sash about what to do about Meow's dependence on me. Sash said that Meow had lost his favorite human when the human was six years old. The human, a girl, was canoeing to the entrance to the cave when she capsized. Meow had been out prowling for food and didn't hear her cries. I would be the same age as the little girl if she had lived.

2

I was able to convince Meow to let me go to town again. He consented when I told him we were low on milk.

"You know, Meow," I said. "Cats who live with humans shouldn't have milk."

"You deprive them of the luscious drink?" He arched his back in disgust.

"Yes. It's healthier for them. Maybe milk is not good for you."

Although Meow communicated with us telepathically, he could vocalize, and I was treated to the longest and loudest hiss I had ever heard.

Sadie came running from one of the other caves with her hands over her ears. "Make him stop, Mom. My ears hurt. I was almost at the underground civilization to play and could hear him. Did you threaten to live somewhere else again?"

"No, I told him milk might not be good for him."

Sadie stomped her feet. "Don't provoke him! I'll never make it to that civilization if I keep having to check on you." Sadie was leery of Meow and jealous of my relationship with him. I had to stifle a laugh. I found it cute, but I did worry that she was having to bear too much adult responsibility on this adventure.

One night before bed, Sadie told me that Meow wasn't my husband. She hated to see me on his lap. Meow and I only cuddled now when Sadie was out exploring the underwater caves or asleep. It didn't always work. Sadie's ability to hear telepathic messages was far superior to mine. She could pick up my thoughts sometimes. I wish she picked up the ones where I was thinking how much I loved her. She seemed to only intercept the ones I had about Meow.

To appease Sadie, I asked her if she wanted to go to town with me. She jumped at the chance.

"You will have no reason to come back," cried Meow. "This is a plot to leave me."

"No. No," I assured Meow, "I'm going for groceries and to get Sadie a library card. I also need to look for homeschool material, since she has been out of school so long. I need science books so I can explain to Sadie why the ocean is like it is. Is there anything you'd like, Meow, aside from milk?" I was tired of catering to his male ego.

"Yes. No one has ever asked me that before." Meow took me into his arms. I braced for the breathtaking hug.

"Enough, Meow. You'll kill her if you hug her that tight," said Sadie flatly.

Meow released me and then began grooming where I had red marks from the hug.

"Oh, geez," Sadie said. "Let's get out of here before you smell like cat spit."

"What is it you want, Meow?" I said.

"Canned salmon. My human used to bring it to me."

I assured Meow I wouldn't forget his salmon. After I washed off the cat spit in a similar shower system to what the other creatures had in their caves, we left. At first, we had trouble adjusting to the sunlight. I had purchased sunglasses, and we drew them from our backpacks.

"I do miss the sun," said Sadie.

"That reminds me. We need to start taking vitamin D. Let's go Walmart." Sadie skipped ahead. Walmart would seem like a treat.

I made Sadie push one of the carts, much to her chagrin. If I had let her go, she would have gotten too far ahead of me. I was still wary of being recognized. I filled one cart with milk. The second had the other supplies we needed. Sadie and I found a deck of Uno cards. We just had to have those. We missed our Uno games. She wanted books to read. I told her we'd use the library. What a mistake. When the librarian asked Sadie what name would be on her card, Sadie didn't use the alias I had given her.

"Sadie Smith," she said.

I panicked, but then I thought, with a name like Smith, we might be okay. I was wrong.

The librarian proceeded to ask Sadie other questions. "Are you new here?"

"Yes, we are on vacation from Cleveland. We've been traveling and staying with crea— Ah, friends. We stayed in Buffalo a while."

Oh, no, I thought. I tapped her on the shoulder. She took one look at me and realized her mistake. Sadie started to shake.

"Well, Sadie," said the librarian. "There seems to be another Sadie with a library card at this library. Let me check with my boss how to handle it." I knew it was an excuse for her to call the authorities.

"Sadie, let's calmly but quickly walk out of here," I said.

"But my card," Sadie said.

"Hush. Walk!" We were halfway to the door when I turned to see what the librarian was doing. She had summoned a security guard. "Run, Sadie," I screamed. We moved as quickly as we could out of the front of the library. The guard was on our tail. Just when I thought he would overtake us, a huge red claw snatched us. Meow! He knew we were in danger. Oh, no, I thought. He has rescued us by putting himself in harm's way.

Luckily, Meow's super speed took us down into the cave system before we were caught. I knew we still weren't safe. The town would be looking for Meow.

"No, they won't be looking for me," Meow said as he groomed himself after his exertion. I had given him a gallon of milk in hopes of calming him. He wanted to cuddle, but I refused with Sadie around. The milk did its magic, and he was asleep.

Once Sadie knew Meow was sleeping, she crawled into my lap. I noticed she didn't fit at all now. Her hair had grown during the months we had been gone. When I bought her clothes, I had purchased a size bigger so she could grow into them, so she fit them perfectly.

"Sorry, Mom," she said as she kissed me on the cheek.

I gave her one back. "It's okay, Sadie. You made a mistake. They happen."

"I think I'm going to take a nap," Sadie said. She went to the cave she had claimed as her bedroom. She'd have a birthday soon. How do you have a birthday party in a cave?

While Sadie and Meow slept, I messaged Bessie and Sash about the incident. I didn't hear anything at first. What I received was a terrifying panicky feeling. They must be worried.

A few hours later, Bessie told me Sash was angry. He didn't understand why we couldn't live as we had with him and Bessie and occasionally visit Meow. Bessie said she tried to tell Sash that we were humans and needed more than a cave and dragon-fire-cooked food. He had locked himself in one of his secret caves and wouldn't come out.

Bessie said to wait a few days. I had her clarify human days or creature days. She said human days. Bessie would contact Guiliana about the breach. If nothing appeared in the papers, we'd be okay. Even if it did, Guiliana said she would deploy her team to the area and allay the area's fears. I felt better after hearing from Bessie. I unpacked the groceries and gathered the ingredients I bought to make spaghetti and meatballs.

3

All was quiet for a few days, and we relaxed a bit. I kept asking Meow about a different place to shop, since I better not go back to Port Huron. He said there wasn't anywhere else, but I knew he was lying. I didn't need provisions yet, but it wouldn't be long the way Sadie was eating. She was in a growth spurt. Meow was drinking so much milk, I had to put it under lock and key. He pouted frequently and refused to let me sleep on his lap. I missed it since I felt so close to Joseph there.

About a week after we were seen, I heard a loud knocking at the entrance door. I had convinced Meow we needed to lock the cave. He hated it because he could not work the lock. I had to let him out when he needed to go. I decided to answer the knocking.

Meow leisurely stretched and moved toward the door. "Meow, no. They might be after us."

Meow gave a little hiss. "Humans, such scaredy cats." Meow opened the door before I could stop him. Whoever was there was caught in a huge Meow hug. I couldn't see who he was hugging; his form completely covered the person or animal. I assumed it was a human—but I'd have seen if it were Bessie or Sash.

Meow finally let go of his captive. "See, it's Esme," Meow said. "Who else would come?"

I felt like the air had been knocked out of me, and I collapsed into one the sofas that I had dragged over from the dump. Esme crossed the room and hugged me. She sneezed. I was covered in Meow's fur.

"Meow, you didn't brush yourself today. You know I can't stand cat hair," I said.

Esme stifled a giggle. "Cat hair. I remember. Don't you, Meow."

"Yes, your mom was quite angry that you came home smelling of cat. That's when I asked Sash to come and build the shower, so you could wash before you left."

"That's right," I said. "You told me you grew up here." I was a bit confused. Hadn't Bessie said that Meow's human had died?

"Yes, and you set off a kerfuffle in my hometown. TV3 sent me here to see if it was connected to what happened in Cleveland and Buffalo. Luckily, they sent me. I can blur the story."

The sighting had made the national news. "How?" I asked.

"I'm not sure yet. Do you have anything to eat? Spitzy flew me here, and she wouldn't stop for snacks."

"Is she here? Is she here?" shouted Sadie.

"No, cutie pie," said Esme. "She turned around right away. She didn't want to be seen."

Sadie was crestfallen. She sulked away to her room.

"And she's not even a teenager yet," I said.

"I did a story recently on what some sociologist call tweens, those aged eight to twelve. The sociologist said that hormonal changes begin far earlier than what used to be thought. From what he described, I thought the tweens were almost worse than teens."

I nodded. As I fixed Esme a sandwich, I asked, "Esme, Sash told me that Meow's human was dead. How could you be?"

Esme sat on the sofa. "The human was my big sister. She was rowing out to one of Meow's caves. Mom had told her not to go to the lake unattended, but my sister was stubborn. A squall came up and tipped her out of the boat. Meow was on land hunting. By the time he heard her distress call, it was too late. Esme wiped a tear out of her eye.

"I'm sorry. I didn't mean to distress you."

"It's okay. I started going to the lake because I knew it was my sister's favorite place. I felt close to her there. One day, I saw Meow. We became friends, but we never had the bond that my sister and him had."

Meow hissed quietly. "I'm in the room. Did you forget about me? If she gets a sandwich, I get milk."

Esme and I laughed. "Just a sip," I told Meow.

"Esme, how are you going to blur the story?" Meow asked.

Esme shook her head. "I'm not sure yet. I came here first thing. I'm going to check into a hotel—I know, Meow, I could stay here. But I need access to the internet and other human things. My first move will be to contact Commander Burke."

"Bessie already has," I said. "I thought it might be her at the door."

Meow hissed loudly. "You were afraid it was someone sinister." He hissed again.

"Okay, okay, but I was hoping," I said, hoping he would stop hissing.

"Esme," screamed Sadie in excitement. She had heard the voices and came to investigate. The two hugged. "Why are you here? Oh, no. We made the news again, didn't we?"

Esme nodded and smoothed Sadie's hair out of her eyes. Sadie's eyes were filled with tears. "It's my fault, isn't it?" Sadie said.

"No, honey," I said. "It was an accident."

Esme swung her backpack off her shoulders and took out a newspaper article:

CREATURE SEEN TAKING TWO PEOPLE

On Thursday morning at 11:18 AM, a librarian reported spotting Sadie Smith and another woman, who she believes is the girl's mother, at the Port Huron Main Library. Miss Summers, a librarian for over 30 years said, "I knew the girl and the woman looked familiar, but I knew once the girls said she was Sadie Smith."

As soon as Miss Summers confirmed the ID of the girl, she alerted the library security team, who pursued the two. "I did a quick Google search to confirm my suspicions. Then I summoned the guard." The guard, who prefers to stay anonymous, stated he was close enough to grab the girl when a huge red and black claw came out of nowhere. "I only saw the claw. And then they were gone. The clawed creature wanted the girl and the woman." The security guard has been hospitalized with a large catlike scratch and PTSD. The doctor fears he will always be afraid of cats.

Janet Smith and her daughter, Sadie, have been associated with creature sightings in Cleveland and Buffalo. One of the creatures is described as a colorful sea-like creature nearly fifty feet long. The other fits the description of a sasquatch: a hairy creature like a human being reported to exist in the northwestern U.S. and western Canada and said to be a primate between 6 and 15 feet tall.

Commander Guiliana Burke of the US Navy found evidence in Cleveland that foreign pollen from an unknown source had caused people to hallucinate the creature. No such pollen is found in Buffalo. Buffalo has had sightings of sasquatches and a colorful sea

creature. A young girl said she had played
with a large red and black cat in the park
near the lake. She appeared unharmed and
reported the creature was large and soft.
The reporting from Port Huron has troubled
the people in Cleveland and Buffalo, who are
wondering if the government has lied to
them.

The reporting couldn't have been worse. "Is this the only article you have?" I asked Esme.

"I have others from the Buffalo paper that say essentially the same thing."

Meow curled in his bed. "You're boring me. I'm taking a nap."

"He's quite a character, isn't he?" Esme said.

"Exasperatingly so."

4

Esme left to find a hotel room while Meow was still sleeping. He demanded the last can of salmon. I was too shaken from the events to argue with him.

"No more salmon now, Meow," I said. "You will have to find me another place to shop."

"Fine. Tomorrow, I'll lead you through the tunnels that end in Canada. You can shop in Sarnia. But you will not take Sadie. I am still shaken and tired from your last adventure." I knew better than to remind him that the event happened weeks ago.

Sadie and I followed Meow through tunnels he had never shown us before. He talked Sadie into staying behind with him with the promise he'd take her to the underground civilization. I was tired by the time I emerged from the ground. Sarnia was a bustling city, much like Port Huron. I asked for directions to a grocery store and found it was so far away that I'd need public transit. When I boarded the bus, I sat next to a man reading a newspaper on his iPad. I glanced at the article. I began to panic. The article had Sadie's and my picture at the top. When the next stop came, I quickly exited. I hoped the man hadn't got a good look at me.

I had a couple of miles to go before I reached the grocery store, but I decided to walk the rest of the way using the GPS on my phone to get there. I gathered what I needed and got in line to pay. There at the checkouts were the tabloids. Sadie and I were splashed on the front of them along with terrible drawings of Sash, Bessie, Chichi, and Spitzy. The drawings made them look like the worst creatures in the world.

I was able to leave the store with our needed supplies. I had purchased one of the tabloids to take to Meow and to be sure what was being reported. I was unsure of the safest way to return to the opening of the cave. I put the coordinates in my GPS. I had nearly ten miles to cover. I called an Uber. It seemed safer than public transit. I stood to the side of the grocery store so as not to be seen by most of the people waiting for their Ubers. The app said it would be a twenty-minute wait. I paced from the front of the store to the back, over and over.

I could see the Uber coming and hurried to the front of the store. I was about to open the passenger door and put in my groceries when I was grabbed and tasered.

I have no idea how long I was unconscious, but it was a few days. The police had brought me food and drink. I must have eaten, since the plates were empty. As soon as I regained my strength, I tried to send a message to Meow, but when I did, my body shook as if it had touched a live wire. When I tried to receive messages, the same thing occurred.

I knew Meow and Sadie were worried about me by now. I decided to explore my cell. I was in a small—maybe eight by ten feet—room with a bed, blanket, commode, and sink. There were no windows, just harsh fluorescent light high in the ceiling. I had hoped there would be a shower, but I was out of luck. I could barely stand how I smelled. I was still in my own clothes.

As I sat on the bed, the door opened by sliding into the wall. Once the officer entered, the door went back in place. I waited for him to talk and felt my best course of action would be none.

"Well, well, well. If it isn't the famous—or should I say, infamous? —Janet Smith, the tamer of monsters," the man said with a sneer.

I kept silent and refused to meet his eyes.

"Look at me," he shouted. I kept my eyes averted. "Feeling uppity?" He took what looked like a taser from a holster on his belt. "Missing Sadie and your crew of monsters? Sources tell me you are in love with a demonic cat. You sleep on his lap. I hear his caves are being searched. They haven't found him or Sadie. Yet."

I braced myself for another electric shock, but he was just clapping the taser on his thigh and circling me. In desperation, I tried to contact Meow, Bessie, Sash, Spitzy, and Chichi. I knew my message didn't go through. I still wasn't feeling any messages coming in.

"You fell into our trap," he continued. "An alert Port Huron Police officer alerted us about you. He knew you had shopped in Port Huron. He had you under surveillance. After you disappeared, he thought you might try to enter our country illegally. The town was blanketed with your picture. Your cashier at the grocery store turned you in."

I swallowed hard. From what he was telling me, Guiliana wasn't in Port Huron yet to calm the public. I didn't know if Esme had filed the report to TV3 that would start to calm people's fears. If I wasn't living this nightmare... No, adventure. Be positive. If I wasn't living this whatever it is, I would be petrified about the monsters. Our nature is to fear what we don't understand. I was just hoping those hunting us would not use violence.

"I'll tell the cook to make spaghetti and meatballs, your favorite, tonight," the officer said, then he left abruptly.

What did this officer know about me? He knew my food preferences. Who was he?

A day or two later, I think—it was hard to keep track of time in a room that was always illuminated—I started feeling a calm fall over me. I took it as a sign that my ability to feel my friends was returning. Who was sending the feeling? It didn't feel like Bessie or Sash. It wasn't Meow; I always heard his purr when he sent feelings. I tried to send messages to everyone, even Sadie, but I could tell they weren't going through.

I didn't sleep well that night. I kept hearing parts of conversations that made no sense. I wasn't even sure who was talking.

"I should go to her."

"No, not you. Me. She doesn't know about you."

"I'm married to her."

"Where have you been?"

"Don't fight. We need a plan that involves the best for the job. We don't have a plan yet."

"The Navy could—"

"No more officials. Let me go."

I heard crying that I knew had to be Sadie.

5

Later in the day, I heard the door sliding open. I tried to prepare myself for the officer.

I heard a woman's voice say, "Thank you, officer. I won't be needing you."

"Are you sure? We do not know if she is capable of strength like the monsters," the officer cautioned.

The woman laughed. It was Esme.

"I'm a seasoned reporter. I've interviewed worse."

Esme stepped out from behind the officer. I knew I better not show relief or smile. "Smith, Ms. Smith, or Mrs. Smith?"

"Mrs. Smith," I answered.

"You won't cause any problems, correct? I'm equipped with a taser, as is anyone who enters this cell. Will you try anything?" Esme said.

I shook my head.

"See, officer, she's not totally unreasonable. Now leave and turn off the camera that is in the corner."

The officer reached up and took down the camera. It had blended so well into the wall that I had overlooked it when I searched the cell. He left and slid the door shut.

Once we were sure he was gone, we embraced.

"How's Sadie?" I asked.

"Fine. Good. Strong."

"Are you telling me the truth? I can't believe I was caught."

Esme gave me a reassuring smile. Then she said, "Sadie was upset at first. The first night, Meow left her alone to search for you. He hated to leave her alone and knew you'd be upset with him, but he felt it necessary. He quickly learned you were in a special holding cell at a Sarnia police station. From my research, I found there is some dispute about who would have jurisdiction. Buffalo, Cleveland, and Port Huron want you. Cleveland thinks you released the pollen. Buffalo's claim was thrown out, as was Port Huron's. Sarnia refuses to send you to Cleveland. Their police want you for criminal mischief. The library system is suing you for the cost of the security guard's time and for his PTSD treatment.

"I found you a lawyer, Aaron Matthew. He knows. Meow wants to come rescue you, but I think it's a good idea to submit to prosecution and clear your name. For Sadie's sake. Aaron is with Meow, Bessie, and Sash. Spitzy and Chichi stayed at their cave. They want to be available to help if any of us are caught.

"I was able to get in to see you with my reporter's badge. TV3 wants a full report. You need to give me something to report."

My head was spinning. I collapsed on the bed. "Say I wouldn't talk."

"Come on, Janet. I need to make a splash."

"You're worried about your career while I'm in danger?" I was angry. I wished I could hiss like Meow.

"No, no," Esme said. "To be able to pursue your story, I must convince my boss it's worth me staying here. I want to be part of the solution."

I nodded. "I wish Joseph was here. I'd gladly surrender in Cleveland if he were here to take Sadie."

"I might have a solution," Esme said.

"No! Sea creatures and sasquatches won't raise my daughter. I don't mind her interacting with them, but I am the one raising her. She'd never have a normal life."

Esme looked thoughtful. She sat next to me and took both of my hands into hers. "I know of an entity that is part human and part sasquatch. Sash tried to save him when he was in an auto accident. He gave the man some of his blood and covered the wound with hair he plucked from his body, hoping the man would be treated at the hospital and be okay."

I pulled away from Esme. I was frightened. "No, no, no."

"Sash has kept this from you. It has been hard for him not to tell you about the mansquat. That's what the sasquatches call creatures who have the fortunate or unfortunate fate to live again by being half sasquatch. Janet, are you okay?"

I noticed I was rocking back and forth on the bed. "Are you telling me my husband is alive, but he's a... what? A mansquat?"

Esme nodded.

I must have fainted, because when I regained consciousness, medical personnel were tending to my vital signs. "I'm fine."

Esme cut in. "No, she isn't. She's not getting adequate light, exercise, or food. She's being detained illegally. She did not break any of Sarnia's or Canada's laws."

The medical personnel said they would have to talk to the police chief. They hustled out of my cell. Esme handed me a glass of water. "Take a slow sip."

I did as she told me. As I took the glass from her, I noticed I was shaking. I remembered what Esme had said about Joseph before I fainted. I let out a long, mournful scream. Esme held me until I was able to get myself in control.

"We have little time," Esme said. "Someone will be back soon. Joseph lives in the underground civilization under Lake Huron. Meow has been trying to keep Sadie away by putting up obstacles to keep her from getting there. She's close to finding a way in. Meow doesn't know if he can keep her out much longer. I suggest we bring Joseph to Meow's cave and introduce him as a nice sasquatch who will watch her while you sort out the legal situation. Joseph will reveal his identity when he thinks the time is right."

I nodded just as Guiliana entered the room.

"Get away from the prisoner," Guiliana barked.

"Yes, ma'am," Esme said.

"I'll be escorting Mrs. Smith to Cleveland. I'm placing a gag order on the press. Nothing should be written," said Guiliana. Then she winked at Esme. Esme got it; she was free to report. Nice—an exclusive for her. "Now leave Ms. Benavides."

Esme left. Guiliana continued the charade by handcuffing and leading me out of the cell.

6

Mom? Mom? I hope you can hear me. I've never tried to use telepathic communication with a human. Esme said you were going to Cleveland to stand trial. I'm worried about you. I'm fine. Meow escorted me to a wonderful city under the lake. I wish you could see it. I love it here. The buildings are different colors of seaweed and coral. The ceilings are high— you know, so that sasquatches can fit in them. When I saw the mansquat though, I was amazed at how short they were for sasquatches. They are bigger than human size—basketball player height. They come in different colors of human skin and patches of hair. Some groom themselves and shave off their hair.

Meow took me to a lavender and green house and introduced me to Jo-Jo. Meow explained that Jo-Jo was a mansquat. He said sometimes sasquatches helped a human too much. When that happens, the human takes on sasquatch qualities, but not all of them. Jo-Jo is seven feet tall with pretty chocolate-brown hair. He's gentle. He shook my hand and made me feel like a lady. I could tell from his grip that he isn't as strong as Sash or Chichi. His voice doesn't sound like a man or a sasquatch. I was surprised he spoke English. Meow says that's why he was chosen for me. Jo-Jo has a huge library and wants to teach me. I told him my mom would be relieved.

He smiled. He wanted to know all about you. I caught him up on our adventures. He had tears in his eyes at the end of my story.

I have my own room. Oh, Mom, it looks so much like my bedroom at home, except that the colors are so much brighter. The room isn't pink, but a nice shade of coral. I have a canopy over my bed like I always wanted. Remember that Daddy said I could have one for my sixth birthday, but he died before he could get?

I'm going to the library now to take my first lesson from Jo-Jo.

I so hope you get this.

Oh, Jo-Jo said to tell you he would like to meet you. He's cool, Mom.

7

I'm under house arrest. When I went before the judge, she was skeptical about the charges—distributing a hallucinogenic drug among a population—and set bail. Esme secured the bond. She was cagey about where she found the money.

My trial is set for three weeks from now. I love being back in my home. It hadn't sold yet, so I was lucky to have a place to stay. I took the house off the market for now. The first thing I did was give the house a thorough cleaning. It had become dusty and stale smelling. I love being able to cook in my own kitchen.

I also feel closer to Joseph here. Of course, Sadie's message was wonderful. I enjoyed hearing about how Joseph had made a home for himself. I was confused how Joseph had changed into a mansquat. Yes, he received sasquatch blood, but I saw him in his coffin, a memory I'd never forget. I sent a message asking Sash for details. He said he dug Joseph up just in time. Joseph had regenerated and was suffocating. He had Bessie take Joseph to Meow, who helped him adjust to the change and installed him in the underground world. I realize that the comfort I felt in Meow's arms had been Joseph's feelings for me. Meow had captured some to share with me.

I also remember well when the cemetery called to say Joseph's grave had been broken into. The man at the cemetery apologized for the security breach and planned to repair the damage. Then the next day, he said he was mistaken, that the grave was intact. I know why now. Sash had fixed the grave after he whisked Joseph away.

I tried contacting Sadie, but I am not sure she received it. I could communicate well with Bessie and Sash. They were in their Lake Erie cave system, available if I needed help. If I'm convicted, they will take me from the courtroom with great danger to themselves. I told them not to. If the verdict is guilty, I'll serve the sentence. Guiliana and Esme, who visit often with Aaron, say that this type of crime is hard to convict for, and even if I am, I'd get a fine and maybe community service. Aaron said it's because I have never had trouble with the law. He is building a case that says no devices that could be a dispersal unit have been found.

Aaron came to my home to begin his trial prep. I was shocked at his height. He must be nearly seven feet tall. I wondered why he wasn't getting his eyebrows shaped. They seemed excessive. He'd be handsomer with them done. Aside from the height and eyebrows, he looked like a serious, no-nonsense man.

Aaron is confident I will be acquitted. I'm not. Public opinion is against me. I have guards outside my home, not because I'm out on bail, but because vandals broke all my windows and trampled my gardens when I moved home. I've never been hated before. It's hard.

Aaron is handsome and looks like he regularly works out. He is close-mouthed about what sasquatch and sea creature he crossed paths with. The only detail I have is that he was vacationing overseas. Aaron told me that he and his wife, Marcela, travel the world between cases. I assume he is a successful lawyer to be able to take trips overseas.

Guiliana was concerned when the police insisted the force investigate the lava tubes for the device. She and Aaron convinced them that the NCIS, the legal branch of the Navy, could do a better job. She never sent NCIS to the tubes, and she falsified a report she forwarded to the police. I hope she hasn't put her career in jeopardy.

In the evenings, Esme, Guiliana, and I meet to play cards and drink wine. Esme does my shopping for me. I am allowed to leave my home, but the first time I did, I was mobbed. I called Bessie, who sent Guiliana to rescue me. I long to shop for myself.

I ditched my cell phone. Too many people were calling to harass me. Guiliana brought me a secure cell phone so she could call me. She gave my number to Esme and Aaron so I can keep in touch. I jump every time it rings. The house is so quiet without my Sadie.

8

Mom, I was so excited when I received your message. I was jumping up and down. Some things fell off the shelves that Jo-Jo made. He didn't scold me but asked that I never do that again. Nothing broke.

Jo-Jo showed me around the city. It has a library, post office, bank—they use US dollars—a theater that produces plays, bocce and pickleball courts, and grocery stores that have ready-made food as well as items you or I could buy in a regular store. I was fascinated with the fashion in the department stores. Jo-Jo said maybe later he would get me some new clothes. He said I was outgrowing the ones I had. I told him you'd pay him back. He said not to worry. I should consider them birthday gifts for the ones he missed. I thought that was weird, but I guess mansquats are different from us and sasquatches. Jo-Jo won't tell me how they get supplies to the city. There is no police station. I want you to come here. If we live here with Jo-Jo, you'd never have to go to jail. He says the punishment for bad behavior is banishment. Tough law!

In Jo-Jo's home, there are many fireplaces and running water. He has several showers, one just the right size for me, and the other for his mansquat friends when they visit. He says Sash helped him with the shower and toilets. Jo-Jo and the other mansquats want flush toilets. When sasquatches visit, they hate to use them. They are used to going in the *woods. Remember the time Sash was sick to his stomach after he ate one of the banana and marshmallow fluffs? Gross!*

The best room in the house is a room for me to paint and draw. I've missed painting during our adventures. Jo-Jo has everything I ever wanted in a studio: canvases, paints of all types and colors, drawing pencils and paper, and lots of light. I have been drawing scenes from our adventures. Jo-Jo says we need to hide them for now. I suppose he's right. He told me my skills have developed. I asked him how he knew. He said Sash had told him, but I think he may have seen some of my drawings somehow.

Daddy—I mean, Jo-Jo. I'm sorry, Mom. I hope my daddy doesn't mind if I slip and call Jo-Jo my dad. You wouldn't believe how much like Daddy he is. He likes the same music, although he has learned to enjoy some ancient Asian tunes. He makes spaghetti and meatballs just like you do. He is also cooking Thai, Chinese, Vietnamese, and Ethiopian dishes. I'm learning to eat different things. It's fun.

I must report to Jo-Jo's library for my lessons. Dad—Jo-Jo—is a rigid taskmaster. Joking. He makes learning fun. Jo-Jo said to send you his love. He's a kind man.

Miss you, Mom. You'd like Jo-Jo.

9

I cried all day after I received Sadie's message. Jo-Jo—Joseph—sent his love. I sent a hurried message to Sadie to tell Joseph that I send my love too. I wanted him to know that I still love him. It's been three years since he died—uh, transformed.

The next day, my eyes were terribly swollen from all the crying. Some of the crying was for losing Joseph a second time. He died as a man. When he came to life, he wasn't a man. I loved Joseph; could I love Jo-Jo? I needed to be ready for the trial. I knew I couldn't dwell on Joseph. My freedom was on the line. The trial started at 10:00. Aaron was picking me up at 9:30. Esme and Guiliana would meet us there. They were being called as witnesses and wouldn't be needed that day. They came to see how the jury would be chosen.

A hundred people were called for the jury. About half were excused because they did not believe there was a monster loose. Another third was excused for seeing the monster. From the rest, a twelve-person jury was seated with little problem. The jurors were matter-of-fact types who rarely watched the news or read newspapers. The judge dismissed the court and set trial for the next day at 9:00. He felt the trial would only take a few hours.

Aaron took me home. Esme and Guiliana brought in Chinese

takeout: egg rolls, lo mein, wonton, sesame chicken, and beef with broccoli. As we sat and ate, I asked Aaron what he thought of the jurors.

"We couldn't have done much better, I think," Aaron stated. "Juror number ten worries me a bit. He's a grumpy man who seems to think the case is wasting his time. He may choose to vote for conviction. If he does, he will hang the jury."

"What does that mean?" I asked.

"If the jury can't come to a unanimous verdict, the jury is excused. The judge will call it a mistrial. The prosecutor then decides if he wants to try the case again."

"Okay, we don't want that, do we?" Esme asked.

"It might be good. It might be bad. The prosecutor may think the case isn't worth trying again and dismiss it, or ask the judge for a new court date."

"No, I want this over. I can't go through this again," I shouted.

Aaron took both my hands and looked me straight in the eye. "It's unlikely that would happen, but I want you to be prepared for the worst. Even if the case is retried, you are strong, Janet. You will be able to do it."

I wanted everyone to leave. Aaron said there was one more thing he needed to tell me. He didn't think I'd need to be called as a witness but wanted to prepare me, nonetheless. After we cleared the dishes, Aaron began to shoot questions at me in rapid fire. After a while, I was confused. I broke down in tears.

"Take a break," said Aaron. Esme broke out the wine. I needed a glass. "I wanted to give you a taste of the type of cross-examination you might have if I put you on the stand. Answer honestly, as you did. Please control your emotions if you can. Tears can sway a jury, and sometimes not the right way."

I nodded. Esme could see I was getting sleepy, so she told Aaron and Guiliana to leave. I was glad they were done. I loved the three of them but needed time to process before the trial.

Once the court was called to order the next morning, Guiliana was the first witness. She explained her role in leading the team to explore the lava tubes. There had been reports of monsters in the area. She detailed the steps the Navy took to ascertain where the supposed monsters came from. She emphasized there were no signs of life. The prosecutor said he was done with the witness. I could see he was upset at Guiliana's answers.

Aaron cross-examined. Guiliana was asked numerous questions about the cave. I knew she wasn't telling the truth; she stretched it. She said she found nothing out of place in the caves and that there was not an infestation of zebra mussels in the lava tubes, a chief concern of the scientists, as they felt it could be a breeding area. Aaron asked if there were signs of life. Guiliana said no. When it was certain that the caves had no information of interest to scientists and the Navy, she ordered the caves sealed. I remembered that new entrances to the caves were created after Sadie and I left to hide with Spitzy. I bet they were disguised as rock walls.

The prosecutor then questioned Guiliana again, trying to get her to say she found a dispersal device. She kept answering in the negative to his questions. Finally, Aaron told the judge the prosecution was badgering the witness. The judge told the prosecutor to end the questioning.

Esme took the stand. She only divulged to the prosecution what she had said in her news reports. When she asked about a dispersal device, she said she never saw one.

At that point, Aaron said there was not enough evidence to send the case to the jury.

The judge said he would take it under advisement, but he would continue the trial. He would let us know his decision tomorrow.

The prosecutor rested his case. Aaron asked if the court could grant a recess, since we had been at it for nearly four hours. He agreed.

Esme had sandwiches delivered, and we all huddled in a room reserved for attorneys and clients. What a dull, sterile room. The walls were a horrible shade of green. The table was mahogany. I was sad to see some people had taken penknives to the table and carved their initials. I wondered how they got the weapons in. I was a bit unnerved by it. The chairs at least were comfortable but well worn. At first, we ate in silence. Aaron was going through the notes he took in court. The three of us didn't want to disturb his concentration.

Aaron said, "I am still not sure I'll put you on the stand. If I put you on, I'll only ask if you had dispersed the pollen or had knowledge about it. Then the prosecutor would have his chance. I am trying to think of the types of questions he would ask that could be a problem. He will ask if you have seen the creatures."

"I lie?" I asked.

Aaron looked thoughtful. "I can't tell you to lie."

Esme interrupted. "What if Janet says she was indulging her daughter in her fantasy of a sea creature. You've seen her drawings."

Aaron said, "Okay, but I would need proof of the pictures."

"There's a ton at my house," I said.

Esme said, "Lunch break is almost over. I'll go get them and be back as soon as possible."

As Esme and Aaron worked out the details, Meow sent a message to ask me if I was okay. I messaged back the situation. Before Esme could leave, the door blew open. A great wind disturbed Aaron's papers. He was rushing to pick them up. Then the door slammed shut. Sadie's drawings appeared on the table.

"Meow," I said.

"How did he know?" Guiliana said.

"Meow asked me how things were going while Aaron and Esme were figuring out the fastest way to get the paintings here. I filled him in. He must have risked being seen to get them here."

The bailiff came in to summon us back to the courtroom. We threw away our lunch things and headed back to court. Aaron had his arm around my waist to support me. I was exhausted from the stress.

We settled at the lawyer's table and waited for the judge and prosecutor. Some time passed. Aaron said he was going to see what the delay was just as the judge and prosecutor came in. The judge didn't go to the bench. He came to our table.

"I have received reports that citizens are gathering at the courthouse after an elderly man reported to police that he saw a red streak go into the courthouse and then back out toward the lake. He has no idea where the streak went. There have been no other sightings that we know of. The fact that the man has dementia makes the sighting suspect. I need to be sure the atmosphere stays calm."

I knew the man had seen Meow. Meow should be back in Lake Huron now, given his speed. I hoped.

The judge continued, "Young lady, why is it wherever you go, strange incidents occur?"

Aaron said, "Don't answer that, Janet."

"No, you better not," the judge agreed. "I'm dismissing the jurors for the day. All of us will gather tomorrow at 9:00 for the defense to present its case. You are putting one on, aren't you, Mr. Matthew?"

"Yes, Your Honor," Aaron responded.

The judge nodded and walked to the jury room to tell them to go home.

"Let's get you home," Aaron said. We all agreed. But getting home wasn't simple. When we reached the front of the courthouse, it was surrounded with people chanting, "Lock her up!"

"They mean me, right?" I asked.

Aaron grabbed me and ordered Guiliana and Esme to get through the crowd and bring the car to the back of the courthouse, where there was an underground entrance for high-profile clients. He and I ran through the halls and raced down the stairs to the basement. I stayed in the stairwell while Aaron checked who was at the entrance.

"It's deserted," he said when he came back. "We'll wait for Esme and Guiliana. It may take them some time."

"I wish we didn't have to come back tomorrow. I have a bad feeling about this," I said.

"Me, too," said Aaron.

10

When Esme and Guiliana came with the car, Aaron said I should get in the trunk. I knew if I were recognized, all four of us would be in danger. I wasn't thrilled. The trunk wasn't too bad. Aaron had equipped it with a light and padding. My home wasn't too far away.

We left the underground garage. I felt the car abruptly stop. My heartbeat quickened. I knew the car was swarmed with people chanting," Send out Janet!" The car suddenly started rocking side to side. Among the shouts of "Send out Janet," I heard Aaron's voice speaking to someone.

"Yes, officer, I'm Janet Smith's lawyer. I'm taking two of the witnesses home."

"Where's Janet Smith," the officer said.

"She left in her own car a while ago," Aaron replied.

I felt a rush of wind and the car rise in the air. I heard Esme and Guiliana scream. What was happening? The car thudded again. It seemed we weren't in the air anymore.

"Run," Aaron said to Esme and Guiliana. "I'll go with Janet."

"What's happening, Aaron?" I asked as I unfolded myself from the trunk.

"Run with me. I'll explain later."

We didn't have far to run. I recognized the entrance to Sash's cave was just ahead. How had we gotten there so fast?

Sash opened the cave door. "Hurry!" We were all out of breath and collapsed on the floor.

"You're safe," said Bessie.

"Yes, Bessie. What's this all about?" I shouted.

"Meow grabbed the car. He says he wasn't seen in the chaos. He knew the car wouldn't do well in the cave—too damp. He dropped you as near as he could to it," Bessie explained. I looked around the cave. Not only were Sash and Bessie there, but also Chichi and Spitz. We had hugs all around.

Spitzy and Chichi had cooked a meal for us. I just wanted water. I was so thirsty after being in the trunk. None of us ate much. The excitement had been too much. We all decided to sleep in the cave that night.

I must have fallen asleep quickly. A few hours later, I heard voices. I looked around. Someone had put me in my nest, which was left from the last time I was there.

"I'm not sure we can chance having Meow take the car to the court. Too many sightings, and there will be questions," said Guiliana. "I can't deploy forces again. My superiors are concerned that my top-secret unit will be uncovered if it goes to any more of the places the monsters have been."

Esme said, "I get it. Your career is on the line."

"It's not that. I would gladly give up my commission. I've been in too long, but my replacement hasn't been chosen and trained yet," Guiliana said. "I have to see it through."

I left the nest and walked to where my friends were gathered. "The three of you take the car to the courthouse."

"How will you get there, Janet?" asked Aaron.

"Sash, take me to my house while it's dark. I'll drive my own car in. The three of you will be out of danger," I replied.

They all fell silent. Finally, Sash said, "I'll alert Meow of the plan.

If you're stopped on the way to the courthouse, he'll take you to the underground garage, and you can enter that way."

"I disagree," said Aaron. "We don't want any more Meow sightings."

Esme was tapping on her phone. She looked up and said, "The media is reporting on the riot at the courthouse. There is no mention of anyone seeing Meow. The chaos must have been too much for anyone to notice."

"Oh, Esme," I cried. "You should be the one reporting this."

Esme shook her head. "My boss knows I'll be filing an exclusive when all of this is over. I assured him I would interview you. I know I should have asked, but I had to explain why I hadn't been making reports."

I hesitated. Did I want Esme to interview me for the entire world to know about Sadie and me? And what about Joseph? Giving her an exclusive was the least I could do. I knew I'd have to lose some privacy. "Of course," I said.

With the plan in place, we all settled in for the night.

11

The plan to arrive at the courthouse went off without any problems. I took my place at the table beside Aaron. I'm glad I left from home. I was able to shower, change clothes, and be fresh for court. Esme and Guiliana looked like they too had been able to shower and change.

The judge called the court to order. He asked if there was any business that needed to be discussed before he brought in the jury. Aaron asked if the judge had made his ruling on dismissing the charges.

"I have a tentative ruling that I was going to read. I've decided that the defense should present its case first," said the judge.

I could tell Aaron was deeply disappointed. The judge asked him for his first witness. "I call Janet Smith," said Aaron.

I walked to the stand and was sworn in. The bailiff said I could be seated. I sat and smoothed my skirt. I heard Aaron whisper for me to look only at him. I set my gaze on him.

"Mrs. Smith, did you have access to a pollen that would erase the memories of your fellow citizens?" Aaron asked.

"No, sir."

"Did you have access to a dispersal unit to release the said pollen."

"No, sir."

"Thank you," Aaron said. "That will be all." He gave me a wink as he sat down.

The prosecutor walked toward me. I looked at the back of the courtroom rather than at him, as Aaron had instructed.

"Mrs. Smith, how are we today?"

"I'm fine. I don't know about you."

The prosecutor said, "I object, Your Honor. She's being combative."

The judge said, "Cut the sass, Mrs. Smith. Prosecutor Winston, stop the condescension, and you won't get sass. Do both of you understand?" We both said yes.

"Mrs. Smith, when did you first meet the sea creature?"

"I was indulging my daughter's imagination. We would go to the lake, have a picnic, and make up stories about sea monsters and sasquatches. When we arrived home, she would paint pictures of the adventures. You see, her father died when she was four. I let her imagine a world with friendly creatures in it. She had so much loss for one so young."

The prosecutor let out a harrumph. The judge banged his gavel.

"Mrs. Smith, I'm not sure that's healthy for your daughter."

Aaron stood and said, "I object. He's editorializing."

"Sustained," said the judge. "Mr. Winston. I've warned you once."

"I have no more questions." I let out a sigh.

Aaron stood to ask the judge permission to clarify my words. The judge consented.

"If it may please the court, I have drawings and painting that Sadie Smith created. I wish to enter them into evidence."

The prosecutor looked like he was about to explode. "I know nothing of these."

Aaron said, "My filing indicated that I would have exhibits of Sadie's artwork."

The judge rifled through his papers. "Indeed, it does. Continue, Mr. Matthew."

"I don't know the providence of these items," screamed the prosecutor.

"If you allow me to question Mrs. Smith, I can provide it."

The judge agreed.

"Mrs. Smith," Aaron said, "do you recognize these paintings?"

"Yes. The one is of Bessie, a sea creature that Sadie said she met at the lake. Sadie drew the creature as a friendly entity. She drew it after we had a picnic at Lake Erie Park in the early spring. You can see she has drawn herself with her spring jacket. She put a hat on Bessie so she wouldn't be cold. The next painting is of Sadie and I visiting Bessie's cave. She must have used the Navy's pictures of the lava tubes and caves to create the cave."

The judge interrupted. "That's enough, Mrs. Smith. The paintings have been authenticated. Do you have any other questions, Mr. Matthew?"

Aaron said he rested his case. The judge asked the jury to leave the courtroom. I tensed up. He was going to rule on Aaron's motion for dismissal.

"I am inclined to grant the defense's motion. However, a jury is empaneled. I'm going to let it go to verdict." Tears welled in my eyes as he asked the jury to return. The judge gave minimal instructions to the jury and released them to deliberate.

"What do we do now?" I asked Aaron.

Esme and Guiliana joined us at the defense table. "We wait. Let's walk across the street to the deli," said Esme. "I scouted the area. There are no crowds. We'd be back in a jiff if there's an early verdict."

Aaron agreed we needed a change of scenery. We made it to the deli without any commotion—for a change. We ordered our food and ate silently. I wanted to contact Sadie but refrained. She would hear the tension in my voice and know the verdict wasn't in yet.

"Go ahead and contact Sadie," Aaron said.

"What?" I said. "How did you know I was thinking of her."

"Just a guess."

Esme and Guiliana looked at each other.

"What do you two know about Aaron that I don't?"

Guiliana said, "Nothing. I met him when I was called in on the zebra mussel case."

"We've crossed paths over the years when I cover the courthouse beat," Esme said.

For some reason, I didn't quite believe them, even though their answers were plausible. I didn't have a chance to question them any further; Aaron's phone rang. There was a verdict.

"At least, it's not hung," said Esme.

Aaron looked tense. "Quick jury verdicts worry me. Especially since the judge granted the prosecution's motion to add the insanity charge. If they say guilty by insanity, we'll have grounds for appeal. I couldn't prepare for an insanity defense. I would have called psychologists."

I nearly collapsed. Insanity? Would I go to a mental institution? Esme and Guiliana walked on either side of me and steadied my gait. I wasn't sure I'd make it into the courthouse, let alone the courtroom. I made it. I saw the prosecutor was at his table already. As soon as Aaron and I took our places at the defense table, the judge entered. We rose. He asked us to sit.

"Bring the jury in," the judge said to the bailiff.

All twelve came in and were seated. I was watching juror number ten. I knew my fate would depend on him. So did Aaron. He was scrutinizing the juror also. I could not see anything unusual in that grumpy juror. "Aaron," I whispered. "What do you think?"

Before he could answer, the judge asked for the verdict slip. The bailiff took it from the foreman of the jury and took it to the judge. The judge opened it, read it, and handed it back to the bailiff so the foreman could read the verdict.

I wanted to cover my ears. I didn't want to know.

"What does the jury say?" the judge stated.

"We, the jury, in the matter of Janet Smith, find her not guilty by reason of insanity."

"Thank you, jurors. You are excused."

Aaron rose to address the court. The judge motioned for him to sit.

"If I let this verdict stand, you will have grounds for appeal. I will read my findings on the motion that you made to the court. I am overturning the verdict."

My heart sank. The judge would find me just plain guilty. Somehow, the mental institution sounded better than jail. Aaron had to help me stand as the judge read this decision.

"Mrs. Smith. I find your lawyer's motion has merit. The prosecution did not provide sufficient evidence that you were in possession of the pollen or the weapon to disperse it. The charges are dropped."

I don't remember leaving the courtroom. Esme was going to drive my vehicle, since I was in no shape to drive. Aaron and Guiliana would follow. I sobbed the entire way home. Esme was about to turn onto my driveway when we saw the mob come out from behind the house. Esme sped by the house and turned toward the area of Sash's cave. I saw that Aaron and Guiliana were behind us. They followed us. I saw Guiliana making calls while Aaron drove.

"I hope Guiliana didn't call in her unit," I said. "She could be in trouble."

Esme didn't answer. She concentrated on her driving, especially when she took the car off-road through the park by the lake. Aaron was on our tail. As we drew closer to Sash's cave, we saw the National Guard had been deployed there.

"What do we do? Why is the Guard here?"

"I don't know, Janet. Call Guiliana."

Guiliana's phone was busy. Darn. I looked at Esme while the Guard surrounded my car and Aaron's. I knew that whatever phone calls Guiliana made would do no good. We were trapped.

I cried, "Joseph." I was trying to alert him to take care of Sadie. He heard. I could tell he heard me. I wished Meow would come and rescue us, even if it risked his life. I heard Esme scream. She was pointing to a tree. Meow was in the tree with a net thrown over him. What would happen to us all?

EPILOGUE

Sadie and Jo-Jo both felt it. The feeling knocked them unconscious. Jo-Jo recovered first. He rubbed Sadie's wrists. When she started to regain consciousness, Jo-Jo had her drink some water.

"Jo-Jo, what was that?" Sadie asked weakly.

"I'm not sure," Jo-Jo said. He did not know how much to tell Sadie about what had happened to her mother.

"It's Mom, isn't it?"

Jo-Jo nodded. "She's alive, Sadie. Remember that. She's alive. I need some time to see what else I can find out."

"Okay, Jo-Jo," said Sadie. "I'll start packing provisions for our journey."

OGUA

PROLOGUE
SOMEWHERE IN THE HIMALAYAN
MOUNTAINS

A few centuries ago, a rumbling in the mountains scared the climbers. They did not know what it was, but they knew it wasn't human. Fire on top of the mountain made them turn back. The fire was only there at times, but the rumbling was constant. The Nepalese government decided to wall off the mountain and forbid visitors.

A brave young man decided to sneak over the wall. He had trained for months to scale the wall and then the mountain. He finally felt ready. The wall was a minor obstacle. He didn't expect the terrain on the mountain to be so dense.

I should have known it would have grown over, Aaron thought. The climbing paths were filled with stones and debris. One time, a smoldering log hurled toward him. He barely got out of the way. After four days of climbing, Aaron thought he could see the peak. It was difficult to tell. The top of the mountain was always encased in clouds, only breaking when the fire appeared. He only had a mile or two to go, when his foot slipped. He tumbled from the mountain into a ravine.

1

OGUA

Ogua heard the distress call. For the first time ever, he was sorry he had adopted the turtle persona after his wings were taken. He had been a young dragon and was impressed with how turtles could be on land and sea. He felt his destiny was to be equally able to conquer both domains. He was faster in water but knew some of his trek would be on land, once he left the Monongahela River. He didn't bother packing and left immediately for Cleveland.

Ogua swam as far as he could, until he had to travel over land. He traveled at night and rested during the day so as not to be seen. The vegetation he found at night was enough to sustain him. Luckily, the trip took only two human days. When he finally arrived in Cleveland, he sensed a crowd had surrounded Bessie and Sash's cave entrance. Janet, the human who needed rescuing, was still trapped in two cars with Aaron, Guiliana, and Esme. They must be dehydrated and starving.

Although Ogua was stepping lightly so his weight didn't disturb the earth, he felt that the only way to save them would be to find another entrance to cave. Sash had told him of other caves in Put-in-Bay, the island in Lake Erie. Quietly, Ogua slipped into the water ten miles south of where the humans were.

Humans, thought Ogua. *They are so much trouble. Whose idea was it to be their protectors? Where did my time with Billy and Patti get me? They just grew up and left.* Ogua swam swiftly and located the cave easily. Sash had sent a good description of it.

Ogua entered the cave. He could see Sash had done human remodeling in this cave also. *Sash and his obsession with humans... Harumph. I never wanted to be a savior to humans, but Mom insisted. She said I'd come to understand the need. What does she know? She's still in a Scottish loch living a comfortable life. She sold her children out by having them travel to a new location and find their destiny.*

Ogua made his way through the underground tunnels. He had to travel slowly. If he went too fast, it might cause seismic waves, and he'd be detected by humans. There was no food in the tubes. Sash had said they were always stocked. What had happened to empty the tubes?

Bessie, Sadie, Chichi, and Spitzy were all sitting around a table communicating telepathically. Ogua could tell their telepathy had advanced further than his. His mom had sent him exercises, but it was too much work with him also having the rivers to patrol to keep humans from having accidents.

Ogua said, "Hi, folks. You called?"

The sea creatures and sasquatches turned to see who was there. Bessie flew into Ogua's arms. "Ouch," she said. "Don't you trim your nails. Now I have scratches."

"Hello, to you too," Ogua said to Bessie.

Sash said, "Who called him?"

Ogua was not the most popular of the sea creatures. He was like his shell. He was always grumpy. "Someone did. I wouldn't make this trip if I hadn't been called."

"I called him," Spitzy said. Spitzy glared at Bessie. Tempers were flaring in the cave. The four of them had been working on a plan to rescue the humans but still had not figured out how to save them. "I thought we needed cynical eyes."

"Well, hello to you too, sister," Ogua grumbled. "I missed you, too."

Spitzy tried to hug Ogua. He backed away and knocked over a couple of nests. His fall was loud, and the earth shook. "See why we don't have you around?" Spitzy says. Everyone except Ogua started to pick up the nests and other things that fell.

"We have to get serious," Bessie shouted. "Janet, Aaron, Esme, and Guiliana have been stuck in their cars for days. Getting supplies to them isn't working well. The humans who surround them have started taking shifts so there's a night guard. From what Bessie could hear, they were afraid they'd escape at night."

"I have it under control," said Ogua. "I can use my spikes to cut the net. I have good night vision. I can lead them into the cave."

"But you are huge," said Chichi. "The humans will see you."

"That's true," said Sash. "However, Ogua, if you make a lot of noise and shake the earth, the humans might run."

Everyone tried to talk at once. "Hush, everyone," said Bessie. "We need to think about the pitfalls of this scheme."

Spitzy gave Bessie a horrible look. "I'm surprised you would even give this turtle-brained idea consideration."

Before the conversation could continue, there was a loud knock at the back of Sash's cave. "Who could that be?" Chichi said.

"Maybe we shouldn't answer," Bessie said.

"Oh, come on, creatures," said Ogua. "Where is your sense of adventure?"

Ogua crossed the cave and tried to open the door, but his claws were too thick to work the lock.

"Do I have to do everything?" said Bessie. She pushed Ogua away, not a small feat, and unlocked the door.

Bessie grabbed the newcomers and began to croon. There stood Jo-Jo and Sadie. When the others, except Ogua, saw them, they rushed to hug them.

"This cave is too crowded. Do you have a room I can sleep in?" said Ogua.

"I do," said Sash. "But don't you want to meet Janet's daughter and hus—Jo-Jo?"

Ogua shrugged, causing much shaking in the cave. Everyone held on to a nest to keep them from falling to the floor. "Hi, Jo-Jo. Hi, Sadie. Where's the room?" Ogua asked.

Sadie ran to Ogua and asked, "May I shake your hand, I mean, claw? We don't know each other well enough yet to hug."

Ogua was stunned. No one had ever asked to shake his claw. Most humans and even other creatures were afraid to go near him. He extended his claw to Sadie. She took it into both of her hands, looked Ogua in the eye, and said, "Pleased to meet you."

"Ogua," said Bessie, "is that a tear in your eye?"

"No way. Direct me to my room."

While Bessie settled Ogua in, the others got out some food and drink for the two travelers. Chichi knew they had to walk most of the way. Even if Jo-Jo had carried Sadie part of the way, they had to be famished.

The creatures and Sadie set down for their meal just as Bessie returned. "Darn it, Sash, you gave the guest room to Meow. Why didn't you tell me? You know Ogua hates cats."

'Sorry, Bessie. In all this chaos, I forgot."

"You don't all love each other?" Sadie asked.

The creatures all turned to Sadie. They looked ashamed that they were bickering among themselves. "Siblings have spats. That's all it was," Bessie said. "Right, creatures?"

They all nodded. Sadie didn't look convinced. "Okay, never mind. How do we save Mom?"

2

JANET

I felt it in my heart. I gasped.

"What's wrong, Janet?" Esme asked.

"Sadie is near," I said.

Aaron nodded. "She is." I looked at Aaron again. His beard was growing faster than I ever saw a beard grow before. He was flicking his eyebrows out of his eyes.

"You are a manquatch, aren't you?" I said.

"Took you long enough," Esme said and laughed. Guiliana and Aaron joined in.

"When were you going to tell me?" I asked.

"We decided to let you figure it out yourself. I maintain a human appearance to work in the court."

"What—who were you before you transformed?" I asked.

"I was Aaron Matthew, a law student who took a vacation in the Himalayas and fell from the mountain," said Aaron. He began to tell his story:

I was attending Case Western Reserve on a scholarship. My dream had always been to become a lawyer. My parents were deceased, but my foster mother stressed keeping up my grades so I might earn a scholar-

ship. I was a running back in high school and hoped football would afford me a scholarship. Even as a full human, I could fly down the field. At the last football game of my senior year, I busted my tibia. The athletic scholarship to Ohio State was revoked. Luckily, Mom emphasized academics. I had applied to Case Western as a backup and to appease Mom. Her father had attended the school. I was accepted and offered a full ride.

I thought my life couldn't get any better. I had a great girlfriend who was as studious as I was. Spring break of my senior year, I decided to scale the Himalayan mountain that I had read about in my mythology class. Mom discouraged me.

"I have a bad feeling about this," Mom said. "I feel it in my heart."

I told my mom it was as safe as when I climbed the Half Dome in Yosemite. There, I had to climb through fourteen miles of rough terrain before even reaching the dome. It only took me a day to make it to the bottom of the dome. I pitched my tent, made dinner, and slept.

At Half Dome, I didn't sleep well that night. The mountain air was colder than I had planned for. I was sore from the few tumbles I had taken climbing the rough terrain. Also, I was too excited to be halfway to the top of the mountain. Even though I was not rested, I was able to reach the top of the half dome. The view was glorious.

I knew if I could climb The Half Dome, I could make it up the walled off mountain. I only had to find the one crack in the wall that the Nepal government hadn't fixed yet. I wouldn't have to scale the wall. I would be rested to climb the mountain and ascertain what the bizarre fire was from.

The weather was perfect for climbing, cool and clear. I stopped many times and took pictures. I wanted proof I had been there. Halfway up, I stopped to eat my provisions. I took a quick cat nap and then started up again. I was five miles from the top when I was hit by a hot, horrifying wind. I tried to hang on, but I fell. I remember thinking how upset my mom would be.

I'm not sure how much time passed, but when I came to, a large, hairy ape stood over me. He must have been over seven feet tall. I could probably sit in his hands—maybe in one hand.

"Don't be afraid," the creature said. "Think hard. You saw me before."

I was groggy and thinking was hard. I vaguely remembered seeing an ape.

"I saw you as I fell. I think you cushioned my fall."

"I did," said the creature.

"What are you?"

"A sasquatch."

"What? A what? Sasquatches are mythical creatures. You can't be one."

I thought I was hallucinating. A talking ape. "What are you?

The creature said, "Many of us live in this world, but we keep ourselves hidden because our appearance scares people. Our mission is to help humans and sea creatures stay safe. You lost a lot of blood. To keep you alive, I cut my arm and gave you a transfusion of my blood. I knew the blood would keep you alive, but only as half human and half sasquatch. You are becoming a manquatch."

I must have passed out again. When I woke this time, I was no longer on the mountain. I was in a house unlike any house I had seen. A manquatch took care of me by preparing human food I was used to, not the nuts, berries, and raw meat the sasquatch had been feeding me.

The manquatch was Jo-Jo. The sasquatch who saved me was Sash. I lived with Jo-Jo for a year, regaining strength at a rapid pace. I was much stronger than I had been as a human. Jo-Jo helped me regulate my strength as I gained it. He introduced me to other manquatches. I learned from them the advantages I would gain from staying in an underwater civilization.

I was young and unruly at times. I still wanted to be a lawyer. I wanted a family. I wanted to let Mom know I was alive. The manquatches saw how unhappy I was. They gathered and devised a way I could live as a human. I had to learn how to cut my massive mane daily. I never did get the hang of trimming my eyebrows. Don't giggle, Janet. I was able to move back to Cleveland and see my mother. The college let me reenroll when they heard of my ordeal in Nepal. I told them I had fallen and the locals had nursed me back to health. I graduated law school. I specialize in cases where humans are deemed crazy from seeing creatures.

I split my time between Cleveland and the underwater world."

We were stunned. "I thought you had a wife," I said.

"I do," said Aaron. "She lives in the underwater world. Chichi had saved her from being attacked by a swarm of bees. She is highly allergic and died from their venom. Chichi sucked the venom out as she poured in her own fresh blood. When I met her, I knew she was the one. I kept encouraging her to learn some grooming techniques so she can join me in Cleveland. She's practicing her grooming, but she doesn't seem ready to see our world again."

"I'm sorry to hear that," I said.

Aaron shrugged. We didn't talk much after that. It was getting dark, and we had a routine worked out to get ourselves ready to sleep. During the day, we moved into one car. Sleeping was better if we split between two cars. As we unfolded blankets and moved pillows around, the earth around us started to move.

"Something is going on in Sash's or Bessie's caves," Aaron said. "It sounds like a big creature."

"All of them are big, Aaron," said Guiliana.

"Bigger than them. Someone has come to join them," Aaron said.

"Who?" I wondered.

"It could be Ogua. I've never met him, but he's a huge turtle, nearly a thousand pounds. He's a grouchy one, not one to volunteer to help anyone," said Aaron.

"I feel Sadie near," I said. "Will he hurt my Sadie?"

"No," said Aaron. "If it's him, he will ask for the best bed in the house as well as the best food. Then he will sleep."

"Isn't that strange for a dragon turned sea creature?" Esme asked.

"I guess," Aaron said. "Ogua never stopped grieving his father. He watched as the sasquatch dragged away his father's body. He was too weak to fight them. From what I heard, he let out the longest and worst scream when the dragons were attacked."

I think I understood Ogua a bit. I know I screamed for the longest time when the doctors told me Joseph hadn't made it. The nurse gave me a sedative, and I stayed in the hospital for a week. My mom, Veronica, was still alive. She took care of Sadie. I think that is when she showed Sadie her pictures of Bessie and told her the stories. I didn't mind. It gave Sadie something else to think about as she grieved for her dad. Not too long after I lost Joseph, Mom died. Sadie was doubly crushed by the weight of losing two of the people she loved the most. By the time Sadie discovered Bessie, I thought she had put aside the stories Mom told her. I guess she hadn't. I think she was secretly looking at Mom's drawings of Bessie. When Sadie said she saw Bessie, I figured she was resurrecting Bessie to be closer to her grandma.

"You look deep in thought," said Guiliana.

"I have much on my mind," I said quietly.

Guliana was in the back seat with me. She drew me into a hug. Esme and Aaron each took one of my hands. The only reason I was hanging on to my sanity were these three wonderful people. We all hugged, and Esme and I returned to her car.

3

THE CREATURES IN THE CAVE

Sadie stood up and yelled, "Stop. You've been bickering for hours. My mom is still a hostage."

All the creatures ceased talking and looked at Sadie. Sadie's eyes were red from crying. Jo-Jo took Sadie on his lap and tried to soothe her, but even Jo-Jo couldn't comfort her.

"Look, I know everyone wants Janet and the others safe," Jo-Jo began. "We must put our egos aside. None of us need to be the hero. Teamwork will help."

As Jo-Jo was talking, Ogua walked into the room, yawning from his nap. "I'm hungry."

Bessie was trying to hold her temper as she took out the greens and seafood that Ogua preferred. She had sent Spitzy out to gather things as the discussion continued. Ogua began munching on his feast.

"Ogua, chew with your mouth closed, and quietly," said Spitzy.

"Harumph," said Ogua as he continued his meal.

"Forget Ogua," said Bessie.

"Just like always, Bessie, you dismiss my intellect," Ogua said. "You all know Aaron, don't you?"

They all nodded, except Sadie.

"Aaron is a manquatch like I am," said Jo-Jo. "What about him?"

"One time, when Aaron was visiting me, he told me of the mountain he was trying to climb when he fell. Before he fell and was rescued, he was trying to determine what was giving off a strange fire-like light. He was close, only a hundred feet away, when the heat of the fire and a terrible wind made him fall."

"We know all that," said Bessie. "Get to the point."

"But Sadie doesn't," Ogua said. The other creatures thought they saw Ogua smile, but they dismissed it. Ogua never smiled.

Ogua picked up another seafood roll that Spitzy had made for him. He chewed it loudly, then burped.

"Gross, Ogua. Now the entire cave smells," Spitzy said.

"Whatever," said Ogua. "I think Aaron was climbing the mountain of our birth."

"There's nothing there anymore," Bessie said. "Even Mom went to Scotland."

"I know. But what about the unhatched eggs?"

An unsettling quiet fell over the group. "They were broken by the sasquatch, weren't they?" said Spitzy.

"We don't know that for sure," Ogua said. "We only assumed. Sasquatches were beasts then. Sorry, Chichi and Sash. But it's the truth."

Chichi and Sash nodded. "No offense taken," said Chichi. Sash nodded.

"We need to explore that mountain and see if any of the eggs hatched and survived. The creature probably flies and breaths powerful fire. Once there, we must convince them we are their siblings and recruit them to shoo away the humans that surround our friends."

The creatures nodded in agreement. "It's the best plan we've heard, as crazy as it sounds," said Jo-Jo.

"Who do we send as ambassadors?" Sash asked.

"Not the sasquatch. If the dragons there even catch a scent of a sasquatch, they will attack," Ogua said.

"You think they remember?" Sadie said.

"We have strange memories, my dear Sadie. We remember things from the past that we didn't experience," Ogua said.

"Ogua, my dear," said Chichi, "what's gotten into you?"

"Nothing," Ogua said. He was embarrassed for showing a strange attraction to Sadie.

The creatures decided to sleep on Ogua's suggestion. As they readied for bed, Sadie asked Ogua if she could share his nest. He agreed.

4

CITY COUNCIL

The mayor was livid. The park was filled with people who wanted to attack the strange woman who had been accused of spreading the memory-reducing pollen. She had been exonerated, but some people still wanted her punished. The other three in the cars posed a bigger problem: Aaron, a prominent and respected lawyer in Cleveland, a much beloved TV reporter, and a Navy commander. His pleas for them to leave peacefully had gone unheeded. The city council met to discuss how to resolve the stalemate.

"Just tear gas them," said the president of the council.

"No," said the mayor. "The hostages would suffer the ill effects also."

"Use the National Guard. They can surround the car, form a ring that pushes back the crowd until they are pushed out of the park."

The mayor pondered that idea. "I'll need to call the governor. He wants this solved immediately. I think he would allow the National Guard to help."

"You will alienate your voters, mayor," said his aide. "There's an election coming up."

"I'm not doing well in the polls right now with this standoff going on for four weeks," the mayor retorted. "A decisive action might show that I don't flinch in a crisis."

"Forget the election," said the council president. "If I have my way, I'll be running against you and unseat you."

"What do you think?" said one of the members-at-large to the council secretary. She had a clear mind and was a voice of reason.

The secretary closed her laptop, where she had been taking notes. After she adjusted her glasses and took a sip of water, she rested her elbows on the table. The council members respected her and looked in her direction.

"Let's offer the crowd a compromise. If they disperse and let the hostages go, the mayor will ask the president of the United States for a federal inquiry into the sightings in Cleveland, Buffalo, and Port Huron."

The council murmured among themselves. "Isn't that passing the buck?" said one member.

The secretary responded, "Yes, that's what politicians do."

The council erupted into laughter but voted unanimously to proceed with the suggestion.

The front-page headline was, *Mayor Asks for Presidential Inquiry into Monster Sightings.*

5

THE CREATURES

I was stunned by the headline in the local paper. Meow found a discarded paper when he snuck into town for supplies.

"We have to move quickly," said Meow.

"Meow is right," said Ogua, who had Sadie on his back. The two had been inseparable. "Let's go over the plan once more."

Bessie said, "I have already contacted Mother. She hasn't left Scotland for eons, but she is swimming to Asia and from there climbing the mountain. I don't like it. She's never left the loch. She's older now."

"Your mother is barely middle-aged," responded Ogua. "Don't sell Mom short."

"Okay, okay..."

"Mom will contact me once she ascertains that the fire could be from the eggs that were left behind," Meow said.

"Bessie, Chichi, Sash, and Spitzy will travel on Meow's back to the spot once your mother lets us know there are siblings," said Sadie.

"I still think it would be best for Mom to greet the newbie dragons first. Dragons know their mother instinctively," Spitzy said.

Sash sighed. "Spitzy has a point. Mom might be able to urge them into action without us. Mom could summon us if needed. I still think we should have Meow fetch the dragons. He's faster."

"Dragons fly almost as fast as Meow," said Spitzy.

"And you would know?" said Ogua sarcastically.

"Please don't fight," pleaded Sadie.

"We will let Mom decide how to get the dragons here." All the creatures nodded.

"Then we have a plan," said Sadie.

6

JANET

The next morning, I was woken by a banging on the car window. As I wiped the sleep from my eyes, I noticed someone holding up a newspaper to the window. The headline blared, *Mayor Asks for Presidential Inquiry into Monster Sightings*.

"Hey, wake up. Wake up," I urged the others.

Aaron stretched. "Where's the fire?"

"Look!" I pointed to the headline.

Aaron motioned to the person holding the paper and mouthed, "Can we have that copy?"

The man motioned for Aaron to put down the window. Aaron grabbed the paper and began reading. "Whoever your boss has writing your stories in your absence is no way as good as you are."

"Thanks." I remained quiet as Aaron read. Esme and Guiliana were just starting to awake.

Aaron said, "The mayor called the president of the United States and asked for a task force to investigate the unusual creature sightings in the Midwest. The president is taking it under advisement."

"That means it won't happen," said Guiliana.

"I'm not so sure," Aaron said. "The mayor has organized a petition drive to get a hundred thousand signatures that he will hand deliver to the president by Friday. The president may have no choice."

"What does that mean for us?" Esme asked.

"The mayor has secured an agreement with the mob to let us go once the task force is formed. That could mean a couple more weeks stuck here. Maybe more."

We all were glum as we began our morning ritual. The police escorts would come to allow us to use the restrooms and freshen up. The Girl Scouts would deliver our breakfast. I'd get my laptop back from them today, since I sent it yesterday to be charged. I planned on writing the rest of the day. Today, Aaron will request law books so he can file motions to have us released. He maintained that we were in police custody for own our safety, but we wanted to be released since there was no warrant. No one dared hope these developments would get us safely released.

7

NESSIE AND HER LOST CHILDREN

Nessie, also known as the Loch Ness Monster, (how she hated that moniker) decided to rest at the bottom of the mountain before investigating whether or not she had more children. She missed the children she had dispersed all over the world. She knew the best thing for survival would be to spread out, but she hadn't anticipated how much she would miss them. Telepathy was no substitute for visits. It didn't allow you to hug or see the children.

Nessie was soundly sleeping when she felt a warmth spread over her. She opened her eyes to see that a teenage dragon had his head on her shoulder. He was so beautiful. She had forgotten what beautiful dragons her children had been. They were now distorted and transformed into unsightly creatures, for the most part. This child brought back memories of how beautiful her children had been. Strong, multicolored, iridescent wings that were handsomely formed. *My child*, she thought. She wrapped herself around him.

"I sensed you were close, Mom," the dragon said. "My siblings sent me ahead to find out if the visitor we detected was you or a sasquatch. For some reason, we all fear that a sasquatch will find us."

Nessie nodded. "Yes, my son. Eons ago, sasquatches cut off our lovely wings. Many of us died. I'm glad the fear of sasquatches was imprinted on you, but much has changed since the sasquatches committed the massacre. They are now our protectors."

The dragon drew away from his mom.

"It's okay," said Nessie. She put her hands on his chest and felt his heartbeat. She imparted the history of the last few eons.

The dragon relaxed. "I will send this history ahead of our arrival."

The dragon urged Nessie to climb on his back. Nessie was much larger than the dragon, but her weight and size didn't bother the young dragon. Nessie was amazed. Her second generation of children possessed more strength than the first. She was bursting with pride.

When Nessie and her son reached the top of the mountain, Nessie saw that her children had received the message the teenager had sent. They had prepared a true dragon feast for them. The delicate eggs of the magical bird were pickled to perfection. The flower blossoms were made into a fresh salad garnished with tender bamboo shoots. Her children urged her to eat before they introduced themselves to her. She marveled at the number of offspring that had hatched. As she hugged each, she learned their names and quirks. When she thought she had seen them all, two dragons went back to the farthest cave from the feast.

"Mother," said the teenaged son who had found her. "We saved the rest of the dragons for last. You will be most proud of them. They are not your sons and daughters. They are your grandchildren, as are we."

Nessie cried tears of joy. She had spent many sad years not knowing if the eggs she had lain were destroyed by the sasquatch. Miraculously, they survived. Each grandchild brought Nessie a perfectly roasted pinecone candy. Her recipes must have left an imprint on them too. As each hugged their grandmother, they told her who their mother was. Meow had the most children, seventy-two. Bessie had twenty-five. Spitzy had fifteen. Even Ogua had fathered five children.

Nessie said to her offspring, "I've come on a mission. You all know what happened to your parents and me. We were maimed and almost died, but the peaceful sasquatches saved us. Your parents are all over the world, but two of them and their sasquatch protectors are in a dire situation. In trying to help the humans, they have been spotted by humans who are unaccustomed to seeing us."

"Mother," said the teenager, "what should we do to save our brothers and sisters?"

"It's not your siblings that need protecting. Humans and a mansquat are in danger." Nessie related how their siblings were seen and the resulting problems. "We must fly to this area and scare away the humans, so the humans and mansquat come to safety and live with us."

The dragons were all murmuring to each other. They were being asked to save siblings they had never met. A few of the older dragons felt it was a trick. Had the sasquatches programed their mother to lure them to their demises? For eons, they lived thinking the sasquatches were the enemy. Had that much changed? A long-held belief is hard to let go of.

The lead dragon, Draconia, said, "Dear Mother, we are finding it hard to believe your story. But we are your children and will honor your request. We only ask that you remain here and see after your grandchildren. I'm only allowing those who volunteer for this mission to go. If a dragon refuses, you cannot cast aspersions on them."

"I accept the terms," Nessie said.

"We fly at dawn," said Draconia.

8

THE PREPARATIONS

The dragons assembled at the top of the mountain. Draconia was surprised how many dragons had volunteered to save the humans and mansquats. Those that didn't volunteer stayed to help Nessie with the children. They would need to gather food and protect the lair. Nessie could impart history lessons to the grandchildren and tell them what their parents were like.

Nessie spent most of the night explaining to the dragons how to reach Cleveland and preparing them for what they would see. Having never left the lair, they might be startled by the wonders of the modern world. It was quite a bit to relay in one night. Nessie did the best she could. When her children left, she was exhausted and slept two human days.

The dragons decided to fly above the cloud cover and stay hidden until they all formed a ring around the mob that surrounded Janet, Aaron, Esme, and Guiliana. The flight would take three human days. Nessie communicated to Bessie that the dragons were on their way. She would need to monitor the dragons' activity and open the cave and lava tube system to hide them in once the humans and mansquat were released. Bessie insisted the hostages be escorted by the dragons to the tunnels. Nessie agreed.

Bessie, Sash, Meow, Ogua, Chichi, Sadie, and Jo-Jo could only wait. Sadie had an Uno deck. She and Chichi taught Ogua how to play. Jo-Jo joined them. He said, "I used to play this with my daughter."

Sadie looked at Jo-Jo. "You have a daughter?"

Jo-Jo realized he had said too much. "I did in the human world," said Jo-Jo.

"Don't you ever get to visit her?" Sadie wanted to know.

"I can't. You see what a problem it is for any of us to be seen."

"I could be your pretend daughter," said Sadie. With tears in his eyes, Jo-Jo nodded yes.

Ogua beat all of them at nearly fifty games of Uno. He loved the game. Bessie and Chichi accused him of cheating. Ogua just laughed and laughed.

"You never laugh, Ogua," said Bessie.

"I love beating my siblings," he gloated.

"Sadie has revealed your soft side," Bessie said.

"She did not. I've always been softhearted." The creatures all laughed.

Bessie was about to say something but stopped. She seemed to be listening to a message. All eyes turned to her, even Ogua's. Bessie shook her head a few times then closed her eyes.

"That was Mom. Upon entering US air space, US Air Force jets were launched to shoot down the UFOs—*our siblings*. The dragons fired on the jets. They crashed. The Air Force had issued an alert that the US is being invaded and attacked with unknown weapons. Draconia was injured. Two other dragons have taken him to a safe place and will return for him when the battle is over."

The cave was silent. Ogua broke the silence, "We must be there when the dragons arrive. They are our siblings." Heads nodded.

"How are you going to do that?" Sadie asked.

"We'll figure it out," Ogua said, placing his hand gently on her head. "I want to suggest that—no offense, Jo-Jo, but I think you and Sadie need to stay here. You'd be an asset, Jo-Jo, but you need to stay safe in case the worst happens."

Jo-Jo nodded. Ogua did not want to leave Sadie without a parent, in case the rescue went dramatically wrong.

"Mom says the dragons will arrive tomorrow. We should be strategically spaced around the crowd tonight. It will be easier to move at night," Spitzy said.

"Of course," said Bessie. "We'll stay hidden until the dragons arrive. They're anticipating an early morning arrival."

Most of the creatures went to their nests early, since they would be up in the middle of the night to move to their positions. Meow and Ogua were sipping their warm milk. "This isn't bad, Meow," said Ogua.

"I hope you aren't lactose intolerant," said Meow. "I don't want to clean up a mess in the morning."

"I have an iron stomach," boasted Ogua.

"What have you been doing with your life, Ogua?" Meow asked.

"I wasn't always grumpy, you know. I never got the hang of being good to small humans. I had bad luck with them," Ogua said. "I thought I had found my human. She was an adorable, inquisitive girl, Alice. Her mother limited her trip to the river, because Alice always got her clothes muddy. If that happened, I knew I wouldn't see her for a while. Then, when Alice reached what humans call their teen years, she told me she couldn't visit anymore. She was interested in boys." Ogua wiped a tear from his eye.

"I have trouble, too," said Meow. "My first one died. Her sister helped me get over it. Esme, one of the ones you are rescuing."

"Maybe I should have been a sea creature like everyone else," Ogua said.

"Me, too," said Meow.

9

THE BATTLE THAT WASN'T

Luckily, the sea creatures could communicate telepathically. They were able to check in with each other to find out where each of them was positioned. Meow was high in a tree north of their friends. His plan was to swoop down when needed and secure the hostages. About fifty yards away and to the south, Bessie had slithered partially under the police caravan of sixteen squad cars. She couldn't be seen. Spitzy waited in a tree just opposite Meow in the south and reignited her fire. It wasn't as powerful as the dragons, but she hoped it would deter some of the mob. Ogua, in the north, was in Put-in-Bay near the opening of the cave system. The two sasquatches were rovers scouting what the police and sleeping mob. Sash told Nessie to have four of the biggest, strongest dragons to swoop in and each take a hostage to Put-in-Bay; it would take the police and mob time to get there, giving Aaron, Emes, Guiliana, and Janet time to enter the caves.

Bessie was first to hear the hum of the dragon wings. She hadn't heard that sound in eons. How wonderful! She wished she had her wings to join in the song. Spitzy was moving her wings to the music; however, it had been too many years since she had used them, and they were out of tune. She hadn't bothered to keep up with the maintenance since she had no one to sing with. Meow purred in the same pitch as the dragons. Even Ogua was humming the tune of the wings. They all had missed being part of a larger group. Although they knew they had an important job to do, they couldn't help but be excited at the prospect of meeting their new siblings.

Out of nowhere, four huge dragons swept in with their flames blazing. They landed on the cars that held the hostages. One of them began to melt the metal roofs, and the others blew the hot liquid away from their intended targets. The ordeal was over in a flash. The mob and police had been blinded by the light of the fires. The four mighty dragons each had one of the hostages in their arms as they flew to Put-in-Bay.

The Navy jets approached the mob just as the four dragons took off with the hostages. The jets were ready to fire, when the other dragons let out smoke and steam. The jets had to pull up and out of the fray, or they would have crashed.

Once the hostages were on their way to safety, the remaining dragons spit fire in strategic areas and caused fires to start. The smoke and flames hid the dragons and the waiting creatures. The dragons and creature friends of the humans and mansquats gathered in mass and flew to Put-in-Bay as a group. Sash and Chichi sprinted to the door that opened to Sash's cave and began the underground trek to Put-in-Bay. Meow was already on Put-in-Bay, having run over the lake to the island. Ogua was making his way through the lake to the island.

10

BREAKING FREE

By the time Ogua reached the caves on Put-in-Bay, Sadie and Janet were hugging. Meow was all over Janet. He hadn't let anyone know how upset he was that she was in danger.

"Meow," Janet said through her tears and laughter, "you haven't been grooming. Look, I'm covered in your fur."

Chichi, Sash, and Bessie waited their turns to hug the four freed hostages. The dragons were introducing themselves to their siblings as soon as they could. The dragons cried tears of joy at meeting their older and maimed siblings.

The entire cave buzzed from the flapping of dragon wings. The maimed dragons, who were now sea creatures, were sending telepathic messages. So many messages were being sent that some were intercepted by the wrong person. Some were garbled. Hours later, the pandemonium was still out of control.

Bessie drew away from the crowd and stood beside Spitzy. "I didn't realize how much I missed being a dragon," said Bessie. Spitzy put his arms around Bessie.

"I can still breathe fire and fly, but not like them. I guess I'm not in shape."

"I guess. Where would you fly without being seen?"

"Exactly."

The entire cave started to fill with wailing. The dragons were saddened by their older siblings' appearances and their loss of power.

"Don't cry," Bessie shouted. "We cried so much when we lost our wings, that we lost our fire. Hang on to your fire!" The dragons turned on their flames to dry the tears. Smoke filled the cave.

"We will burn up, dear siblings, if you don't turn off those flames," said Meow. "I don't want my beautiful red fur singed.

"He's always so vain," said Bessie to the dragons. Everyone had a good laugh.

The mayhem settled. The dragons and sea creatures talked in small groups; some slept.

Chichi and Bessie started to prepare a celebratory feast. Esme wanted to help but was shooed away. The four who were rescued were given nests, which had been pulled into the common area of the cave, to rest in while the food was being prepared. There was no shortage of flames to cook meat for the humans and the creatures who had become used to cooked meat.

Aaron wandered over to Jo-Jo. They embraced. "You need a shave, Aaron," said Jo-Jo.

"Yeah, I sure do if I'm going to stay in Cleveland. I'm thinking I might just shut down the law practice and live in the underworld from now on. All of this was too much," said Aaron.

"I have a favor to ask you, Aaron."

"Anything," said Aaron.

"Teach me how to groom for the human world."

Aaron could see Jo-Jo staring longingly at Sadie and Janet. "Janet knows you are a mansquat."

Jo-Jo nodded. "I can't ask her to live in my world. I need to reenter the human world as much as I can."

"Sure, we will get started as soon as things calm down."

"Aaron, Jo-Jo, come eat," urged Chichi. The two mansquats walked over to where the feast was spread. Jo-Jo kept hiding behind the huge creatures. He stared at Janet from afar; he did not approach.

She had experienced enough shock in the last few months, he thought. Jo-Jo went to a nest in another part of the tunnel and curled up to sleep. At least, he hoped he could sleep. Seeing Janet had been overwhelming.

The dragons sang all night for their siblings, who had been starving for the sounds of wing music. Some dragons and sea creatures were dancing. Sadie was creating words for the songs.

Ogua said, "Sadie, let's create a ballad that will honor this epic battle."

"I love that idea," squealed Sadie. "Let's start at the beginning of the adventure. Bessie, you and Sash could help with the early history, and then I can add on what I know."

"Great idea," said Chichi.

"Let's get started," said Sadie.

Bessie provided paper and pencils for Sadie to write the words. Everyone was talking at once, giving ideas. Sadie struggled to keep up. Janet saw Sadie's eyes struggling to stay awake."

"That's enough for now," Janet said. "I'm assuming none of your aunties and uncles enforced bedtimes for this little one."

The creatures looked ashamed.

"Jo-Jo did," said Sadie. "Hey, where's Jo-Jo?"

Janet's heart beat faster. She wondered if she was ready to see her transformed husband.

Bessie looked concerned. "Ah, Sadie, I think he went to bed early."

Sadie looked crestfallen. "Mom, I wanted you to meet him today. He's so cool."

Janet had to take a deep breath before answering her daughter. "I am sure he is. We can meet tomorrow. Now you need to go to bed."

"Sleep with me," Ogua said.

"No, me," said Meow.

Sadie giggled. "Let's have a pajama party, and the three of us can cuddle together. Mom, join us."

Janet smiled and agreed.

11

MEANWHILE

The mayor was livid as he paced the room. "How did they get away? Who set the fires?"

The chief of police was speechless. "We are investigating."

"Do it faster," screamed the mayor. "How can I tell the president the crisis is over?"

"Technically, it's not. We do not know where the four hostages are. My squads have found no charred remains. There are no footprints to tell us which way they left."

The mayor sat down and began typing on his computer. When finished, he read it to the chief.

> From the office of the mayor.
> I regret to inform you that the hostages are dead. The fire in the park incinerated them.
> The crisis is over.

"What do you think?" said the mayor.

"It's the most plausible explanation," said the chief. "But what happens if they're hiding somewhere and reemerge with their sea monster friends?"

The mayor said, "I don't know. I don't know."

12

JANET

Although cramped, with three other creatures in the nest, I slept the best I had in many nights. My Sadie was with me. I hadn't realized how much I had missed Meow. Ogua took some getting used to. My goodness, his snoring! Bessie told me Ogua was the youngest of the first generation of dragons. He was spoiled. Nessie spoiled him, giving him whatever he wanted. Her husband decided they needed more children so Nessie wouldn't fuss over him so much. They had lain the eggs just before the sasquatches came and took their wings. Nessie lost so much—her husband and her eggs. She was overcome with joy when she found they had survived. I can't wait to meet Nessie. Bessie wasn't sure Nessie would be heading our way. She was staying in the Himalayas, playing with her grandchildren.

The dragons were my heroes. They were beautiful creatures. The scales were iridescent in all the colors of the rainbow. I noticed some dragons changed colors with their moods. They were more comfortable flying than walking. Luckily, the cave walls were high for the sasquatches. The dragons had enough room to maneuver.

The others in the nest were still sleeping. I crept out quietly and entered the main area of the cave. Many dragons were buzzing around. The sweet sound of the wings humming was soothing. When

I entered the room, they stopped and bowed. "What's this all about?" I asked.

"I am Draconia," said the largest of the dragons. His wing was bandaged, and he seemed to be in some pain. "We heard what you have done for our older siblings. It is a great honor to meet you."

"Oh, no. It's my honor. You are my saviors," I replied. When the dragons sent the telepathic messages, there was a distinctive hum with it; whereas, their older siblings sent feelings with theirs. I was mesmerized by the dragon sounds. The creatures who had been maimed were calmer and gentler than their younger siblings.

I looked around the cave and saw we were all there except for Aaron and Jo-Jo. I guess grooming a mansquat takes time. Then I realized I didn't hear Meow's purr. "Where's Meow?" I asked.

"He went out to find a newspaper to see how our rescue was reported. I'm hoping the fire and smoke kept the humans from seeing what we did," said Chichi.

"Oh, boy. We could be in more trouble. I wonder what the Navy pilots saw," I said.

"I know. The dragons said they've used the smoke and fire as camouflage many times when humans were near. Not too many people have seen them," said Chichi.

"It's so good to see you again, Chichi," I said.

"We're excited to have all of you here," Chichi said. We hugged.

We stayed in our embrace for a while until I felt something smaller hugging me. Sadie. Chichi and I included her in our hug. Before I knew it, Chichi, Sash, Bessie, Sadie, and I were hugging and crying.

"Hey," said Spitzy. "I want in on this hug."

I don't know how long we stayed that way. And of course, it was Ogua who interrupted us.

"Geez, you humans and creatures, all you do is hug," groused Ogua.

"Just join us," I said.

He didn't have to be asked twice. We all squeezed into the best hug ever.

I heard someone enter the room. I looked up from the hug and saw Jo-Jo. My heart seized. I couldn't breathe. I knew without a doubt, Jo-Jo was my Joseph. I could see that Aaron was looking like a man not a mansquat. I wondered why Jo-Jo didn't groom. If he did, maybe we could be friends. At least friends.

Before I could release from the hug, other dragons, Esme, Guiliana, and Aaron entered the room. They looked refreshed from their night's sleep, too.

"I have to report to the base," Guiliana said.

"Of course," I said. "What can we do to help you?"

Guiliana looked a little dazed. "Somehow I need to get back to the mainland."

Bessie looked frightened. "It's not safe there. The police and Navy are investigating a strange occurrence where the mob was."

I laughed. "Of course, they are."

Aaron said, "Now that I've groomed, I can go to the courthouse to see what the buzz is."

"Come on, Aaron," said Jo-Jo. "Your eyebrows are still shaggy. I have a kit with me." The two of them headed to a side cave. I was relieved to not have to talk to Jo-Jo. The trauma of captivity, the exhilaration of the rescue, and the joy of seeing Sadie again frayed my nerves. I wasn't up to a reunion.

Meow entered with the latest newspaper. His normal red color had faded to pink. "Bad news, folks," he purred. Bessie took the paper from Meow's paw.

"The police are saying they woke up to bright lights. Then when the lights left, all of you were gone," Bessie said. "The mayor is saying the four of you disintegrated from the heat. I don't think there should be any fallout from this rescue."

I was devastated. I could never return to my world. Neither could Esme and Guiliana. Aaron would be okay; he could live in his underwater world.

"You are safer if the world thinks you are gone," Bessie said.

Ogua didn't seem convinced. "I think we all need to go to my river. It's quiet. Not too many people. We can travel by lake and lava tubes. We can all lay low there and figure out how to restore their lives."

The other dragons started to wake, demanding breakfast. Chichi and I started to prepare a meal. Sadie wanted to help. Jo-Jo had taught her to cook while I was held hostage.

"This is all my fault," I said to Chichi as we roasted the bacon using the dragons' fires.

"There's no time to assign blame," Ogua said. "I think we need to return to our homes and hide for a century or so. Mom's plan was working before we gathered to save humans."

Bessie nodded. "If we separate, we won't put each other in danger."

"But, Bessie, all of you are so joyful now that you are together," I said. "Isn't there some way you can all stay together?"

Bessie crossed the cave and hugged me.

"You're going to be okay," said Sash. "We'll work it out."

I didn't share Sash's optimism.

Aaron came into the cave with Jo-Jo. I could tell Aaron had fussed with his eyebrows. The brows still didn't look human. Jo-Jo hadn't groomed at all. I guess he didn't need to, since he was going back to his underwater world.

Aaron, Esme, and Guiliana were talking. Aaron said, "We want to return to Cleveland and out ourselves. We'll turn ourselves in to the mayor and give an account of the rescue. The newspaper didn't report any unusual disturbance when the mob left. I want to be sure the town is settling down. We'll tell them Janet was incinerated. If the mayor and town think you're gone, then you'll be safe, Janet."

"No, I should go too," said Janet. "I'll face the consequences."

The creatures sent messages to Janet all at once. Janet couldn't unravel the ideas. "Stop! You're confusing me."

Jo-Jo quieted everyone with a message of calm. "Janet, you will always be a pariah. How will Sadie have a normal life with you being ostracized?"

"I'll live in the caves the rest of my life," I said, crying.

No one spoke.

Sash broke the silence. "Is it so bad living with us?"

I sensed I had hurt all the creatures' feelings. "I don't mean to hurt your feelings. I have lost my life."

Jo-Jo said, "Janet, we have all lost the lives we had. You are one of us now."

"I sound selfish," I said. "I'm sorry."

They all gathered around me. While they comforted me, Aaron, Esme, and Guiliana prepared to leave. Each was given a replica of a lava tube.

"It's functional," said Sash of the gift. "If you ever need us, blow into the tube. We will come."

Everyone was in tears now. I felt like I was losing family as Sash left with Aaron, Esme, and Guiliana on his back. I was sad to see them go. They could return to their lives before the creatures were found. My future was not certain.

13

JANET

All the dragons and creatures had returned to their homes except Meow and Draconia, one of the newer dragons. He would need an escort home once he got stronger. His wing had been broken by the Navy jets. Meow kept making excuses about why he hadn't taken off for Port Huron. I had a feeling he would become my house cat. I'll need a big house. Sadie, Jo-Jo, and I were the only humanoids left in the caves on Put-in-Bay.

After they left and we all pulled ourselves together, Sadie said, "Mom, have breakfast with Jo-Jo and me. We haven't eaten because of all the goodbyes."

"That's okay, Sadie," said Jo-Jo. "I need to return to my home. Now that your mom is back, she can care for you. I was just babysitting." Jo-Jo looked directly into my eyes. I had to turn away. I thought that Jo-Jo—Joseph—would stay with us. I knew he had been gone several years and probably wasn't sure he wanted to live in the human world. It had been so long that he probably has another family there. I knew I was going to cry, so I left the main cave and returned to the nest I had slept in last night. I don't know how long I'd been crying when Meow came to the nest. He enveloped me in his furry arms and purred until I fell asleep.

When I woke, Meow said, "He still loves you, Janet."

"Then why hasn't he groomed? Why is he talking of going back to the underwater world?" I didn't like the idea of living in an underwater civilization. Sadie needed a normal life after the last six months. What would I do there? I'd be the only human. I could not see a life for me there.

"It's hard to keep groomed enough to have a full-time presence above ground. Mansquats are much more comfortable with their own. The underground city is wonderful. I have visited there several times. You should see it for yourself. There are schools, stores, churches, organized sports, and many other human things. The manquatches made the world as they had it in their past world, but they left out the negative forces. It's a peaceful place to grow. Maybe your life is in the underwater world."

"Maybe I could visit and see what it's like. Sadie doesn't seem negatively affected by living there."

"Good plan, Janet," Meow said. "I can whisk the three of you there today."

"Today! I must think. I don't even know if Jo-Jo wants me."

"He wants you, dear one. He doesn't know if you want him."

I stayed in Meow's nest with him for a while thinking. I wasn't sure how to approach Jo-Jo—Joseph—about visiting the underwater world. Did I even want to give the world a chance? He didn't know I knew his real identity. "I need to fix Sadie breakfast."

"Let Jo-Jo," Meow said. "They need time to say goodbye if you don't stay with Jo-Jo."

I nodded, and Meow wrapped himself around me. I had no idea how long I slept in Meow's arms. Did I have the right to take Sadie from her father? Did I have the right to deprive her of the normal world? My dreams were restless. I failed to decide anything.

When I returned to the main cave, I smelled something burning. Sadie was helping Draconia learn to play Uno. "No, no, Draconia," Sadie said. "When you lose, you don't burn up your cards." I laughed.

"It's not funny, Mom," Sadie said. "One deck is completely gone."

"Once we know where we are going, I'll get you another deck."

"Where are we going, Mom?"

"I don't know. Let's take some time to rest here. I'm sorry, Sadie, that I didn't have breakfast with you. I'm still shaken by all that has happened."

"Jo-Jo made it for me," Sadie said coldly. "You were rude to Jo-Jo, Mom. I wanted you to eat with us, so you see how cool he is."

"Where is he now?" I tried to keep my voice even, but it cracked.

"Mom, what's wrong?"

"Nothing, Sadie," I snapped.

"You can tell me. We're both hurt. I was scared I'd never see you again. I had only sea creatures, dragons, and mansquats to take care of me. I was scared too."

Sadie went back to her game with the dragons. I was a mess. I was rarely short with Sadie. I took a chair at the table where Sadie was playing and hugged her. She pulled away and gave me a hard shove.

"We've started the game. You can't join us," said Sadie. "In fact, you are crowding the table."

I was still fragile from my ordeal. I knew I had to discipline her, but I burst into tears instead and went running from the cave and right into Jo-Jo, who was entering as I was exiting.

"Whoa," said Jo-Jo. He put his hands on my shoulders. A jolt ran through me as our skin touched. I looked him in the eye and saw his love for me. I collapsed into his arms. He embraced me for a long time and then guided me back to the table and sat me beside Sadie. He knelt beside me and took both my hands into his.

Sadie stared at us. She shook her head and looked bewildered. "I'm not talking to her, Jo-Jo," Sadie said. "She was rude to you this morning."

"She's your mother. You respect her. Time out," said Jo-Jo. He stood and led Sadie by the hand out of the room the way he used to when I asked him to discipline her. His body language and gestures hadn't changed. His approach with Sadie was the same. Was he just a bigger and hairier version of Joseph? Sadie tried unsuccessfully to break from Jo-Jo's grip. "No, Sadie," Jo-Jo said. "You must respect your mother." Sadie looked into Jo-Jo's eyes and gasped.

"Daddy!" Sadie threw her arms around Jo-Jo's—Joseph's—large frame. She let out a deep sob. Joseph picked her up and held her in his arms. I could see tears in his eyes as he looked at me. I smiled, stood, and joined the hug.

No matter what my future held, I had to have Jo-Jo and Sadie in it.

YOWIE

PROLOGUE

The banner said, *World Famous Author Elizabeth Alias Here Tonight.*

"Wow, Mom, look how big the banner is," Sadie said. She was going by Sophie now. Our identities had to be concealed.

I was overwhelmed. I had hoped the books I wrote about our adventures with the sasquatches and sea creatures would provide a modest income to support Sophie, Johnny—aka Joseph—and me. I was shocked when the first royalty check came. $438,127! The book continues to trend at the top of the Amazon and New York Times book lists.

I dreaded book signings but had to showcase the book. Sophie and I were in Port Huron hawking the book. I was nervous. I hadn't been here in years.

1

"Ouch," said Jo-Jo.

"I'm sorry, honey. I don't understand how the clippers work," I said.

Sadie said, "Let me do it, Mom."

My now nine-year-old thought she knew everything. She surprised me when she took the clippers and deftly shaved Joseph's entire back. Joseph could take care of most of his own grooming, but the back was tricky.

"Turn around, Dad," said Sadie. Joseph did as he was told. "You look like my daddy now."

The three of us had been living in the underwater world in Lake Huron near Meow's cave. Joseph and I decided we would give his world a six-month trial to see how Sadie and I adjusted. Sadie adjusted just fine. I wasn't so sure.

I was happy that I saw Meow, Bessie, Sash, and Chichi often. I missed Ogua's presence even though he could be gruff sometimes. Esme had just left after a month's stay. She won a Pulitzer for her reporting on the sightings of Bessie and Sash in Cleveland. Meow was with us. He and Esme had been close since Esme was a child. For the most part,

Meow had bonded with me. He caused a kerfuffle between me and Joseph. Meow always wanted me to sleep in his nest. Joseph was jealous. I had to wean Meow from wanting me there all night. I could now tuck in Meow, and he would let me go. It had taken almost six months.

Sadie was excited that the three of us were going back to Cleveland. My boss wanted to see my stories. I wanted Sadie to enroll in a human school. Joseph was going to resume his photography career. From what my boss said, I still had my job. I still had the alternate identity, credit cards, and money that Sash had given me. I figured we could live three months in Cleveland. If neither Joseph nor I could earn a living, we would have to go to the underwater world permanently. Joseph and I decided to split our time between the two lifestyles if all went well. All I was concerned about was getting Sadie in school. Joseph assured me that Sadie wasn't behind, but I wasn't certain. The underwater world had a good school system. It was mind-blowing how many professors and teachers had been saved by sasquatches. Most of them opted to stay in the underwater world to educate those born here.

The underwater world had its good points. You didn't need money. Your work was supporting the community. If you did your fair share, you had everything you could possibly need—clothes, food, a home, entertainment, civic clubs, and a multitude of places to worship. I knew Joseph was happy in this world. I was adjusting, sort of.

Sash came to see us a few days before we were going to depart for Cleveland. He and Joseph were arguing and had been since Sash arrived. I stayed out of it. I had no idea what they were so angry about. I was busy working on the book and overseeing Sadie's homework. I didn't remember math being so hard.

"Janet," Joseph called. "Come in here. It seems Sash and I have a disagreement that maybe you can solve."

Oh, boy, I thought. I reluctantly entered the central room in Joseph's underwater house. "Sadie, I'll check your work when I return. What's this about?" I moved to Joseph's study.

"Sit," said Sash. He had fixed a platter of goodies and opened some soda. "Enjoy."

"Don't try to bribe her, Sash," said Joseph. But his eyes were dancing with laughter. Whatever the disagreement, it seemed less serious now.

"The three of you are going to try to live in the human world. In Cleveland. Where you aren't wanted. Correct?" said Sash.

I nodded.

"It's been less than year since all the trouble began. You were put on trial and exonerated. But the people of Cleveland have long memories," said Sash. "You will be recognized. Others will be shocked that Joseph, or what sort of looks like Joseph, has returned. Have you thought this through?"

"We have," I said firmly. I looked at Joseph. We had discussed our return at length. I got my old job back. My boss was hiring my new partner, Joey, as a photographer. I had the paperwork done for Sadie to enter school.

"Your looks haven't changed. You know, your picture was plastered all over Cleveland when you were wanted," Sash said.

"Sash, you are a good friend, but humans need a human world," I said. "It's been decided." I looked to Joseph, now Joey, for support. He wouldn't meet my eye. "Joseph, it has been decided, right?"

Joseph slowly looked up at me. He took a long time to respond. "Janet, Sash pointed out an error in our thinking. You and Sadie are recognizable. Maybe it's time you assume a new identity and change your hair. I'm supposed to be dead. How do we explain it?"

"No. I've lost too much already," I said, crying.

Neither Joseph nor Sash responded.

"There is an alternative, but it's not the best plan," Sash said. "You can keep your identities, but you would need to go to a new place, where you aren't recognized."

"That's impossible. I was all over national news," I said.

"It would have to be a place where the news is less likely to be reported." Joseph took both my hands in his.

"Where?" I asked Joseph.

"Brisbane," Sash said.

"Where is that?" I asked.

Sash explained Brisbane was in Queensland, a colony in Australia. I opened my mouth to protest, but Sash put up his hand, ordering me to stop. Brisbane, capital of Queensland, is a large city on the Brisbane River. South Bank is the cultural precinct where the Queensland museum and science center are located. In addition, there are art galleries like the Queensland Gallery of Modern Art, and major contemporary art museums. The climate is subtropical with temperatures in the upper seventies to low eighties. It can get quite humid. Brisbane, an urban city with a population of four million, is a global center for research and innovation. It is a transportation hub, being served by large rail, bus and ferry networks, as well as Brisbane Airport and the Port of Brisbane, Australia's third-busiest airport and seaport. Aside from good primary and secondary schools, three universities are located there.

"The sea creatures held a special conference about where you should go. Australia speaks English. You would understand the people, even if the culture is different. I implanted in your boss's brain the idea that you need a sabbatical to write your book and that you need rest. He will call you with an opportunity to be a stringer on a local paper with plenty of time to rest. Joseph will become one of its photographers. The schools are excellent."

"There are lots of places like that."

"I'm not finished," Sash said. "Does she interrupt you like that, Joseph?"

"Pleading the fifth," said Joseph with a twinkle in his eye.

"Diplomatic answer," I said as I playfully tapped his knee.

"Brisbane is the home of Moha, another of Bessie's siblings. Moha was close to Ogua. She was so impressed by Ogua's transformation that she began the process. It didn't go as expected. I'll let Moha tell her story. Her sasquatch is my sister, Wilhelmina—Willie for short. The caves are in the coral reefs off the coast of Queensland. All of us are envious of their beauty. Willie is lonely most of the time, creating a special bond between Willie and Moha. You'll be safe with them and—"

I stood up and screamed, "I am not living with sea creatures and sasquatches again."

Joseph put his hands on my shoulders and forced me to sit down. He looked deeply into my eyes. He said, "Janet, Willie has found us a nice home—three bedrooms, offices for you and me, a playroom for Sadie, large country kitchen, and two living rooms, one formal and one informal. She discovered the best school for Sadie and will enroll her. "

"Stop," I said. "I have to think." Sash nodded at Joseph. They left me alone with my thoughts.

I sent a message to Meow, who is usually around. I wanted his warm lap to think in. He avoided me this morning. He knew what Joseph and Sash were planning.

Instantly, Meow appeared and swooped me into his lap. I didn't even have time to pour him some milk. "Shh, my dearest Janet, I can have the milk later." He always read my mind.

"I don't want to talk right now," I said. "I need to be alone with my thoughts."

"Okay. But I'm here when you're ready. I've always wanted to see Australia and spend time with Moha. She is a pleasant soul. Does she know what milk is? She never gave me any. Is there milk in Australia?"

"Meow! Quiet!"

Meow curled into a sleeping position. Now I could think.

2

I must have dozed off, because when I woke up, I saw an empty bowl with milk residue. Someone had given Meow his coveted drink. He was in a milk stupor and snoring, making it easy for me to leave his lap unnoticed. I looked around and didn't see Sadie, Joseph, or Sash. I started to prepare dinner, when the three of them burst into the house.

"Mom," squealed Sadie, "we've been shopping for Brisbane. Look at my new bathing suit and school clothes. I'll be the poshest one there with clothes you'd never find in the US or Australia. Look at my haircut."

And there my nine-year-old stood, in an iridescent, mint green and sea blue mini skirt, with her hair all in layers. She didn't look nine. I'm not ready for her to grow up. I lost two years with these creatures.

"She looks great," Joseph said. "Sash picked it out."

Sash looked embarrassed. I loved the look he had chosen for her but wanted her to stay a baby longer. Joseph came over and hugged me. "I know. I missed so much of her childhood."

Then I felt terrible. I'd had Sadie during the creature years. Joseph had lost much more. Was I being selfish? My decision had been to say no to Brisbane, but I knew I couldn't if I were to see if Joseph and Joey could live in my world.

It was decided. Meow would take the three of us to South America, directly across from Australia. Then Draconia would fly us to Brisbane. I was relieved there was no water travel. At first, Sash suggested that Ogua take us so he could see his sister. Joseph vetoed the plan. He hated water travel. I started to pack. We would leave in three days. Australia. At least, I'd still be Janet.

3

I slept through the run with Meow. I was a bit disappointed. I had hoped to see the country. Joseph said there was nothing to see but blurs. How silly of me. Sadie was hungry. I broke out the picnic I had packed, the last meal left from the United States. I had hot dogs, potato chips, potato salad, pickles, and fruit. I tried not to cry as she ate. Would I be able to find American food in Australia? Sadie was losing her heritage.

We didn't have to wait long for the dragons. Draconia arrived with his two brothers. I flew with Draconia. Joseph was with Sadie on another dragon, and Sash claimed the last. The flight was beautiful. The Pacific and Indian Oceans were sights to behold. The waves in the Pacific were peaceful; no wondered it was called pacific. Draconia circled all of Australia so I could see its different terrains. The continent looked beautiful. I was glad we were not near the deserts.

Taking me on a sightseeing tour meant I was the last to see our new home. From what I gathered, Sadie had already claimed a bedroom. Meow wanted the same room, so they played rock, paper, scissors for it. Sadie won. I told Meow his claws meant he wouldn't be able to play the game.

When Meow announced he'd build his nest in the room Joseph

and I would share, Sadie saw the horror on her father's face and said, "You take it, Meow. I don't' like it so much anymore."

"Sadie, he's manipulating us to get the room," Joseph said.

"Would you do that, Meow?" asked Sash.

"Of course." Meow licked his paws and pranced into his room. *Cats.*

Joseph convinced Sadie the bedroom at the front of the house had more light for her painting. She agreed, ending the kerfuffle. After that grueling trip, I didn't want confrontation.

Most of our belongings had been brought by dragons a few days before. I was pleased to see how nicely the rooms had been arranged.

"That wasn't the dragons," said Sash. "Moha and Willie tried to make the place humanlike."

"I can't wait to meet them," Sadie said.

"Tomorrow," her father and I said in unison.

"I'm outnumbered. I'll get ready for bed," Sadie said. "It's easier to manipulate one parent. Now I have two to listen to." She had a sweet grin on her face.

Once Sadie left, Joseph, Sash, and I burst into laughter. "Life is hard at nine," I said. I fixed warm milk for Meow, and then we all retired for the night.

4

When I rose the next day, I saw that Sadie had already eaten, but I could find no sign of her. Joseph appeared to be missing, too. Meow slinked into the room demanding milk.

"I think Joseph gave you some," I said, looking at the milk dish.

"I see what Sadie meant by having two parents now."

I laughed, walked to the fridge, and poured him a small amount. "You have a way of manipulating. It takes two of us to keep you honest."

Meow patted his lap, and I climbed into it with my coffee. "Where is everyone?"

"Sash, Joey, and Sadie took off early this morning," he said.

"I can see that. Where did they go?"

Meow said, "I was sworn to secrecy."

"Meow, you never keep a secret."

Meow purred. I guessed he was going to keep this one.

After my leisurely cup of coffee, I began giving my new home the once over. I thought I would rearrange things to my liking but found myself satisfied with Moho and Willie's job. I decided I'd make a nice lunch for my wayward family, when there was a knock at the back-door. I went to answer and only found a note tacked to the door. It said to go into the basement. Having experienced many weirder situations than this, I went down the basement stairs. I was shocked at what I saw. The basement was fully finished and had several bedrooms, a kitchen, bathroom, and a sitting room that doubled as an eating area.

"Surprise!" shouted Joey, Sadie, Sash, and two creatures I couldn't identify.

"What's this all about?" I asked.

A large female sasquatch moved to my side and put her arm around me. A half-turtle creature was on my other side. The creature was not as large as Ogua. She had a similar face but with sharp teeth. Like Ogua, her tail was twelve feet long, nearly half of her thirty-foot body. "Welcome," said the sasquatch. "I'm Willie. How do you like your new home?"

The half-turtle creature introduced herself as Moha. I embraced both creatures.

"The two of you did a magnificent job with my home," I said. "Thank you."

I heard noises in one of the bedrooms and a distinctive snore. "Ogua?"

"Yes," said Moha. "I'm so excited to see him again."

"Ah, yeah. Why isn't he in your cave?" I asked.

"He thinks our caves are primitive. He decided to sleep here. For many years, I have owned this house and used the underground access to come and go. I never put in human plumbing or other human things like Sash did. Didn't feel I needed them. It seems someone spoiled my brother," Moha said of Ogua.

I felt like Moha was blaming me. But I knew he had learned his hygiene from Sash, the cleanest sasquatch. He'd been taking showers since long before I met him.

"Janet, this basement is our failsafe. If we are ever discovered in Brisbane, we can scurry in here and stay a few days. We had to use it years ago," said Moha. "I'm not being a good hostess. Sit, sit, and I'll tell you my story. Sash, grab some beers from the fridge."

I frowned. "It's too early for beer."

Willie laughed. "It's not human beer. Try a sip."

I didn't want to offend Willie, since I just met her, so I took a small sip. I can't describe what I was tasting, but it wasn't human beer. It was delicious. "Yum," I said.

"And you won't get inebriated," said Moha. "Sadie, you're still too young for it." Moha took a bottle from her hand. "It's for grownups." Sadie pouted.

"I want to hear the story, don't you, Sadie?" I asked. Sadie took a chair next to me and lay her head on my lap."

"Now, where was I?" Moha said.

I was young when the sasquatch cut off my wings. Mom didn't think I'd make it, since I was only ten centuries old. When our species was maimed or hurt and under an eon old, we died. Ogua was comforting Mom as she held me tightly in her arms. Ogua changed the bandages. You must remember, Mom and Ogua were maimed and in pain too. They took shifts watching over me.

Ogua was still a maimed dragon then. He spent hours rocking me when I cried in pain. Every morning, Mom, as hurt as she was, went from nest to nest checking on my siblings. She gave them hope that they could have a life after the maiming. She had not yet devised her plan for us to disperse.

Mom's wounds were infected from her traveling, but she wouldn't rest until she felt all her children were going to survive. Now we had to minister to her to keep her alive. If Spitzy hadn't returned, I am not sure she would have made it.

While Mom was recovering, Ogua and I became best pals. We learned to walk by helping hold each other up as we slowly got our land legs. Both of us mourned the loss of our wings and the freedom they had afforded.

Ogua and I were thrilled when Bessie found we could breathe underwater. Ogua and I swam daily, trying to outperform each other with our tricks. Mom then told us her plan to have us live underwater and find homes throughout the world. Ogua and I begged Mom to let us stay together, but she wouldn't allow it.

The best Ogua and I could do was to take on the same persona so that when we visited, we could do the same things. Ogua was obsessed with the turtles. He wanted to be able to live on land and sea. I saw the advantages.

Ogua and I traveled together all over the world. He was obsessed with a river called the Youghiogheny, which flowed through a small town outside Pittsburgh. I couldn't see the attraction. He consented to travel with me to view other places. Ogua wanted me to look at other lakes and rivers near Pittsburgh. I couldn't stand the hills. Yes, I had lived in mountains before, but I wanted a change of scenery.

We had just made our way to an area that would be called Australia when I fell in love with the coastal waters. I wanted to live here in Brisbane, but Mom preferred the cave system in Sydney called Chillagoe. I hated it. It didn't have the color of the caves here in Brisbane. The paths were confusing. Ogua and I obeyed our mom, and I settled in those caves. Our first order of business was creating a map of the cave system. We built nests thinking Ogua would need one when he visited. We would transform into turtles there. Ogua would have an easier time getting home if he could swim and walk.

Transformation is a complicated process. First, you must find the species that you want to be. For us, it was a turtle and easily obtained. We had to live with the turtle strapped to us for a century. My turtle never took a liking to me. She was always chewing through the leather straps we used to secure her. Some part of her body had to always touch my skin.

For the most part, Ogua and I could do whatever we wanted. We traveled to the caves and set up housekeeping. We stocked up on food for the last stage of transition, which was napping for an eon. Ogua told Mom our plans. She approved but worried about us transitioning at the same time with no one to monitor us. She sent Spitzy to take care of us.

Spitzy arrived two days before we would hibernate. She approved of the supplies and our cave remodeling. We helped Spitzy build a nest so she would have a place to rest. She built it at the cave opening so she could fight off any intruders.

The day came for us to sleep. To rest comfortably, we took great care of our nests. We checked and rechecked our turtles' straps to be sure they would stay in place. I easily fell into slumber. Ogua didn't, but I was unaware of it.

Ogua woke up before I did, fully transformed into a sea turtle. He told me later that he tiptoed out of the cave so as not to wake me. Spitzy had a feast ready for us. Ogua wanted to wait to eat until I woke up. Every hour, Spitzy or Ogua checked me. Ogua was too hungry to wait for the feast, so he devoured all of it. Spitzy worried something was going wrong in the transformation. He contacted mom, who said he should make sure the turtle had contact with me and that its straps were secure.

Spitzy was horrified at what she found. Half the turtle had come loose from my body. The other half did not get the nourishment it needed from me. I had only transformed into a half turtle, half fish. Spitzy, unsure how to wake me, contacted Mom again. She said she was coming.

Mom arrived a century later. She said the only way I might wake up is through her singing to me. Ogua left. He hated singing. Spitzy and Mom stayed and sang to me for another century.

I was groggy when I woke. I had no idea why Mom was there, but I hugged her fiercely.

"What happened?" I asked. I suspected something was wrong when I saw her. "Where's Ogua?"

I panicked, convinced that Ogua hadn't made it through the transformation. "Where's Ogua?" I screamed.

Before Mom or Spitzy could respond, Ogua arrived at my nest. "Hey, sleepy head," he said with a smile. The smile didn't last long. Ogua stared at my half turtle, half fish body. He let out a howl that shook the entire cave. I was slowly getting out of my nest. I crossed to where Ogua and tried to hug him. Ogua backed away and fled the cave. He had rejected me because of my incomplete transformation.

Mom and Spitzy hugged me tightly. I could tell Mom was angry with Ogua, but she concentrated on soothing me. "I'll have a talk with that boy," Mom said.

Spitzy led me to the food she had prepared, anticipating my waking. I had no appetite, but I ate. Spitzy would have been hurt if I hadn't. I started feeling better with food in my belly.

Mom sent Spitzy home. She left a century later once sure I could function in my new body. She while I tried several times to contact Ogua. I sent a message to him, saying I wasn't mad at him. That's the truth. I wasn't mad, just hurt.

After Mom left, I explored the cave system and found a way to commute between Brisbane and Sydney. I have been seen many times, but the Australians are used to seeing me. I am careful. You never know how attitudes can change.

Moha wiped a tear from her eye. "I was happy to see Ogua. It's been eons since our split. I thought he was visiting to heal our relationship. It seems he was just worried about Sadie."

Angry at Ogua, I walked into his room and tried to yank him out of the nest. "You! You! You!" I couldn't articulate my feelings.

"Good to see you again, too, Janet," Ogua said.

"You know what I mean. How could you do that to Moha, your sister, and the species closest to you?"

Ogua hung his head. "I hoped you would never find out what an idiot I was. I came here a few centuries ago to apologize, but Moha wouldn't accept it. When I went back to my home, I sent daily messages to her. She finally accepted my apology when I returned home after you were rescued by the dragons."

I had calmed a bit. I gave him a hug. "I missed you," I said.

"Harumph," said Ogua. Typical Ogua, the grouch.

5

Joey, Sadie, and I settled into an easy routine. The people of Brisbane were welcoming. Sadie had already made a few friends in school. She hosted a pajama party for her friends last weekend. I thought it went well. Most days after school, she comes home with her friends, or she is over at a friend's house. I am finding long stretches of time to focus on my book. Joey has been active with the local paper, taking photos for news stories. The boss assigns me a story here and there.

Joey seems to be readjusting to human life. He gets up early in the morning to start his grooming, which takes nearly an hour. He leaves his back till last, for Sadie or I to shave. Joey drops Sadie off at school most days before he reports to his boss for his assignments. Willie is a reliable sitter, and I have her watch Sadie at least once a week so Joey and I can have date night. I had my life back. Or so I thought.

When Sadie came home from school today, she was crying. Her best friend, Chloe, told her that she couldn't play with her anymore. Girl friendships are hard to navigate. I assume by tomorrow, all would be made up. Sadie asked if she could call Tammi, another friend. I gave her permission. I heard her calling Tammi; then I heard more tears.

"None of my friends will talk to me. Tammi, Chloe, and Jessica. Their parents won't let them play with me."

I put my arm around her and led her to the couch. Once we were snuggled, I asked, "Why do you think this happened?"

Sadie became still and wouldn't look me in the eye. I gave her the "out with it" look. Then she said, "I told them about my other friends."

"What other friends?"

"Bessie, Sash, Spitzy, Chichi, Meow, and Ogua."

I was incredulous. "Sadie, you know you can't talk about what happened when we were the creatures."

"I didn't tell them they were creatures, Mom. I swear."

"Then how did they find out?"

"Chloe's dad is a lawyer. He read an article on your trial in his law journal. When Chloe mentioned my friends to her dad, he figured out who you were."

I sighed. "I don't know what to say."

"Let's just go to the underwater world. My friends there didn't mind if I was friends with the creatures."

Joey walked in from work and saw that Sadie and I were huddled together. He came to join us on the couch. I briefly outlined the problem. Joey looked at Sadie, then me. "This is a problem."

"Then solve it, Daddy," said Sadie.

"I don't know how, but I'll contact Sash for ideas," said Joey as he walked to his office to send a telepathic message to our friend.

"Mom, I'm sorry. I thought if I just told my friends about Sash and Bessie as if they were human, it would be okay."

"I know, sweetie, but you must be careful. No one can know of the adventures. I know you enjoyed them, but no one must know," I said gently. "Come on, help me make Sash's chili recipe."

6

Before Joey received any word from Sash, the crank phone calls started. "I'd like a sauteed dragon. Please deliver to 650 Main Street." You could hear the giggles in the background. "Could I borrow a sasquatch to trim my trees?" "I'd like to take Spitzy to prom. She'd light up the place." Joey turned off all our phones. The only ones we wanted to hear from were our creature friends, with ideas on how to handle the situation.

All of us were stressed and decided to go to bed early. As I was preparing Sadie for bed, we heard a crash and glass breaking.

"You two stay here," Joey said. "I'll investigate."

Sure enough, our front window was smashed. Our garage door had been spray-painted *creature lovers*. A mob was carrying signs outside our home. They read, *strangers go home*; *you can't trust Americans*; *how big are your monster cat's furballs*? I won't repeat the nastiest.

Joey called the local police, who dispersed the crowd. They gave us advice: Leave.

Moha and Willie were in the basement getting it ready for the incoming crowd of creatures. I tried to help but found they could handle it. I felt bad because Moha and Wille had taken the cave path to Sydney, where they spent time in the beautiful caves. I was still impressed with the caring and generosity of these creatures. Why can't humans be that way?

Sash, Spitzy, Chichi, Bessie, and Aaron all arrived in the basement of our home the next morning. I had sent Meow to whisk them here. I thought the number of bedrooms was excessive, but there was a room each of them. I was non-stop cooking, laundering, and cleaning. I didn't mind. It took my mind off our problems.

Joey called in sick to the boss so he could meet with the creatures.

Aaron's solution was a legal one. Sue the parents for defamation? Joey and I hoped it didn't come to that. We wanted a less radical solution.

The creatures argued for hours. I let Joey handle the negotiations. I took Sadie to school that day. She usually took the bus, but I wanted to be sure she made it to her classroom without interference. As she and I entered the schoolyard, a rather large man with a balding head stopped us.

"I'm Principal Flynn."

I wouldn't let him continue. I said, "I trust you will see my daughter is safe in your school."

My forwardness rather confused him. "I, uh, I..." he said.

"Spit it out, Mr. Flynn."

"It's Principal Flynn. Your daughter will face a barrage of teasing today. Do you really want her to go through that?"

"It's up to you, Mr. Flynn, to not let that happen." Principal Flynn stood there with his mouth agape. "She is enrolled in this school. Unless you expel her, you are responsible for her safety on campus." I was glad Aaron had directed me on what to say.

"Mrs. Smith, with all due respect, your daughter isn't wanted here."

Sadie was tugging at my sleeve, clearly uncomfortable. I had no idea how to respond.

I bent down to Sadie. "What?" I listened and then nodded.

"Principal Flynn," Sadie said. "I have an active imagination. I can't believe my friends thought I was talking about real creatures. I shouldn't be punished for their error."

I could see Mr. Flynn was befuddled. Once he regained his composure, he said, "Well, Katie, sometimes people are misunderstood. I take it this is not the case."

Sadie said, "Mr. Flynn. My name is Sadie."

Mr. Flynn was angry now. "Leave now. Both of you, or I'll call in the authorities."

Sadie let go of my hand and walked toward the school entrance. "Bye, Mom."

I didn't know if I should let her go in or if I should stop her. I was the speechless one now. I finally offered, "Take good care of her, Mr. Flynn. I work for the local paper. I'll be writing a full report." I turned, walked to my car, and drove off. I tried to hide my fear. What would happen to Sadie today?

7

I shook as I drove. I needed to get home and see what had been decided. Meow was out of milk; I had switched him to 2%. He wasn't happy. I needed to get greens for the vegans. I pulled into my regular grocery store, grabbed my wallet, and tried to exit the car. The door wouldn't open. I looked out the window and saw that my car was surrounded. Then, the car began to rock. I couldn't open the door. I was trapped. After a few minutes, my vehicle was on its side. Then it was upside down. I didn't know whether I should take off my seatbelt and use my legs to kick out the window or stay as I was. I sent a telepathic message to Joey. In a flash, I was pulled out of the car by Meow. Within a minute or two, I was safe at home.

Joey wouldn't stop hugging me and saying he should have taken Sadie. I reassured him and the creatures that I was fine. I had a few bruises. I was sore. I'd live.

Willie gently pulled Joey away and rubbed a salve on my body that instantaneously stopped the pain. I was amazed at all the sasquatches knew. "Thanks, Willie," I said. Willie blushed.

Sash was pacing the room. I went to him and hugged him. He allowed me to rest my head on his chest—well, really his waist. "We'll figure it out, Janet," he said. "I promise."

Meow, now sulking in his nest, had been quite upset with me since I failed to bring home milk. Joey urged me to nap after my ordeal. He escorted me out of the basement and to our bedroom. "Rest, my love," he said.

I smiled. "I'll try." I told him about what the principal said. Joey wanted to go to the school and have it out with Mr. Flynn. I urged him not to, feeling Sadie would be punished for it. He eventually returned to the meeting in the basement after I pretended to be asleep.

After Joey left the bedroom, I snuck down to the basement to eavesdrop.

I could only catch a few words since I was afraid to get too deep into the basement. Sash was advocating we move. Bessie wanted us to come live with her for a while. Meow was begging for more milk. Chichi said she would support whatever Spitzy decided. Moha was crying because she was growing attached to us. Willie was comforting Moha. I couldn't hear what Joey said in reply to them since he was speaking. The creatures, I could hear telepathically.

I went to the kitchen to make them food platters, when my phone rang.

"Hello, Mrs. Smith," said Principal Flynn. "You must pick up your daughter now. She is a disruption to the entire school."

"Mr. Flynn, you are inflaming the situation. How can a nine-year-old disrupt the entire school?"

Mr. Flynn shouted into the phone, "Children are passing notes to her, wanting her to tell more of the stories. She obliged at lunchtime. She attracted a crowd. Some children didn't eat their lunches because they wanted to listen to her."

I paced the kitchen, wondering how to respond to this odious man. I turned to walk into the living room, and there stood Sadie. I sent her a telepathic message asking how she arrived home. She sent one word back: Meow.

"Mr. Flynn, my husband just retrieved Sadie. She's here with me."

"She's suspended indefinitely. The school board will hold a disciplinary meeting in one week. Be there." He ended the call.

After I told Sadie to do her homework in her room, I scurried down to the basement. Meow had already told them about Flynn's call. "What do we do?" I asked.

Willie began to explain the plan. "Moha and I will escort you to the beautiful caves in Sydney. Humans have explored these caves, but they don't know all the intricacies. We can put you there until Aaron and Joey travel to Sydney and arrange a new life for you there. We will supervise the moving of your things."

I was getting dizzy. Another move. Hiding again. "I don't want this life!"

Bessie wrapped herself around me. I let her comfort me. Of course, moving was the only recourse. "Okay. Let me pack what Sadie and I need."

"No," said Sadie. "We can't keep moving. We just can't. I want to face the school board and the consequences they decide on. I'm tired of hiding my friends."

Joey and I looked at each other. What a strong girl we were raising. "I'm not sure that's wise," I said.

"The last two years of my life I've spent in hiding. I'm going to tell my tale."

I knew the creatures were talking among themselves but had blocked the words from me.

Sash said, "Joey, Janet, can you leave Sadie with us for a while. Alone?"

Joey and I left the basement. I prepared sandwiches for Joey and me. Neither of us really wanted them. "Sadie," I said. "We wanted her to be spunky."

We both laughed. "I am sure the creatures are explaining to her why her plan is not feasible," Joey said.

"You're right. I'm not hungry. Let's pack for our relocation."

8

Our relocation was painless. Sadie and I hid in the caves. They were spectacular. "Oh, Mom, I need my paints," Sadie squealed.

Before I could answer, Sadie's painting supplies arrived. I assume they were courtesy of Meow since we saw nothing. She settled down to paint. I had my laptop, so I continued my writing. A little later, Joey arrived, saying our new home was set up. New identities would take a few days. I asked Bessie to take us to the new house immediately, but she refused. She wanted our identities in place.

My life had become a series of relocations. I couldn't believe I was on the lam, hiding until creatures who most considered monsters could keep me safe. I had a series of bruises down my arm, where I regularly pinched myself to see if this world was real.

The three of us settled into our new home the day before the school board meeting. Meow came to fetch the three of us. "Meow," said Sadie, "Be careful. Don't wrinkle my dress."

"Harumph," said Meow. Great. Meow was picking up Ogua's grumpiness.

"Sadie, shh," I said. "It will only be a few minutes." Just as I finished my sentence, we were in Moha's cave. After living in a colorful setting for just a few days, Moha's cave looked dreary. No wonder she spent time in Sydney. Before Willie took her hand, Moha menaced the waters in Sydney. There were numerous sightings reported. Willie urged Moha to stay hidden. Moha didn't like to be hidden. Since she had a fish tail, she couldn't walk the land and angrily patrolled the coast.

All the creatures were assembled in Moha's cave, making it quite crowded. I was perspiring. Sadie looked scared. "You don't have to do this," I said.

"I must," said Sadie.

When it was time to appear at the school board meeting, Meow took the three of us and Aaron. Aaron felt Sadie needed legal representation. Joey and I agreed.

The boardroom was packed. Standing room only. The chairperson of the board asked Sadie to step forward. Aaron went with her.

Principal Flynn erupted. "She can't have counsel. No!"

The chairperson banged her gavel. "I think it's wise, Mr. Flynn, for her to have legal advice."

"It's Principal Flynn."

What a petty man, peeved when someone doesn't use his title. My palms were sweaty. I could see Joey shaking with anger. None of this boded well for us. After the chairperson read the charges against Sadie, she began her defense:

Madam Chairperson, Principal Flynn, and school board members. I am Sadie Smith. Two years ago, I didn't have any friends—until I met Bessie in Lake Erie. Bessie had been a playmate of my grandmother's when she was young. At first, Bessie thought I was my grandmother, since I look like her. When Bessie realized I was her former playmate's granddaughter, Bessie introduced us to Sash.

For years, Lake Erie had the legend of Bessie as one of its folktales. The first recorded sighting of Bessie occurred in 1817, and more sightings have occurred intermittently and in greater frequency in the last three decades. Bessie is reported to be snakelike, thirty to forty feet long, at least a foot in diameter, and grayish in color. I beg to differ with the internet reports that Bessie is gray. To most people, I assume she is, but to those she loves, she radiates a kaleidoscope of color. But I digress. An extraordinary sighting, covered by local newspapers, took place. In July 1892, the entire crew of a ship bound from Buffalo, New York, to Toledo, Ohio saw a large area of water about 0.5 miles ahead of them churned up and foaming. As they approached, they saw "a huge sea serpent" that appeared to be "wrestling about in the water, as if fighting an unseen foe." They observed as the creature relaxed and stretched out full length—estimated at fifty feet long and four feet in circumference—with its head sticking up above the water an additional four feet. The brownish creature's eyes were described as "viciously sparkling," and large fins were also noted. Let me introduce Bessie. She speaks telepathically. Sit quietly. You will hear her.

I gasped. Appearing on the stage was Bessie. She addressed the crowd: "I live in Lake Erie and have special friends who keep me company. My best friend is Sash, a sasquatch. Don't be alarmed at his size. He is strong but gentle. His heart is bigger than a human heart, not only because it has more blood to pump, but also from his giving nature."

In a moment, Sash appeared, giving peace signs with each hand. The crowd chuckled.

"Wait just a darn minute," Mr. Flynn yelled, jumping from his chair. "What kind of sorcery is this? What are these things—puppets, marionettes, wax figures?"

The chairperson banged her gavel and asked Mr. Flynn to sit down. She urged Sadie to go on.

"Janet, this won't be good for us. Summon Meow to take the three of us to Sydney," said Joey. I sent a message to Meow. He didn't appear, and he didn't respond.

"He's not answering. Do you think all the creatures are going to appear?" I asked.

"Probably," said Joey with a sigh.

Joey was right. For an hour, Sadie introduced one of our friends, who communicated with the crowd. The crowd was eerily quiet. I nudged Joey, "The crowd is listening. Do you think the creatures put a spell on them?"

Joey shook his head. "No, we don't have magic."

"Whoever is talking in the audience, please restrain yourself. You are disrupting the creatures' thoughts," the chairperson said. Joey and I stopped talking.

As one creature took the stage, the one there left. It sounded like they were all going to the football field for a meet and greet later. Then Sadie introduced the last two creatures.

Now, as a special treat, I'm going to introduce you to Brisbane's and Sydney's own creatures. Moha and her sasquatch, Willie.

As Moha took the stage, the crowd panicked. Everyone was trying to flee through the doors in the back of the auditorium. Chairs were thrown out of the way. Children and babies were howling. Moha and Sadie called for calm. It didn't help.

"What did you say to them?" Sadie screamed at Moha.

"I apologized for being a menace when I first moved here. I was distraught over losing Ogua and took out my bad temper by terrorizing residents."

"I told you not to do that," said Sadie through her tears.

Meow, who hadn't appeared on stage yet, blew into the auditorium and picked up Sadie, Joey, and me. I expected to land in the caves below the surface, but we were taken to the football field. The audience was milling around the creatures and communicating with them. It was the strangest sight. Sadie jumped out of Meow's claws and joined the crowd. Joey told me to do the same. He had something he had to do.

"How many of you gathered here have seen these creatures before and were afraid?" said Sadie as the town and creatures all gathered on the football field.

Nearly half of those attending raised their hands.

"I'm so sorry," said one person. "Willie, do you remember meeting me in the caves when I was working on my dissertation?"

Willie nodded, moved toward the man, and gave him a hug. The floodgates seem to open then. Willie and Moha became celebrities overnight as those who had seen them before waited in line to talk to them. The day turned to night, but no one wanted to leave the field.

"Disperse! Now! This is the Sydney Police. Leave this area at once."

"What's going on, Joey?" I said. The atmosphere that had been so full of love and caring was now being assaulted with floodlights. The night's peace was broken by sirens and police vehicles. Joey didn't answer. I could tell he was getting messages from some of the creatures.

"This is Principal Flynn. I did not give permission for the creatures to gather here. This is an illegal protest."

"Meow is coming. He may have to make a couple trips," said Joey.

Before he completed his sentence, Joey, Sadie, and I were in Moha's cave labyrinth. Within ten minutes, we were all together.

"That man. Flynn," Sash said. He was fuming. I was afraid he would hyperventilate from breathing so hard. Bessie noticed and cuddled Sash in her grasp.

"How are we going to explain our departure?" said Sadie. "Meow, you ruined everything."

"Sadie," said Joey. "Apologize to Meow. He was protecting us. Flynn is not going to embrace the creatures. We need to stay out of sight for a while to let the town adjust to our presence."

"No," said Sadie. "We should have stayed and stood up to Flynn." She stomped out of the cave and to another branch that no one had explored yet.

"Sadie," said Sash, "get back here." But Sadie didn't comply. Sash went after her.

I was worried she might encounter something awful in the uncharted caves. Joey followed Sash. I didn't know whether I should stay with the other creatures or follow my child and husband. Willie laid a large hand on my shoulder. "Stay," she said. "Sash will make it right."

I leaned into Willie for support. The day had been stressful. I just wanted to rest but couldn't with Sadie and Joey in danger. Willie led me to an unused nest. "Lie here," she said. "I'll help you sleep."

I am not sure what Willie did, but I slept soundly. I woke in the morning expecting to see Joey and Sadie, but they were nowhere to be found. "Willie? Moha? Where is everyone?"

Willie entered the cave with my breakfast. "Eat," she said.

"No. Where is my family?" I asked.

"We don't know," Willie said.

I was stunned. I didn't know if I should cry, scream, or search. "Willie, what are you saying?"

Meow entered the room and pulled me onto his lap. I craved his support and warmth.

"Sash came home in the early morning hours without Sadie and Joey. Sash was unfamiliar with the trail Sadie took. From what Sash described, Sadie knew where she was going. Joey was just behind Sadie within reach to grab her. Then they both disappeared."

I burst into tears. Coming to Australia was supposed to keep us safe. Instead, my husband and child were missing.

Moha entered the cave. "I should have finished the mapping. Then we'd know where went."

"Are you looking for them?" I cried. All the creatures had entered the cave. "Why are you all standing here? Why aren't you looking for them?"

Willie quickly explained that Sash, after packing provisions and a brief rest, had started the search. The creatures had decided to stay here and go to Sash when he called. "You must understand, Janet, that there are creatures living everywhere that we might not know about. We must be careful."

I didn't want to hear it and left that cave. I wasn't sure where to go. I paced through the labyrinth, not even noticing its beauty. I kept tripping over potholes and rocks. The caves here were primitive, not like the ones Sash, Bessie, Chichi, Spitzy, and Meow had. I have no idea how long I paced. Meow came after me. "I want to be alone," I said.

"You can't travel these caves alone. This part of the world is unknown. We all grew up in Asia but never realized there was a land mass so far south. Mom never directed us to the rivers or coast of Australia. Ogua and Moha had discovered it and wanted to stay. Mom said it would be okay if they made accurate maps of the area. When Moha's transformation went wrong, Moha and Ogua didn't finish the maps. They never told Mom," said Meow.

I didn't know what to say. Sash and the others had sent us here before the area was fully known. "What type of creatures might Joey and Sadie encounter?" I asked.

None of the creatures answered.

"What aren't you telling me?" I demanded.

Moha began her story:

After Ogua left, I had to map the caves alone. Although I had been menacing to the humans in the area, I was a gentle soul. I was a bit afraid on my own but explored further every day.

One day, I smelled something that made my eyes water. I was blinded by my tears and, while I kept traveling, sensed a dreadful presence. I must have fallen and passed out. Evidently, the trails in these underground caves are difficult to traverse. The area smelled so bad that I was easily confused. When I woke from my stupor, I saw a hairy beast—not a human and not a gorilla. I felt like I could see through him. I figured I was hallucinating. How can anyone see through someone? The creature sensed my stirring and hit me on the head. I passed out again. This time when I woke, I was in a cage of some sort. I tried to shake the bars apart, but whatever my jail cell was made of didn't budge. I heard the creature coming, so I pretended I was still sleeping. This ruse wouldn't work forever; I had to think of an escape.

I opened my eyes halfway and saw that I was surrounded by many of the hairy beasts. I tried to communicate telepathically but could tell they didn't have that skill. I tried some sign language. The creatures backed away from me. I wondered if I had said something offensive. Their language skills were primitive. I knew I could not communicate with them. I was in despair. How was I going to escape?

The beasts approached me again. When they did, they had spear-like tools that they stuck into my skin. They clipped pieces from my fin, cut chunks of my hair, and forced my mouth open to take a saliva sample. I felt so violated. A few hours later, one of the beasts brought what I assumed was food. I refused to eat. Aside from the horrendous smell, it looked like worms.

The next day, the beasts released me. I'm not sure how I understood them, but I knew I was not to travel into these areas again.

Moha looked exhausted after relating this story. Chichi went over to Moha and hugged her. "Moha," Chichi said, "you saw the yowie." Moha went pale. Her usual bright colors turned gray.

"What's a yowie?" I asked.

Chichi and Willie looked at each other cautiously. "You tell her," said Chichi.

Willie said, "Yowies are a distant cousin. A yowie is usually described as a bipedal, hairy, ape-like mythical creature standing upright at between six and twelve feet high. Yowie feet are described as much larger than a human's, but their tracks are inconsistent in shape and toe number. The yowie nose is described as wide and flat. Behaviorally, some report yowies as timid or shy, but most recount it as violent or aggressive. I'm sure some Australians thought I was a yowie when I first showed myself."

I started to shake. "Then Joey and Sadie are in danger?"

"Maybe," said Willie. "I know the locals here fear the yowies. I keep a low profile to avoid being confused as one."

"Were you harmed because you were mistaken?" I asked.

Moha answered, "Willie would rather not talk about it."

I nodded and gave Willie a hug. "Most here know how many toes a sasquatch has and can identify a yowie footprint."

"What do we do?"

Meow stretched and arched his back. "I'm going into the caves. I can travel faster than any of you. I can explore quickly, rescue, and leave before a yowie can do anything."

My creatures asked me to leave the area so they could communicate privately. I was insulted but did as they asked. No mistakes could be made.

10

The creatures found me drinking sasquatch beer with Chichi. I had developed a taste for it. Chichi wouldn't tell me what it was made from. The creatures each grabbed a beer and made a circle around me. Willie said, "Sash is already looking, but we have concerns he may have been captured by the yowie. We are almost certain that Joey and Sadie have been captured too. Meow's plan seems the best. He's already left to find them."

I didn't know how to respond. I couldn't just sit and do nothing. I lied to my friends and said I was going to nap. Instead, I snuck out of the cave and went in the direction I'd seen Joey, Sadie, and Sash go. I was surprised at how well lit the caves were. I hadn't taken a flashlight, water, or any provisions. I was only concentrated on finding my family.

I walked the main path for almost an hour before I realized the folly of my ways. I retraced my steps and started to explore the branches of the path. These paths were less lit than the main one. I realized that Moha and Ogua had lit the areas of the map they had explored when they first came here. I had a hard time walking the paths. There was at one time a path, but now it was broken with potholes. I had to slow my pace. I was frustrated. I realized I wasn't accomplishing anything. I turned back toward the main path. I was almost back to the main path when I stumbled and fell into a large hole. I have no idea how deep in the hole I was.

I landed on a stone floor. I was bruised and scraped. I tried to stand, but I was pushed down again and surrounded by yowies. I must have fainted, because the next thing I remember is that I was strapped to a table and blindfolded. As terrified as I was, I could hear telepathic messages, but they weren't coming from the area I was in. The messages were garbled.

I felt hands with many fingers roaming all over my arms and legs. Some seemed to have three fingers, others up to ten. The hands were enormous and hairy. I knew I had been captured by the yowies. I hoped the garbled messages were from Joey, Sadie, or Sash, saying they were near. I felt what I thought was a knife blade where my shoulder was. I screamed. I felt the blade move away from my body, but I kept screaming. I couldn't stop. I was out of control.

I felt a wad of something being forced into my mouth. I started to gag and choke. "No," I tried to scream. Then the object was in place. I could scream no more. I sensed that the yowies had left the room. I tried to regulate my breathing so I didn't choke. I tried not to focus on the fact that Joey, Sadie, and Sash must be enduring the same fate.

I must have fallen asleep. When I woke, I was starving and thirsty. The gag was still in my mouth, and I was still bound. The messages I thought I heard were gone. I panicked. Maybe the yowies had hurt my family and friends. My heart started to race, but I immediately tried to get it under control. I had to keep a clear mind. Slowly, I tested my restraints. Whatever the material, it stretched some. I moved my wrists up and down slowly. I didn't want to draw attention to what I was doing in case the yowies were watching.

I have no idea how long I worked my hand restraints, but I felt one give. My one hand was free. I took the gag out of my mouth. What a relief. I moved my hand to the other restraint in search of a clasp but found none. I used my free hand to pull my other hand harder on the restraint. I had it free in no time. The cave was dark, so seeing things was difficult. Then I remembered I was blindfolded. I took off the blindfold. The light was dim, allowing me to see outlines of what was in the cave. I sat up slowly so as not to make myself dizzy. Once up, I got to work on my foot restraints. It was easier to break them with both hands working together. I moved off the table slowly, testing the ground to see what kind of surface I would land on. It seemed the same as I had been walking on. Carefully, I inched out of the cave by using my hands to find the exit.

Once I found the opening, I ran in the direction I had come. Once I thought I was far enough away from the yowies, I stopped to catch my breath and leaned against the wall of the path. Once calmed enough, I sent messages to Joey, Sash, and Sadie explaining how to break the restraints. I had no idea if they heard me. I was hoping at least one received it and could break free.

Quickly, I made my way out of the cave system and back to where my friends were. As soon as Chichi saw me, she screamed, "Janet is back."

The creatures gathered around me. I had no idea what they were saying; they were all talking at once. "Where's Meow?" I asked.

"He left as soon as we discovered you had the harebrained idea to look for Joey and Sadie by yourself," said Willie.

I admitted to my friends that it had been a bad idea. I related my ordeal. Chichi sent a message to Meow with the info I provided. I could only hope he got it. I asked her to send messages to Sadie and Sash. She agreed.

I was famished. Chichi and Willie manned the kitchen and produced a feast.

"Slow down," said Willie. "You'll make yourself sick."

"Okay, but I'm starving. How long was I gone? A few hours?"

Willie and Chichi exchanged looks. "Don't overreact," said Chichi.

"Just tell her," said Willie.

"Three weeks."

I spit out the bite of food. "What? How long has my family and Sash been gone?"

They both assured me I had left only a day or two after they disappeared.

"It felt like a day," I said.

"You were in a place where cyrtid time takes over," said Aaron. He came into the room and gave me a big hug. I noticed he was freshly groomed.

"You mean, I experienced time as cyrtids do?"

They all nodded.

"Then Sadie and Joey are experiencing it?"

"Probably," said Chichi.

I sighed deeply. "Have you heard from Meow?

Chichi and Willie shook their heads. Chichi said, "We fear he lost his speed when he went near the cyrtid time machine. It overloaded his senses. We are afraid he was caught."

My only hope to rescue my family was trapped, too. I shouldn't have left the caves. I should have looked for them. I was such a coward.

"You're not a coward," said Willie. "You took the most prudent choice—to get to safety."

Aaron explained he had been researching yowies in the local library. Not much was known about them. "Yowies are spirits that walk around at night. They sleep during the day. Reports from South Wales say that they have long white hair hanging down from their head over their features so as not to show their flat noses. They try to impersonate sasquatches, which most people in Australia feel are harmless. Their arms are extraordinarily long, furnished at the extremities with great talons, and their feet are turned backwards, so that, on fleeing from humans, the imprint of the foot makes it look like the being had gone in the opposite direction. They describe it as a hideous monster of an unearthly character and ape-like appearance."

I explained to Aaron that I hadn't seen them, that I was blind-folded. Aaron said that was typical. They were afraid to be seen. Aaron went on, "Though many, naturally, doubt the existence of yowies, some Aboriginal cave art seems to depict tall, hairy creatures painted alongside Aboriginal humans. Some have suggested that this is a sign that yowies were an early hominid that since went extinct—or perhaps merely disappeared deep into the Australian Outback, away from human eyes. This explanation is what the government told the settlers in order to prevent panic."

"How do they attack?" I asked.

"There hasn't been an attack in years. Most scientists feel that the yowies are deep in the Outback living away from humans. I'm thinking they just went underground," said Aaron.

"How does any of this save my family?" I asked.

Aaron shook his head. His search didn't uncover any place to look or methods to capture them. "Meow isn't back?" Aaron asked. We all said no.

"What I'm worried about is the report that yowies have super-powers—speed and shapeshifting," said Aaron.

Now I was worried about Meow. Were the yowies faster than him? "I think the reports are true about the speed. I had this feeling that I was in one place, and then in the next second, I was tied down. But shapeshifting," I said.

"That's what bothers me," Aaron said. "The record is vague as to what kind of shapes yowies can take."

We were all quiet, alone with our thoughts about what shapeshifting might mean for finding my family. Could they impersonate humans and other cyrtids? Did they become inanimate objects? The more I thought, the more upset I became.

A breeze blew through the cave. Meow appeared. I was relieved. If he had been caught, he'd gotten free. There was hope my family would too. I ran to Meow and curled up in his lap. I needed his comforting purr. He seemed surprised I was there. "What's wrong, Meow?" I asked.

"Nothing. I'm not used to having someone in my lap," Meow said.

All of us were surprised. "Very funny, Meow," I said. "I'll get you some warm milk."

While I went to fix Meow's milk, Chichi and Willie pumped him for information about what he found. "I'll tell you after my nap,"

Meow said. He looked at the bowl of milk I put beside him. "Why would I want that?"

This was not Meow. It was a yowie. Willie, Chichi, Aaron, and I exchanged looks. Willie said, "You nap, Meow. We will let you rest."

We went into the cave paths and walked far enough away that Meow the yowie couldn't intercept our thoughts. For once, I was relieved to know telepathic communication.

"What do we do now, Aaron?" I asked.

"The yowies seem able to take the form of other cyrtids, but not their personality. The personality we are seeing in Meow must be the yowie's," Aaron hypothesized. We nodded. "Let's pretend it is Meow and see what we can learn."

We all agreed it was the safest plan. When we returned to the cave, I planned to crawl into the nest that the fake Meow inhabited. As I started to climb in, Willie shouted, "No! Look."

The fake Meow had now taken the form of a yowie. I guess sleeping made it harder to keep the disguise. Aaron sent a message to us to find something to tie down the yowie with. I didn't think anything could hold him. He had super strength and speed. I only hoped the strength of Willie and Chichi would keep the yowie restrained. Aaron returned with a steel rope and locks. The three bound the faker tightly to the nest. We didn't know what to expect when the yowie woke up.

11

The creatures took turns watching the yowie. We slept in shifts. For three human days, the yowie slept. No sound emerged from him. I noticed he was shedding all over the nest, something Meow never did. I spent time sweeping up the yowie fur. Aaron took it to a scientist who lived in the underwater world for examination. He had no idea how long it would take the scientist to draw any conclusions.

"I just hope his findings show that those yowies are no relatives of us," said Willie.

"Yep," I said. "These creatures cannot be related to sasquatches."

On the fourth day, the yowie woke. Chichi was on duty and marveled at how the creature had turned back into Meow. Chichi sent me a message saying to bring him milk. I warmed it the way Meow liked it and brought it to the yowie.

"Oh, Meow, I was so worried. You slept so long. Here's your favorite," I said as I set the bowl next to him. I petted his fur, trying not to gag, and gave him a hug.

"I'm a cat. Don't touch me. Don't you know cats don't like touched?"

"Meow, you are hurting my feelings. We used to be so close," I cried

"Oh, geez, humans. Such babies," Meow answered. "Get me some fish, not this odious liquid."

Moha was best suited to collect fish. She took off to catch and prepare a meal for this creature. When Moha returned with a colorful sushi plate, she set it beside the fake Meow. He sniffed it.

"It's not that fresh," he said.

"Oh, Meow, you always say that," said Moha. "Eat."

In a flash, the sushi was gone. "Mediocre. You'll get used to my tastes. Moha, you must be quicker at serving me, so the fish isn't spoiled." I could see Moha seething, but she graciously told the yowie she would do better next time.

"Do you want me to brush you?" I asked the imposter.

"Don't touch me. I'm a cat," the yowie said.

I figured that the yowies had researched cats and was mimicking normal cat behavior. I wondered if the yowies didn't like touching and had seized on the cat characteristics that fit them best. "I'm sorry. I just missed you," I said.

"Oh, humans. And these cyrtids. You all smell."

"Meow, there is no reason to be mean," I admonished.

"There's no reason to be mean," mimicked the yowie.

I had to leave the area. My Meow would not act like this. It was hard to see a creature looking like Meow behaving that way. I ran down the path to the uncharted cave. When I entered the area where I was captured, I screamed, "Yowies! I'm not afraid of you. Gimme my family back. Gimme Sash and Meow. You know nothing of their character. Your version of Meow is all wrong. Just looking like us doesn't make you us. Stop impersonating us." I was out of breath and shaking in anger. I expected to be swooped back to where I had been held captive. I received no answer. I kept walking. I would find my family alone if none of my friends would help.

I had blisters on my feet from walking, but I persisted. I knew my family had to be close. I reasoned that the yowie had taken me before I came too close to where they were holding my family. No one was around to take me now. Were the yowies gathered to torture my family?

The path through the labyrinth narrowed. I could touch both walls without extending my arms. I hoped it wouldn't get too narrow. I would crawl if I had to.

I felt something land on my heart. I looked around. Nothing was in the passageway with me. I then realized it was Sadie trying to contact me. I stopped and listened carefully.

"Mom, we're okay. Walk a little farther, and you'll find us," Sadie said.

I was elated. My Sadie was okay. Then I paused. Was it Sadie, or a yowie pretending to be her? Instead of rushing to where I felt Sadie was, I stopped to think. The yowie that was impersonating Meow didn't use telepathy, did he? He spoke. Why hadn't we picked up on it? I believed it really was my Sadie. I ran toward where I thought the telepathy had come from.

Something stopped me. I realized it was Sadie leading me to where she was. I looked around and saw three different branches in the path. Which one would take me to her? I chose the one closest to me.

12

I slowly entered the area where I thought my Sadie was. The cave was dim. Once my eyes adjusted to the low light, I saw a table much like the one I had been strapped to. I rushed to it. Sadie was strapped down like I had been. "Sadie," I whispered.

"I knew you would come," Sadie said. With the two of us working together, the bonds broke easily.

"Do you know where your dad and Sash are?" I asked her.

"I know where Meow is," she said. "He couldn't believe a creature was faster than he was. He's miserable."

I asked Sadie to show me the way to Meow's confinement. He purred loudly. "It's my Janet. I knew you would come," he said. Sadie and I freed him quickly. He wanted to whisk us back to our caves, but I refused to go without Sash and Joey. "I can come back for them," Meow said indignantly.

"Meow, I love you for thinking of us, but you were caught. It could happen again," I said.

"We all could be caught. At least you and Sadie would be safe," he said.

I allowed Meow to take Sadie to the home cave. He was back in a flash. Confinement hadn't ruined his speed. He picked me up to quickly take me to Sash.

"Janet," said Sash, "you shouldn't be here."

"We'll talk about that later," said Meow. In a minute, Meow had Sash freed and flew him to the home cave.

"Where's Joey?" I asked Meow.

Meow wrapped me in his paws. "Janet, I don't know. The last message I received from him was garbled. I think the yowies were experimenting on him. Where he was taken, I can't find."

I gasped. Joey... experimented on? Meow took me in his arms and purred until I was calmer. "We will look. I have some ideas."

The next thing I knew, Meow was whirling around the cave paths and caves looking for Joey. "What if the yowies see us?" I asked.

"They won't. I learned how to disguise myself. They shapeshift. I try to do the same thing. I take on the appearance of a yowie when they are around. I'm not good at it, but I evaded them for a while before they caught me."

I have no idea how long we searched. Then I felt it. "Meow, he's in there," I said.

Joey was lying on a slab much like I had. He seemed unconscious. Meow had him free in an instant. An instant later, we were in the home cave.

Joey was still unconscious. Willie and Chichi started to minister to him. The rest of us were jubilant. We were safe. Sash, Willie, and Chichi took off to wall off the branch of the caves that led to the yowies. I was beginning to feel safer when they returned.

Willie and Chichi, who had been working on Joey, came into the cave. They were pleased the cave was walled off. I was waiting for them to tell me about Joey.

"How is Joey?" I asked, scared to know. Would I lose him again? For good?

Willie took me in her arms. Chichi took Sadie. I knew it was bad and started to sob.

Sash, who had been helping Willie and Chichi, spoke first. "He's alive."

Sadie and I sighed in relief.

"He's not a mansquash anymore," Willie said. "The yowie performed some sort of procedure on him. He's a man."

Sadie and I leapt from our creatures' arms and embraced. We were laughing and crying. Willie, Chichi, Sash, and the others were flummoxed. "You are glad," said Sash.

"Yes, we can be a true family. No cyrtid in our way," I said.

Sadie and I danced, laughed, and cried. Then I noticed the looks on my friends' faces. "Oh, no. No. I love all of you. I need all of you. You saved me, Sadie and Joey—Joseph—so many times. You will always be family."

Sash said he would lead us to Joseph. The rest of the cyrtids said they needed to sleep. What I said wasn't enough for my friends to forgive me. I was torn between going after my friends to beg forgiveness or going to see my normal husband. Sash steered Sadie and I toward Joseph.

13

Joseph, Sadie, and I settled in Sydney. We wanted to be close to where our friends gathered in case they forgave me for my outburst when I realized Joseph was a human again. We found work at a local newspaper. Joseph took pictures for the paper. He hoped to start his own studio. I worked part-time to spend time with Sadie and my writing. I wanted to finish the book and have it published. I would send it to my cyrtid friends as a peace offering. I missed Meow the most. I cried almost daily that I couldn't snuggle in his lap. Joseph was patient with me. He knew how much Meow helped me handle the strange happenings.

My life was normal again. I should have been happy, but I missed my friends. They were my family too.

Sadie was excelling in school. When she entered high school, she took as many science classes as she could. She wanted to become a scientist who documented cyrtids. Joseph was concerned about her obsession. I encouraged it. Maybe her work could reconcile all of us.

My book was published in Australia. It became a bestseller. I was reluctant to have it marketed in the US. Right now, we are happy in our new home. The US seemed like a distant memory.

CADDY

1

Mom and Dad are sitting as close to the stage as they could. I know they are brimming with pride as I am conferred my PhD in science. I'm not in my robes yet. They may be proud of me, but I am so proud of them. They endured more than most couples and were still able to raise me to be a functioning adult. It was iffy at times. When I was seven and living near Lake Erie, Mom and I met and befriended cyrtid creatures who changed our lives. My mom and I thought my father was dead. We went to the beach many times, and I met Bessie, a sea creature. Most people thought Bessie was a legend. I learned that legends have facts in them. If Sash, a sasquatch and Bessie's best friend, had not given his blood to my father, he would have died. He would not have lived as a mansquat for many years before the strange cyrtids, the yowies, made him human again, allowing me to live a normal life. Many times, Mom's life was in danger. Mom was arrested and put on trial for befriending Sash and Bessie. She lived in a car for weeks, because, even though she was acquitted, the mobs wanted her to pay. The worst experience was when Dad and I were captured by yowies. If Mom hadn't risked her life, I am not sure Dad and I would be here to enjoy this day.

After Mom, Dad, and I escaped the yowies, our lives were normal

—normal in the sense that I was able to attend school, and Mom and Dad could continue their careers in journalism. Abnormal would be that family vacations were to visit our sasquatches and sea creatures. We also had a pet, Meow, who really was a dragon who had been maimed and turned into a water cat. My family settled in Sydney, near some of the cryptids. I was able to complete my education and went to the University of Sydney. My undergrad was in science. To earn my PhD, I studied the myths of cryptids and merged it with science. My work had been called groundbreaking. My post-graduate studies, which I would start in the fall, were to further human acceptance of cryptids

2

_____

After the graduation celebration with our human friends, the dragons took us to the Himalayas for the real celebration with the cryptids. Draconia transported me while his brother, Dragoon, took Mom and Dad. Draconia and Dragoon made the flight spectacular by doing loop-the-loops. When we approached the mountains, they flew us up to a peak, soared straight down to the valley, and then back to the top. Mom was nauseated when we reached our destination. Dad and I wanted another ride, but Mom said no. Party pooper.

When we dismounted the dragons, we were swept into a crush of sea creatures, sasquatches, and dragons all begging for hugs. Meow had arrived earlier because of his super speed. As soon as he saw Mom, he grabbed her and settled her into his lap. She brought out the milk she had smuggled on the dragon. Meow lapped it up and fell promptly asleep.

Once we were settled, the dragons staged a magnificent fire/flight show that lasted over an hour. During the show, Sash told me their original dance was a century long; he urged them to shorten it to conform with human time. I stifled a laugh. The difficult part of my dissertation was trying to explain in human terms how cryptids handle time.

After the fire/flight show, we sat down to an amazing feast. Nessie, Chichi, and Willie made every dish imaginable: mashed clams, roasted squirrel, barbequed dodo, and wild boar with berries and nuts. There were salads, nuts, and fruit for the vegans. I know I ate too much, because I couldn't sleep—too much heartburn. I always eat too many dodo birds.

Mom and Dad left on dragons early the next morning; Meow stayed a little longer since he could zip home in half an hour. I was never fond of Meow. As a child, I was jealous of the time Mom spent with him. He and I bonded over my dissertation, because Meow could transport me across the world faster than any other mode. I know Meow still didn't trust me.

Although the next part of my research was to start in the fall, I decided to begin it early since I was already in the Himalayas. I didn't share the subject of my post-doc with Mom and Dad. They would have opposed. In fact, Sash thought it was ill-advised. My original work focused on cryptids who befriended humans. I felt to be a thorough researcher, I would need to document those that didn't. Sash was sending a guard dragon and a sasquatch with me for protection. Draconia was the best guard in the dragon community. Sash wanted to be the sasquatch, but I insisted he was needed to lead his family. He suggested his brother, Quatty. Quatty and I worked well together. When Sash was unable to come with me on a cryptid safari, Quatty was a capable co-worker. He had learned from his human how to read and write a bit. He learned more when he helped me.

I rested and played with the dragons for over a week. They complained it was too short. I kept explaining my time was shorter than theirs. The next week, Quatty, Draconia, and I set out on my new adventures. I'd miss my parents, but we all had mastered telepathic communication and could easily send messages.

Draconia was a great colleague. He provided transportation, fire for cooking, and diversions, if needed. Quatty and Draconia were the best of friends, so I didn't need to worry about internal squabbles. I slept on our way to the Pacific coast of North America. The trip took longer than usual because we were carrying cold-weather gear. Even though it was summer in North America, the area had cold snaps. We settled on an island west of Seattle, Washington, to set up a base camp. Quatty and Draconia would share a tent. I had a smaller one beside theirs. There was also the research lab. Quatty got it up and running quickly. Draconia caught and roasted a few squirrels for our dinner. Squirrel meat wasn't my favorite; remember Rocky the Squirrel? Draconia talked about catching a moose for its skin and meat. I grew up watching Rocky and Bullwinkle cartoons, Mom's favorite. I could never eat Bullwinkle.

I was up early the next day. I prepared the video cameras on the tripods. From where we camped, we had a 360-degree view of the ocean. The video would record while we explored the area. Draconia flew us off the island and to the coast to Ape Cave, the third longest lava tube (2.5 miles long) in North America, where the cave temperature is 42 Fahrenheit, or 5.6 Celsius, year-round. My theory was that a sasquatch lived in lava caves near a sea creature, just as I found Sash with Bessie. I sent a message to Sash asking if any of his siblings lived here. He didn't know of any who had settled there. Draconia hadn't been alive during the diaspora of Nessie's first family. I had no idea if the creature that lived there was one of Nessie's children. The creature sounded menacing.

A Victoria lawyer and his wife were cruising in their yacht in 1933 and spotted a horrible serpent with the head of a camel and menacing teeth. The creature showed itself again in 1934 when two members of the Canadian Provincial Government reported seeing the creature, the same description as the first. Later that same year, two fishermen saw two monsters in the bay, one about sixty feet long, the other half that size. A rather interesting sighting was made by two hunters as they tried to recover their wounded duck. The monster rose out of the water, swallowed the duck, snapped at some gulls, then resubmerged. They noted the six-foot-long head with saw-like teeth. There were other sightings that were explained away as whale carcasses or pipe fish. I concluded that the creature ate more birds than fish. Now I could test my hypotheses.

Draconia led the way through the lava tube using his fire as a flashlight. Quatty was in the rear. Either could fight off danger should it occur in the tubes. We moved slowly as I gathered soil samples and anything unusual. I would examine the specimens in the lab when we returned to the island. I was exhausted by the time we arrived back at camp. I had no sightings of sasquatch-type creatures. Tomorrow, I would use scuba gear to examine the life in the ocean near the last sighting of the sea monster. Quatty was reviewing the video while I safely stored the specimens. I'd examine them in the morning before we explored the ocean. I decided to prepare dinner—rice and beans—before Draconia brought home more squirrels.

"Sadie," said Quatty, "come quickly!" I guessed dinner could wait.

I hurried to Quatty's side. He was viewing a video of a creature that looked exactly like a Cadborosaurus. A Cadborosaurus resembled a serpent with vertical humps in tandem behind the horse-like head and long neck. It had a pair of small, elevated front flippers, either a pair of hind flippers, or a pair of large, webbed hind flippers fused to form a large fan-like tail that allowed it to move forward. I instructed Quatty to capture some photos of the creature and to be sure there were reference objects to help me determine size. If I knew the measurements of mountains, cell towers, and other objects, I could estimate the cadborosaurus' size.

"Where's Draconia?" I asked.

"Out hunting," Quatty said as he began the screen captures.

"No, not squirrel again," I cried.

"No squirrel or moose. I told him you were a picky eater," said Quatty with a grin.

"I'm not picky."

"Right, uh huh. He's looking for ducks and quail."

I sighed in relief. At least dinner would taste like chicken.

3

I woke up before my companions the next morning. I grabbed a duck leg out of the cooler to gnaw on while I worked. Mom said my eating habits bordered on disgusting from spending so much time with cryptids. She doesn't remember the years we were on the lam with them and ate with our hands. She maintains we always used flatware, but Spitzy didn't have any. Sash and Bessie kept utensils for us, but none of the others ever did.

I started my work by looking at the still shots Quatty had captured for me. He did a good job. I had more than enough reference points to determine Caddy's length. (I decided to give the creature a shorter name for my reports.) I determined that Caddy was at least sixty feet long, as earlier sightings had recorded. I believed it was much longer. Caddie had humps along its length that went above the water. I could not ascertain if there were similar humps below. If those humps were the same as what showed above, it was sixty feet long. If the humps were longer, then it could be much longer, maybe a hundred feet.

I started on the specimens next. I was excited to discover that one strange rock I brought to examine was fossilized dung. I also found some DNA samples that would need to be compared to the other cryptid DNA I had discovered in past research. I summoned Meow, who came in a jiff. He was to take the specimens to my lab in Sydney and instruct my grad students to use MRIs, X-rays, and other short-spectrum means to see what was inside. The DNA would be run and compared to the DNA samples I had of other cryptids.

"Aren't you forgetting something?" said Meow.

I gave him a quizzical look. "Right." I went to the cooler and poured him a bowl of milk.

"It's not warm."

"No, Meow, it isn't. Draconia isn't up yet to heat it. Don't be so darn cantankerous."

Meow begrudgingly drank his cold milk and then left. Why did Mom adore him? I have no idea.

Draconia entered the lab tent rocking from side to side. "Was that Meow flying by me?"

I nodded. "You should have been here earlier. He was angry his milk was cold."

"Spoiled."

"Yep." Quatty came in behind Draconia. "Meow just left to take specimens from my lab in Sydney."

Quatty stretched his long arms and put a hand on each side of the tent. "I thought so. I felt a breeze."

"What's the agenda for today?" asked Draconia.

I told Draconia he was to stay near base camp to monitor the video cameras. He couldn't scuba dive for obvious reasons.

"Can I hunt?"

Both Quatty and I said, "No." Poor Draconia. Quatty's and my diet were similar. Dragons killed and charred whatever they could find.

Quatty and I went back to our tents for scuba gear. We planned to follow the lava tube to where it ended in the ocean. From there, we would explore the ocean floor, look for an underwater cave that Caddy might use, and gather water samples. We worked side by side for a few hours. I gathered my water samples easily. Quatty scoured the ocean floor and grabbed some of the matter on the ocean floor. As I got ready to surface, I saw something that looked like a tail—a large, webbed flipper that almost hit me in the face. Quatty caught the message I sent to him. He whipped out the underwater camera and started clicking. I was trying to see the other end of the creature to see if it indeed had a horse head with menacing teeth, but the creature appeared to go on and on forever.

We surfaced and swam to the island. Draconia had caught and prepared some fish for us to eat. Famished, I dug right in. Quatty wanted to download the pictures first. He brought the new pictures to compare to the stills from the video. I wiped my hands. I took the pictures and made a column of the ones from the video and one of today's pictures. Caddy's tail had been under the water when it was caught on the video. The pictures that Quatty took of the tail showed me my calculations of its size were not accurate. The tail itself was at least ten feet.

"Seventy feet long, at least," I mumbled. Quatty nodded.

After lunch, I took a short nap and then examined the water samples. I summoned Meow again after alerting Draconia he had to stay near to warm his milk. I wanted Meow to bring the water samples from other cyprid sites and the analysis of the samples I sent earlier to my lab in Sydney. Meow arrived about an hour later with everything I asked for. Draconia warmed his milk. Meow lapped it up and then bedded down in my tent. I'd have red cat hair all over.

Draconia and Quatty left me alone in the lab to continue my work. Looking over the water samples from past studies and the ones from this location, I noted six similar markers. Five or more of these markers in one location signaled a pod of cryptids. I hadn't examined the ocean floor samples taken yesterday. I began comparing those to floor samples from other cryptid locations. I realized I had picked up Caddy eggshells, much like other cryptid finds.

I had worked so long, it was dark when I emerged from the lab. Draconia had a nice fire going. Quatty was roasting some kind of bird. I was afraid to ask what kind. Meow was enjoying a nap by the fire.

"Meow, why are you here?" I asked.

'I decided to stay. You were going to summon me again, right?"

"Well, yes, Meow. In fact, take the pouch of materials I left on the lab table to my lab and wait for results. Tell my grads to get in a supply of milk. You'll be there a few days." Meow was gone.

"What did you find?" asked Quatty as we began to eat dinner.

"Definitely cryptid. Same markers in the water. Eggshells on the floor. I don't think I have actual DNA from the creature, but I do have it from the shell. I had Meow take the shells to Sydney and told him to wait for the results."

"Am I related to it?" asked Quatty.

I knew it bothered many of my friends that I was looking for cryptids who were not kind. They hated thinking there was a version of their relatives that were hostile to humans. I'd have to choose my words carefully. "I think that Caddy and his kind are distantly related. The Caddy seemed less developed. I wish I had a way to MRI its brain."

"Don't even think about that," Draconia said. "It's too dangerous."

"Yes, Dad," I said sarcastically.

"You better revere me like your dad. He put me in charge of your safety."

"Okay. Okay."

The three of us turned in early. I wanted to do more underwater exploring the next day. Quatty and Draconia would further explore the tunnels looking for nests. They also wanted to see if the creature made tools or used implements of any kind. I doubted they did. I was guessing Caddy's brain wasn't developed enough.

4

I first thought the rumbling and shaking of the earth was in my dream, until I found myself upside down. Something had grabbed my tent and was shaking it from side to side. I tried to calm myself and send a message to Quatty and Draconia. I could tell they didn't receive it. Once the caddy—I assume it was the caddy—slammed my tent down, I struggled to exit it. My right foot was broken and bleeding. I managed to crawl from the tent to where Quatty and Draconia's tent was. It was missing. My lab had been destroyed. There was no Caddy in sight.

I knew I would have to summon help. I could hear my parents thinking, *I told you it was dangerous*, when I summoned Sash. He had sent them my distress call after he assembled a team of sasquatches and dragons. Sash, Bessie, Chichi, and Spitzy were on the way.

Luckily, our fire was undisturbed, and some fish were left over from last night's dinner. I crawled to where my lab had been. I was glad I sent Meow to Sydney when I did. None of my work was lost—just the equipment. I found the first aid kit untouched. I dragged myself to it and cleaned the wound. I had never seen a wound like this before. There were tiny, thin spikes sticking out of my ankle on both sides, where the blood was leaking from. Teeth. The creature left its teeth in wounds to enhance the bleeding of its prey. I tried to pull out the teeth, but they didn't budge. The more I pulled, the more I bled. I tried to move around the site looking for my pliers to pull the teeth out. I couldn't find any. Feeling weak, I lapsed into a deep sleep.

I woke in my tent. Someone had set it up and put me in it. My ankle was bandaged. I couldn't tell if the teeth were under the bandage. My foot was swollen. I felt dizzy and was thirsty. I sat up slowly. I was too weak to send a telepathic message. I couldn't stay sitting up. I must have fallen back asleep.

When I woke again, I was shaking from the cold. I felt a blanket being laid over me. I passed out again. When awake, I felt like I was drowning, which made me fall back asleep. I could hear voices but not recognize them. I have no idea how long I slept.

"Hey, sleepy head," a voice said. "How are you feeling?"

I shook my head. "Water, please," I managed to croak out. Someone helped me sit up and supported me. Someone else held a glass of water and helped me take a sip. My eyes couldn't focus. I asked for another sip. I almost choked.

"Take it easy," said the voice. "You were poisoned by the bite."

"Who are you?" I asked.

"Oh, honey, it's me, Mom. Dad's here, too."

I smiled and went back to sleep.

The next time I woke, I felt much better. I felt a bit stronger. When I opened my eyes, I could focus if I concentrated hard. Dad was holding my hand. I had a red blanket over me—wait. It was Meow.

"Don't try to sit up yet," Dad said.

"Okay. What's going on?"

Dad explained that Sash had contacted them when the group Sash assembled found me unconscious. Chichi was able to remove the teeth from my ankle. Bessie sucked as much poison out of the wound as she could. The ankle wasn't broken. It was traumatized by the poison.

"How long was I out?" I asked.

I saw Mom come into the tent. "Four weeks, honey," she said. She moved Meow a bit so she could sit beside me.

"I was asleep," griped Meow. "Oh, wait!" He saw that I was conscious and started to purr and paw at my chest. "She's alive. She's alive." Meow was brimming with glee. He jumped off the bed and then started his zoomies. All we could see was a red blur going in circles.

"Calm down," said Mom. "Warm milk?"

Meow stopped, jumped on my bed, and waited patiently for his warm milk. Dad looked at me and smiled. We hugged. After Meow had his milk, Dad and Mom filled me in on what had occurred after I was found. Dad said:

Sash received the distress call and assembled his team. The fastest dragons flew them here. Once Sash understood the seriousness of the wound, he contacted us and sent the dragons to bring us here. By the time we arrived, Chichi had removed the teeth. Bessie had sucked out the poison, and Spitzy had cauterized the wounds to stop the blood flow. Mom and I needed to give you blood transfusions. Willie reassembled your lab and called for the dragons to replace the equipment that was ruined. She took samples of your blood and noticed under the microscope you had additional antibodies not normally present in human blood. Meow fetched the lab result from Sydney. Willie was able to determine that the antibodies had the same DNA sequence as the lining of the eggshells. The only thing we could do was give you transfusions with high concentrations of an anti-viral that your grad students made. We were able to replace enough blood and anti-viral that the caddycells stopped growing in your body.

None of us knew if it would heal you or kill you. Your mom and I decided you'd never come back to us if we didn't try to counteract the caddycells. Your dissertation supervisor was summoned, since he had a medical background, and administered the IVs of blood and fluids. At first, your body rejected the transfusions. Meow was dispatched to find a blood purification machine to filter the blood. The machine took out many of the caddycells. Some, however, had started working on altering your DNA. The doctor tried a lower dose of the anti-viral with my blood. Nothing happened. Then he tried the anti-viral with your mom's blood. The tests were showing that the caddycells stopped growing. We don't know what will happen with the dead caddycells. We will have to be patient and vigilant.

"What does that mean?" I asked.

"Weekly blood tests. The doctor trained Willie to draw and test your blood. She'll be joining your team for the remainder of your research."

"You aren't going to make me abandon my research?" I asked my dad. I thought for sure they would order me back to Sydney.

Dad laughed. "And when have you followed our orders?"

I laughed. "When I was three or four, I assume."

"Not even then, Sadie. Not even then."

5

_____

I agreed to return to Sydney for an extended time while I regained my strength. My team stayed on the island to send me specimens for analysis. Mom was on me constantly about the time I spent in my lab. She thought I was doing too much. I put a cot in the room adjacent to my lab and told her I'd take frequent naps. I am not sure Mom believed me. I needed two significantly long naps a day.

I was comparing my DNA with that from Caddy's eggshells, when Meow blew into my lab. "You scared me, Meow," I said.

"I slowed to half speed when I got here," he said. "It didn't help?" I shook my head. Meow agreed to stop at my lab door next time and walk in.

"I needed to be here pronto. Sash and Quatty did an underwater dive and snapped great pictures of Caddy."

"Oh, wonderful! Oh, wait. Were they harmed?" I asked.

"No. They think the caddy was so long that he couldn't see where they were. Quatty said they were somewhere in the middle of its body."

"Interesting. Ask them to explore the eyesight issue. Tell them to stay away from its mouth."

"I have something else."

"Just tell me, Meow."

Meow pulled a specimen vial from deep in his fur.

I gasped. "Caddy DNA?" I was jumping up and down. Meow had a case of zoomies. Then we collapsed in each other's arms.

"Quatty said he stuck a needle into Caddy about twenty feet from its tail. Caddy didn't feel a thing. Or, if she did, the pain didn't register with her until Quatty and Sash were out of the way."

I was exhausted from our celebration dance. I still wasn't a hundred percent. I told Meow I was going to prepare the slides for the DNA. I began dropping the sample on several slides. When I came to the last one, I dropped it. It broke. When I picked up the pieces, I accidentally cut my finger. I sucked on it to stop the bleeding. I decided to leave the lab early and get a fresh start in the morning. I couldn't wait to see what the DNA showed.

My parents were surprised I was home so early. The three of us decided to go out for dinner and enjoy our time together. I know both my parents were disappointed that they didn't see me more often. I knew I was obsessed with cryptids. Mom was saying I needed to find balance. I would find balance once I proved my hypothesis.

We picked our favorite Italian restaurant. The staff knew us well and showed us to our favorite table overlooking the street. We liked to people watch. I was always comparing human movement to that of my cryptids. I hoped to find markers in the cryptids that matched human markers. I had employed AI in my computer program to speed up the process.

"Sadie," Dad said. "Mom and I are worried about you."

"When aren't you, Dad?"

"Hear me out. You're twenty-six years old. You can't spend all your time with the cryptids and ignore your private life. You almost died. We thought you would reassess your priorities."

The same old argument. Dad and Mom wanted me to settle down and give them grandkids. That wasn't my goal. "I'll have a private life once I crack the cryptid DNA sequencing and show a link between us and them."

"Joseph," said Mom, "not now. Let's enjoy our evening."

"All right," said Dad.

I ordered my favorite, baked ziti. As usual, Mom and Dad split a pizza. I took a big bite of my food and choked. I couldn't breathe. Dad grabbed me and started the Heimlich maneuver. The food wouldn't dislodge. Mom was screaming to call 911. Something inside me told me to push Dad away. I gave him a hard shove, and he flew through the window and out onto the sidewalk. Mom screamed some more. I pushed her down and sat on her head to stop the screaming.

I knew what I was doing, but not why I was doing it. Something had taken control of my body.

6

I heard sirens in the distance and knew I had to leave the scene. I got up from Mom's head and went out the restaurant door. The entire door frame went with me. I couldn't figure out why I had broken the door. I was being compelled to run. My pace made me dizzy. Everything around me was a blur. Mom or Dad must have summoned Meow, because I found myself surrounded by fur. I couldn't move. My parents were now on the street with me and Meow. He grabbed them. With his super speed, he took us to the island in the Pacific Northwest.

I tried to explain to my team what had happened to us at the restaurant. I found that I could no longer use my telepathic skills. I opened my mouth to talk to Mom and Dad. Gibberish came out. Sash came at me with a needle. Willie and Chichi held Sash while he poked me with it. I screamed. I felt like my body was not me. I was trapped in a body I couldn't control. Whatever Willie and Chichi gave me made me feel like I was far away from them. Yet, I could hear and understand them.

"I don't know what happened," said Meow. "I gave her the DNA. She started to prepare the slides. I know she dropped one and cut herself." Sash, Chichi, and Willie listened carefully.

"Was there DNA on the slide that broke?" asked Sash.

"I assume so," said Meow. He was jonesing for some milk. I could tell. They seemed oblivious to his needs, and I couldn't tell them.

Sash looked thoughtful. "If there was DNA on the slide and some entered Sadie's system, it may have reactivated the caddycells."

I gasped. My friends turned to me and tried to communicate. I couldn't decipher the telepathic messages. Mom's words seemed garbled. I wanted to tell them I had been exposed to the caddy DNA. I never thought being near it could harm me .

"Let's try the anti-viral again," said Chichi.

Sash seemed skeptical, but there was no other solution. Chichi, Sash, and Willie had to hold me down while Draconia put the needle in my arm. I felt needles enter my arm. I growled when the needle entered my arm. When I growled, I understood. I was a Caddy now.

I don't know how much time passed. I know I slept a long time. Mom was sitting by my bed when I came to. "Mom," I said.

Mom turned toward me. "I can understand you now, Sadie." She and I embraced.

"Thank goodness. What is happening? I think I know, but I'm not sure of anything anymore."

"You were exposed to caddy DNA. The anti-viral is working slowly and killing the caddycells that were reactivated."

"What do I look like?" I asked. I was fearful that I looked like a Caddy.

"You were no more than half caddy. You looked like a mermaid with a fan tail. Your head and shoulders were you. You looked lovely, except—"

"Except I was huge," I interrupted. Mom nodded. "Am I still huge?"

"No, you are your normal size, but you don't have legs yet."

I felt my body. It seemed like skin until about my waist. I could feel where my skin turned to scales. I sobbed. Mom just held me and allowed me to grieve.

7

I spent most of my time in the water once I had my strength back. The swimming helped me regain my strength. I could also explore underwater without a breathing apparatus. I felt so free underwater. I strapped myself in a backpack with all the equipment I needed and gathered specimens all day. Mom and Dad were worried I might encounter caddycells or DNA. I took precautions. I had gloves on, a swim coat, and flippers on my tail. I was a sight to behold. Not really; I looked ridiculous.

After my morning swims, I worked in my lab with the samples I had gathered. Dad had fashioned a chair to accommodate my tail so I could sit comfortably for hours. I was in the lab one day when I just felt so overwhelmed. I wanted my legs back. I wanted to be human. Was there anyone on Earth who had experienced being half fish, half human? I wished there was someone I could explain my feelings to. None of the cryptids nor my parents could understand what I felt. I shed a few tears, wiped them away, and went back to work. I worked another hour and decided to close the samples for the day. I got up and walked to the lab door.

I screamed, "I'm walking!" Sure enough, I had legs. How did it happen? I have no idea. My friends and parents were there, instantly responding to my screams. Sash was the first to see what I was screaming about.

"She has legs," yelled Sash. Everyone crowded around me. I felt almost claustrophobic with all the hands and legs surrounding me. The next thing I knew, I was on the ground. The tail was back. I heard my friends groan.

"What happened?" I cried.

I could hear them all sending telepathic messages to each other, trying to figure it out. The only one not communicating was Sash. Though glad to haved my telepathic powers back, I worried about Sash's demeanor.

I slithered over to Sash. He held me in his arms. "What's wrong, Sash?" I asked.

Sash smiled at me. "Try thinking of being a frog."

"What?"

"You heard me. Be a frog."

I did as Sash said. I began hopping all over the island. It was so much fun. My head was mine, but my body was a frog. Meow laughed and joined me in my hopping. My friends were not amused. They were calling for me to stop hopping and be sensible. I obeyed. My friends and parents had experienced so much pain with my transformations, I knew I had to be sensible. The minute I thought of being sensible I was human.

Mom said, "Sadie, you are you." I looked down, and there I was. Legs. Skin. No scales. A jubilant cheer went up from everyone but Sash.

"Sash," I said. "What are you thinking?"

"You can shape-shift."

Sash was right. I could shape-shift.

8

S ash started training me so I could stay human for long periods. I had to train my mind to remember I was human while living my normal life. Yeah. Right. Sash shadowed me in the lab to be sure when I was working with cryptid samples that I stayed human. It was tough at first. I was half sasquatch, half human for a while. Being a Bessie-type creature made it difficult to move around. As the training continued, I could stay human for five-hour stretches. After five hours, I turned into a mermaid-like creature. I would swim for a while and continue underwater research. I made sure to turn human for dinner with my team. When I slept, I was a mermaid.

Until I could find a way to rid myself of the caddycells, I had to work from the island. I couldn't risk becoming a creature where I'd be seen. Dad was sure I'd never be cured. He knew what it was like to be another creature. He was a mansquat for nearly four years. I had someone to talk to about the problem with. Meow set up a dragon-Uber to transport items between my island and Sydney. He was only used for urgent needs. Some of those needs were supplies. I didn't want Draconia killing our dinner. We were upsetting the ecosystem enough just by being here.

My biggest fear was working with yowie DNA. If I didn't maintain focus on human traits, I could become a yowie. Yowies were horrible creatures that Mom, Dad, and I ran into on our adventures with the sasquatches, sea creatures, and dragons. The yowies we ran into held Dad captive. They were experimenting on him. I have never been able to figure out what they did. I felt indebted to the yowies, since the experiments took the DNA of the sasquatch out of Dad. He was human again. I grew up with both parents as humans. Sash was afraid; since my heart had a soft spot for yowies, I'd be vulnerable to changing and might not be able to change back.

As I was sequencing the caddy DNA, I noticed a similar sequence to what I found in Bessie and her mother, Nessie. Were the sea creatures a cousin to the caddy? I asked Meow to transport Willie to Ogua, Spitzy, Nessie, and Moha so she could extract a blood sample from each. I couldn't believe I had failed to sequence the DNA of those close to me. Meow wanted to give the assignment to one of the courier dragons, but I wanted lightning-fast speed. I promised him an entire gallon of milk.

As soon as I received the blood samples from Meow and Wilie, I began sequencing the DNA. I then compared Ogua's, Spitzy's, Nessie's, and Moha's DNA to the caddycells. I heard a terrible yowl. I raced from the tent to see what was wrong. Meow was caterwauling, as if he were dying.

"Meow, you got your milk. What's wrong now?" I asked him once I calmed him with another pint of milk.

"You never asked for my DNA," he cried.

"Oh, you silly beast," I said. "Willie will take yours today." And the crying and caterwauling stopped. I realized I had missed testing him because I think of him as a cat rather a sea creature.

Meow rubbed his head against my legs then stood up and put his two front paws on my shoulders to lay his head on my chest. I had never seen him more pleased.

When I had the DNA sequenced and compared, I saw a definite lineage between the caddy and the sea creatures. I asked Meow to take me to Nessie. Mom and Dad didn't want me traveling in case I shapeshifted abroad. I explained to them that I needed to ask Nessie some personal questions. Meow said he'd take me if Sash went with me to continue my concentration exercises.

9

Nessie was so happy to see me, Meow, and Sash. I had to tell her the results of my dissertation. She listened carefully and nodded. Then I told her about sequencing her children's DNA. I saw Nessie go pale.

"The Evil One," said Nessie. Meow, Sash, and I looked at each other confused. Nessie said:

I never told my children about the one dragon I abandoned. He refused to quell his fire when we were all together. At meals, he'd char his siblings' food. My children were all young then. Most of them didn't get out of their nests. The Evil One never stayed in a nest. I'd find him at the top of the mountain freezing and unable to get himself home. Once I had to rescue him from the few remaining dinosaurs that were still here. It takes a long time to cook a T-Rex. Dessie and I made the hardest decision of our lives when we took him to the bottom of the mountain and clipped his wings. He could still fly but half as high as his siblings. I also sealed part of this throat, where our flames come from. He had a meager fire. I didn't think the sasquatches who clipped our wings had also taken his. I heard rumors from my children once we dispersed around the world that somewhere in the northwestern part of the US, there was a menacing sea creature. Dessie's brother, Lenny, decided to look for himself. He wanted to dispel the rumors. Instead, he found the Evil One, who immediately recognized him. TEO, as Lenny called him, thought his father had come to welcome him back into the family. Lenny never let TEO explain that he had outgrown all the behavior that got him banished. TEO gave up his wicked ways to rejoin the family. When he realized Lenny was not asking him back to the mountain, TEO reverted to his bad behavior.

I was riveted by the story and a little angry at Nessie. When I interviewed Nessie at the beginning of my dissertation research, I asked if she knew of any sea creatures who were not kind. She never told me. I didn't show my displeasure. I could see she was ashamed of her past behavior.

Meow flew me home. Sash and I discussed how much of this story we wanted to share with the other sea creatures. The offspring of Nessie thought of themselves as forgiving, helpful, peaceful beings. News such as this would alter their beliefs. I felt we should leave out details. Sash wanted to share it all.

"Hello," said Meow, "I'm here. I'm a sea creature. Was I upset about hearing I have an evil brother? It might come in handy someday to tell people I have a brother who can enforce my will."

"And why didn't Nessie banish you, Meow, if you were behaving like TEO," I said.

"Because I was the sweetest baby dragon there ever was."

Sash and I roared with laughter. Meow decided to fly us upside down the rest of the way.

10

We told Bessie the news when we arrived home, and she wept for her lost sibling. She did not recall knowing TEO as an infant. She agreed with Sash that they all deserved the entire story.

"Where there is good, there is also evil," said Bessie. "I knew deep down there had to be an evil sea creature out there." Sash hugged Bessie tightly as she sobbed on his shoulder. Meow took his paws and hugged the two of them. The creatures needed to mourn without me there. I crept out of the tent and to my lab.

I wondered, if I injected DNA from the sea creatures into Caddy, would there be a change in his personality? I also wondered what this new finding meant for me. Would the DNA stop the shapeshifting?

As I was considering uses for the DNA, Sash, Bessie, and Meow walked into the lab. They looked solemn. I gave them a questioning look.

Bessie said, "Meow and I feel we need to convene all the sea creatures in the Himalayas to announce this news." I was about to object, but Bessie sent me a message to stay quiet. "First, Meow and I will travel to Nessie and see if she is comfortable having this secret out. If she consents, we will convene. If she wishes to tell the story, we will let her."

"Good plan," I said. "I'm concerned about the difference in our time calculations. If this takes a century or two, I'll never know what you decided. Worse yet, I won't ever see you again." I was near tears.

Bessie came and put her arms around me. "We discussed it. We're going to turn off the time maker and try to have it wrapped up in one of your weeks."

"Thanks," I said. "I guess I'm selfish. I just want to live out my life with you."

Mom and Dad heard I was back and walked into the tent. I know they heard me say I wanted to live the rest of my life with cryptids. I hadn't told my parents about my plan.

"Mom. Dad. I was going to tell you when my research is done," I said.

They didn't reply. "Bessie, what's your plan?" asked Mom. Bessie filled Mom in. They made a plan that organized the logistics of such a huge gathering.

"If you're going to start planning, do it outside or in another tent," I said. "I have work to do." I was furious at Mom for giving me the silent treatment. I needed to do one more DNA comparison—the yowies and the caddies. I hadn't touched yowie DNA for fear I would be contaminated and shapeshift into a yowie. I knew I couldn't put it off any longer.

I put on a protective outfit I hadn't used in years because of its weight. I sweat profusely in it. I knew I better wear it for this comparison. I was zipping up the front, when Willie entered the lab.

"Heard you were back. What's this getup?" said Willie.

"I have one DNA comparison left to do, but it requires I sequence the yowie DNA."

Willie's eyes grew wide. "Does Sash know?" I shook my head. "Do you have another of that monstrosity for me to wear?" Willie asked, pointing to my safe suit. I nodded toward the closet.

"Maybe it should be Sash helping me," I said.

"Sash won't let you do it," Willie said. "You need me." She was right. Sash did not want me to sequence the yowie DNA at all.

Willie prepared the slides for the yowie DNA and started the machine. We both took off our suit helmets to get a little air. We walked outside of the lab. I looked longingly at the ocean and felt my tail starting to appear. "Quick, Willie," I said, "send me human thoughts. I'm slipping."

Willie started talking about my favorite things: microscopes, roasted dodo, research, walking... I kept thinking, *Legs... Legs... Legs...* Nearly a half an hour passed before I felt my legs forming.

"At least turning you back into a human made the wait go quickly," said Willie. We walked back into the lab. The sequencing was almost done. Willie brought me the printout while I organized the caddy DNA and Bessie's. What I saw didn't surprise me. The yowie DNA had a similar sequence to the caddy's. The partial sequence in the yowie had two differences. Both sequences were nearly identical to a partial pattern in Bessie.

Willie and I stripped out of our suits. We were dripping in sweat. When a sasquatch sweats, buckets of it land on the floor. "Watch your step," said Willie. I carefully walked around the puddles toward the tent door.

"Willie," I said. "We didn't remove the slides."

"It can wait until tomorrow."

I figured it could. Willie and I joined the others at dinner. Mom and Dad ate in their tent. They still weren't speaking to me. Sash and Bessie told us the convention would be next week. Good! The loose ends were being tied. I could publish my research and retire from the Sydney lab. Then my life would start.

All of us talked until late. We said our goodbyes and went to our tents. The lab was on the way to mine. Those slides were bothering me. I never left a lab unsecured, and I wouldn't start now. I entered the tent and switched on the lighting rather than asking Draconia to provide light. I put on the gloves from my security suit and the helmet. I couldn't bear to put the entire suit on. I had my most vulnerable places covered.

I took the tray of slides from the machine. I saw a red blur. Then the next thing I knew, I was standing in glass and blood. Every slide had broken when I dropped them. Pieces of glass had hit my lower legs and drawn blood. I froze. Meow grabbed me and ran into the ocean. He pulled out any glass embedded in my legs and used salt water to cleanse the wound. I was crying, not from the cuts, but because I might have been exposed to yowie DNA.

The others heard my cries and Meow's obvious caterwauling. They left their tents to see what was going on. Mom knew immediately. She plunged into the ocean and took me from Meow. My teeth were chattering. Mom and Meow dragged me from the ocean. Sash and Bessie had grabbed all the blankets they could to put around me. Willie dressed my wounds. I tried to fight, but I fell into a sound, deep sleep.

When I woke, I could tell a considerable length of time had passed. The trees were losing leaves. I could feel a nip in the air. Summer had turned into fall. I got up—at least I had legs. I walked to the bathroom where there was a mirror. I was terrified to look but needed to know. I saw my face had transformed into that of a yowie. I opened my mouth and saw my menacing teeth. I was covered in hair. Appearance aside, I felt fine.

I walked out of my tent and into the ocean. I swam until my arms could no longer hold me up. Mom was sitting on the beach with towels. She helped me dry off, then embraced me. We cried.

11

I insisted the sea creatures still have their convention. Sash and Mom wouldn't let me attend. I spent the time they were away trying to make an elixir that might allow me to look like myself. I was also confused by the DNA. The yowies and Caddies had the exact same sequence in some places. Both groups shared dragon and sea creature DNA. I was frustrated I couldn't figure out the patterns.

I knew a geneticist who might help me. Except... he and I were not speaking. Jonas McGregor lived in Scotland. He was sequencing the DNA in different regions to see how closely they matched. His work was groundbreaking. I guess I would need to swallow my pride and contact him. No matter what, I wasn't apologizing.

I wrote a letter to Jonas that explained my predicament. He expressed sympathy and said he'd catch the next plane to the Pacific Northwest. I offered a dragon or Meow's services. He said to pick him up at the airport in Seattle. I advised against it.

"It's risky to have a creature go to an airport, where he can be easily seen. I've been through the aftermath of such sightings. It's just not a good idea," I cautioned.

"You worry too much. Your groundbreaking work made humans a lot less fearful of these wonderous creatures," Jonas countered.

"I know. I'm just too stressed to be involved in a sighting again." I sighed loudly into my phone.

Jonas didn't reply for a minute or two. "Send a dragon. I get less motion sick on a dragon than on Meow."

Meow was not pleased that Jonas preferred a dragon for his transportation. "Jonas is just jealous of our relationship," said Meow.

"Our what?" I said.

"Our closeness."

I had to stifle a giggle. "Right, Meow. Right."

Two days later, Jonas arrived. Jonas embraced me and kissed me on the cheek. I was surprised. I looked like an overgrown ape. "You make a great yowie," he joked.

"Thanks, I think."

"Seriously. You do."

I spent time with him explaining where my research stood. I could tell he was impressed with my findings. I was relieved he didn't see any mistakes in my work.

We had a nice feast for him the first night. The dragons who were functioning as Uber drivers put on a light show after dinner. I could tell Jonas was impressed. After the dance, I introduced Jonas to my parents. I could tell Mom was planning a matchmaking scheme. I would have to talk to her. I was not getting involved with Jonas again. Meow had worked on Jonas' tent and accouterments. Jonas was quite impressed with how Meow made his quarters welcoming. "Meow, this was more than I expected," Jonas said. I swear I saw Meow blush.

"If anything is amiss, let me know. I can have it to you within a minute."

Jonas laughed. "Yes, you could."

The next morning, I showed Jonas around the lab. He was quite pleased to see I had state-of-the-art equipment and had the DNA organized in an order that pleased him. I'd remembered how exacting he was and had tried to conform to his standards. I left Jonas alone with my findings. I decided to swim.

The beauty of being a yowie is that I could hold my breath underwater indefinitely. I wanted to relax in the water and be mentally alert for Jonas' questions.

I hated swimming as a yowie, even though I could stay underwater as long as I wanted. My body was bulky. Drying my fur took forever, and if I didn't use a hair dryer, the fur stood up all over. I surfaced and leaned against a sandbar. Jonas hadn't emerged from the lab, so I took one last swim around the island.

As I leisurely backstroked, I thought I saw something flash past me. I figured it was Sash or Meow checking on me. As I broke into a front crawl, I felt my legs being held. I couldn't move. Something coiled around me. Once I was bound, the creature started swimming so rapidly I thought I'd be sick. I passed out and woke up in an underwater cave, being cuddled by the caddy, who I think was singing me a lullaby. I looked into the caddy's horse-eyes. I swore I saw love. Caddy saw that I was awake and began talking to me in a language I didn't know. He seemed stressed that I didn't understand. I tried telepathic communication, but Caddy didn't seem to receive it.

Caddy fed me some fish stew and then tucked me into a nest. I think he expected me to sleep. Did he think I was his baby?

I was able to sleep. I felt like I had been rocked all night. I realized I had been. Caddy had stayed up and rocked the nest like a cradle. Yes, he thought I was his baby.

By now, my colleagues on the island would be wondering where I was. I didn't have a good sense of time underwater. I sat up and climbed out of the nest. Caddy applauded. Then I began pantomiming what I wanted to do. I explained I needed to go to the surface. Caddy understood. He was shaking his head vigorously. I decided I would make a break for the cave door while Caddy prepared my breakfast. I left the cave and swam as quickly as I could. Just as I broke through the surface of the water, I felt something grab my foot. I screamed. Sash, Chichi, and Willie were on the beach and heard me cry. The three of them jumped in the ocean and swam to me. Chichi and Willie were tugging me away from whatever had my legs. Finally, they pulled me free and took me to shore. My parents, Jonas, and the other cryptids were running toward me. Jonas, who had a medical background, examined me to see if I was injured. Mom brought me cocoa.

Sash surfaced about half an hour later. He looked exhausted.

"Was that the caddy?" he asked.

I nodded. I explained how the caddy took care of me. "He wasn't menacing at all. He thought I was his baby."

"You understood him?" Sash asked.

"No, and he didn't understand my words, but I acted out what I was going to do."

Once everyone calmed, Jonas took me aside. "I think I see the areas where you have pinpointed the similarities. I saw dissimilarities in other strands of DNA. The yowie and the caddy had mirror images in some strands."

"That's it!" I cried. I ran to the lab. Mom, Dad, and Sash ran after me, telling me to rest. I didn't listen. I pulled up some calculations I had made before I was kidnapped by the caddy. Jonas followed me into the lab.

"What are you thinking?" he asked.

"I was working on an elixir that might turn me back into a human. I was playing with the sequences you said were mirror images. I knew they were important, but I didn't know why. Jonas, take my blood and sequence the DNA."

"Won't it be caddycells?" he asked.

"No, I don't think so. I think the yowie DNA is wrapped around my own DNA. I'm able to talk and think like a human, so my DNA is still there. There are two DNA profiles warring with each other. That's why I was shapeshifting. Unfortunately, if I stay a yowie long enough, the yowie DNA will eat the human DNA, and I won't be able to become human."

I should have been overjoyed at my hypothesis, but I knew I had limited time to rid myself of the yowie DNA. Jonas agreed with my two-strands theory. He took more of my blood and put it in a centrifuge to separate the DNA strands. Then he ran the blood through the filtering machine. The blood was clear of yowie DNA. We grabbed each other and jumped for joy. Our reverie attracted a crowd outside the lab. I went out to explain what we had discovered. They all cheered.

"Don't be too happy yet," I cautioned. "We don't know if I am transfused with the clean blood that I will be healed."

Jonas joined the crowd. "We need a blood filtering machine that cardiologists use. I'll call in a favor. Meow, take me back to Scotland."

Fifteen minutes later, Meow and Jonas were back. Meow helped Jonas set up the machine. Then Jonas had me lie on a table and started a line between me and the machine. "You'll be cold at times. Let me know," said Jonas. "I can bring blankets as needed."

"Jonas," said Meow, "I'm the only blanket she needs." Jonas and I laughed.

As the machine started to work on my blood, Jonas started an IV line with a saline drip. He didn't want me to become dehydrated. The entire process took eighteen hours. When Jonas disconnected me from the machine, he had me lie still for a while. He brought me a bowl of stew and fed it to me.

"You need to eat and drink to regain your strength," Jonas said.

"I can feed myself," I said.

"That's right. You are an independent woman."

"Not that again."

Jonas held up his palms to me. "I surrender."

I laughed. Jonas never surrendered.

After I had eaten enough to appease Jonas, I joined my friends around a campfire. We always kept one going now that fall temperatures were here. Meow wrapped around me like a cape. I didn't mind. I was still a bit chilly. Willie and Chichi wanted to know more about the procedure I just experienced. Jonas supplied the details. I was just happy sitting with those I loved and enjoying the banter.

After a good night's sleep, Jonas drew my blood. I was too nervous to help him sequence the DNA. I paced outside the lab tent for what seemed like hours.

Jonas stepped out of the lab. I stopped pacing and looked carefully at him, trying to read his body language. There was no mistaking the results. Jonas had a huge grin on his face. He handed me a mirror. The reflection was of my human face. I was free of yowie DNA.

"Mom, Dad, Sash, Meow," I cried, "come see me." I thought Mom was going to faint. She was so joyous that she was lightheaded. Dad brought her some water. The dragons got out the dragon beer. We celebrated the rest of the day.

I slept late. I realized that Jonas was leaving today. Had I missed telling him goodbye? I put on actual jeans and a sweatshirt and went looking to see who else was awake. Jonas was sitting on the beach, throwing shells into the ocean. I sat down beside him.

"I will never be able to thank you," I said.

"Seeing you whole is thanks enough," Jonas said.

I smiled. "Leaving today?"

"I plan on it. I have a proposition for you."

"And it is...?"

Jonas outlined a series of papers that we could write for the *Cryptid Scientific Journal*.

"What's the *Cryptid Scientific Journal*?" I asked.

"Our joint publication. We can work from our own labs using email and other methods."

"You mean you don't want Meow running my ideas to you."

Jonas laughed. "I will be back in Scotland and can use traditional means of communication. I assume you'll return to Sydney."

"The plan is to break camp tomorrow and return home."

"What do you think of my plan?" he asked quietly.

"I'm not sure, Jonas," I said. "It didn't go well before."

"I know. But we won't be sharing the same resources. We won't even be on the same continent. I want a strictly professional relationship."

My heart sank. Professional relationship. "Okay, let's try for three months," I said, holding back tears.

We talked about for an hour longer about the logistics of our partnership. He summoned Meow, and off he went. Then I really cried.

12

We broke camp the next day. I let Meow take the heavy things back to the lab and took a dragon-Uber home. Meow was bugging me to start a dragon-Uber business. "Just think of the money rolling in from businessmen that want to go halfway around the globe and still be sleeping in their own bed the same day." I just shook my head.

Draconia took me home. He asked me if there was any place I wanted to see before he deposited me in Sydney. "No, Draconia, thanks. I've seen enough of the world for now." I settled down to nap the rest of the trip.

Mom and Dad came home on a dragon-Uber. They arrived a few hours after I did. I had time to take a long shower and sort through my mail before they arrived.

"Mom, come sit at the kitchen table," I said.

"Did you make dinner?" she asked.

"Heck, no. I don't cook," I said. "Look at the table."

On our kitchen table was a bound copy of my dissertation. Mom squealed with joy. "That's not what I want you to focus on. Look at the envelope."

The envelope was addressed to Mom. She looked at the return

address. "It's from a publisher," she said. I nodded. "It's a rejection, I'm sure," Mom said. She opened the envelope slowly. I wanted to rip it from her hands. Finally, she took out the letter and read.

Dear Ms. Smith,

We are pleased to offer you a contract for your series of books about cryptids. Please call at your convenience. In the conversation, we can discuss the details.

Tallyho Publishing

Mom and I embraced and started to jump around the kitchen. Dad came in and said, "You'll wake the dead." I grabbed the letter out of Mom's hands and handed it to my dad. With tears in his eyes, he took my mom into a warm embrace and kissed her.

EPILOGUE

The banner said, *World Famous Authors Janet Smith and Sadie Smith Here Tonight.*

"Wow, Mom, look how big the banner is," Sadie said.

I was overwhelmed. The books Mom wrote about our adventures with the sasquatches and sea creatures would provide a modest income to support her and Dad. The publisher had been so taken with Dad's photos of the creatures, the pics were used to illustrate Mom's book. The publisher also had me revise my dissertation for the public market. Mom's book and mine were marketed as a pair; Mom provided the human interest. I provided scientific evidence.

I dreaded book signings, but I knew I had to showcase the books. Mom and I were in Cleveland, where the entire adventure started, hawking the book. I was nervous. I hadn't been here in years. The people of Cleveland were hostile to us when we first appeared with the cryptids. The mayor assured us that all was forgiven. He wanted our books to showcase Cleveland. Neither Mom nor I were okay with it. We only agreed to the signing.

The bookstore owner gave us the signal that she was about to open the doors. As the people filed in, they lined up as instructed. For three hours, we signed books. Dad took photos.

As we drove to our hotel, Dad wanted to drive past our former home. Mom and I were anxious to see how it looked. As Dad pulled up to the curb, I spotted a for-sale sign in front of the house.

"It's for sale, Dad," I said.

"Afraid not," said Mom, pointing to the sold sign.

"It's not like we were going to settle here. We have our home in Sydney," I said.

The three of us sat there for a while reminiscing about our time in Cleveland. We had good memories of the time before Dad sort of died and Mom and I encountered Bessie and Sash.

Someone came up to Dad's window and motioned for him to put the window down. He handed Dad a key and some paperwork. "Enjoy your new home," he said.

"Joseph, what are you saying?" Mom asked.

"I want a home here. The home I was cheated out of when I became a mansquat. We don't have to live here all the time. A vacation home, if you will."

Mom and I looked at each other. "Dad, Mom, I have an offer from Case Western to start a cryptid program there. I'd have free reign in hiring, choosing equipment, applying for grants, and the direction of the research."

"Why haven't you told us?" Dad said.

"I didn't want it to overshadow the book signing and homecoming."

Mom had tears in her eyes. "I guess we are moving."

"Well," said Dad, "let's go into our house."

We opened the front door. "Surprise," said all our cryptid friends. I looked around the room and saw that our friends had moved us while we were at the book signing.

Mom was so thankful the move was taken care of. "I'm so glad you're here. Thanks for moving us. Willie, I bet it was you."

Willie blushed.

"Now, if you had moved my lab, everything would be perfect," I said.

Meow walked over and hugged me. "Who said we didn't?"

DRAGON CELEBRATION

PROLOGUE

"Where are we?" asked Sadie. They had both landed on a hard surface, butts first. Sadie was rubbing her behind and checking Jonas for injuries. "Where's Adam?" she asked.

Jonas shook his head and pointed. "Look! There's your mom and dad. Your mom has Adam in her arms."

Sadie rushed to her mom and took Adam in her arms. He giggled. "My butt hurts."

Joseph looked stunned. He was the only one who had not landed on his butt, but on his head. Jonas saw Joseph bleeding a bit from his scalp and held a handkerchief from his pocket to Joesph's head.

"Thanks, Jonas," said Joseph. "Is anyone else hurt?"

"I don't think so. Sadie is okay. Janet, how are you?"

"I'm fine," Janet said. "Sadie, what did you do to get us thrown here?"

"Why do you always think the adventures with the cryptids are my fault?" said Sadie.

"Janet, stop," said Joseph. "How could you think Sadie was involved?"

"Easy! Since her studies with the cryptids, we can no longer visit our friends without some sort of calamity."

Jonas took Sadie in his arms and whispered, "This is not the time to argue." Sadie nodded.

None of them had ever seen a space like the one they were in. Janet thought it looked like her childhood dreams of what the Age of Aquarius would have looked like. Joseph mused that the serenity surrounding him was much like the underground of mansquats. Adam loved running through the space. He was lightning fast in this new environment. Jonas, ever the scientist, took out a pocket gadget he always carried with him to test air, ground, and water quality. It wasn't working.

Janet asked, "How did we get here?"

The rest shook their heads. The space seemed to go on indefinitely. Joseph and Jonas told Sadie and Janet to stay with Adam. They were going to explore.

"You're going to leave us alone?" Janet said.

"We'll be fine, Mom," said Sadie, shaking her head in disgust. "You used to be adventurous. What happened?"

"I grew up."

They all laughed.

Jonas and Joseph didn't get far, maybe a half a mile, when they ran into an invisible wall. Joseph suggested that, since they had found the wall, they should follow it to check out the perimeter. They determined the circular space was half a mile across. Jonas fiddled with his pocket gadget but still couldn't get a reading. They returned to the two women and Adam and reported what they found.

Janet had found what she thought was a flowerbed and starting smelling the pretty coneflowers and black-eyed Susans.

"Mom, whatever are you doing?" Sadie asked.

"Smelling the flowers."

"What flowers?" they all asked her.

"The flowerbed here."

Sadie said, "Ah, no. We're in the woods. See the stream?"

They shook their heads.

Jonas thought they were in a blank space. Joseph told them it was like his home in the city under Lake Huron.

"Okay," said Jonas. "We aren't on earth."

Janet cried, "Are we dead?" she buried her head in Joseph's shoulder.

"I don't think so," offered Jonas. "Whatever or whoever put us here has made it so we see what comforts us. I think we are in another dimension."

1

Sadie looked frantically for Adam. She and Jonas had split up to cover more ground at the Dragon Fairgrounds. Sadie knew it would be hard to keep track of an active three-year-old at the Cyrtid Convention. Mom and Dad had offered to keep Adam with them, but Sadie couldn't bear to be away from her son for even a few hours, let alone a three-week convention in the Himalayas.

The convention was the culmination—a celebration—of Sadie and Jonas' work on cyrtid DNA and its relationship to that of homo sapiens. After their work was published, cyrtids were accepted into society. Major advances in eco-friendly transportation were on the rise. The dragons and Meow were making money hand over fist by providing anyone, not just VIPs, with rapid transit. A dragon train had been developed that could take hundreds to a specific area in less than two hours in most cases. Sasquatches were hired as security guards, making workplaces, transit stations, and homes more secure. Crime had dropped everywhere around the world. Ogua was training sea turtles to explore underwater areas too dangerous for humans. Discoveries of new species of animals and cyrtids abound. Spitzy was working on training dragons to provide energy that was renewable and safe for the environment. Meow was beside himself. He couldn't clone himself to have a fleet of supersonic seacats that would outstrip the dragons. He was finally appeased when Jonas suggested he study cats and see if they could be trained. Spitzy had trained dragons to provide a grill-lighting service and to light up memorial vigils. Chichi and Willie now had a chain of restaurants that cyrtids and humans both frequented. Moha was giving tours of underground caves in Australia. The economy of every country was booming. New treaties were signed; fewer conflicts arose. If war was threatened, mediators Bessie and Sash negotiated a truce.

Sadie and Jonas were in the Himalayas to be honored for their achievement. They had already been awarded the Nobel Peace Prize and other humanitarian prizes. They had a room in their home full of their accolades and awards. They fought over bringing Adam with them. Jonah did not think it was safe. Although the cyrtids were widely accepted around the world, terrorist groups had formed to disrupt the cyrtid economy. The groups wanted the proceeds of the enterprises. The cryptids had agreed they did not need the financial compensation and were donating their proceeds to those in poverty and in need of food and/or education. A thriving economy was leading to smaller working-poor and homeless populations.

Sadie and Jonas had hired sasquatches to discover who these terrorists were. Sadie was convinced it was the caddies or maybe even the yowies behind the attacks. As much as Sadie tried, she could not find anything positive about the existence of these creatures. She had hoped her DNA discoveries would yield a way to tame the malevolent beasts. Sadie felt her failure to find a way to tame caddies and yowies tainted her career. The sasquatches were still investigating the case.

At times, Sadie was overwhelmed with the positive changes that transformed the Earth. She couldn't believe the world had over-whelmingly embraced the cryptid population. Jonas oversaw intro-ducing each cryptid slowly to the world by highlighting the good the cryptids could do for the human population. Sadie was worried she had created a subservient class by employing the cryptids as human servants. She wanted the cryptids to be seen as equals to the humans, not as their servants. As the cryptids gained wealth, they had purchased land and started businesses. There had been some back-lash to these developments, even though the proceeds improved life for humans and cryptids alike. To Sadie, this was progress, but a small number of humans and cryptids thought the developments were dangerous.

Under threats of demonstrations, the convention went on. Sadie feared that the first action of the anti-cryptid humans would be taking her son. First, there would be a trade show of the cryptid busi-nesses. Any attendees could peruse the industry booths and sign up for cryptid innovations. Although admission was free, there was a screening process to keep hostile humans and cryptids away from the event. The process had created some protests from those opposed to the incorporation of the cryptids into mainstream society.

Sadie feared the worst when she heard Jonas' cries.

"He's here," said Jonas.

"Where?" Sadie said. Jonas and Sadie were using the telepathy they had learned from sasquatches. They were afraid their voices would alarm the crowd. Sadie rushed to Jonas' voice.

"Meow," shouted Sadie, "why didn't you tell me Adam was napping with you?" Her anger was readily apparent, sending Meow into a tizzy. Meow and Sadie had a love/hate relationship. Right now, Sadie was in her hate mode.

"What?" said Meow. "You told me to keep safe. How could he be safer than napping on my chest? Oh, boy, having him nap on me is almost as good as having Janet in my lap."

"Yes, Meow, but when I asked you if you knew where Adam was, you didn't answer."

"Oh, dear sweet offspring of Janet, you are not Janet, but I love you and Janet's grandson. Do you really think I'd let anyone touch this precious child?"

Adam, sensing Meow was awake, yawned and stretched. "Hi, Mom. What's up?" He flashed his biggest grin, which always melted Sadie's heart.

"Nothing, honey. I didn't know where you were," Sadie said.

"You told me to stay with Meow. What did I do wrong?"

"Nothing, honey."

"Okay. Are Grandma and Grandpa here?"

"Not yet, sweetie," Sadie said. "Why doesn't Meow get you some lunch?"

"Yum," said Meow. "Have you ever had roasted dodo? Your mom loves it."

"Sounds good," said Adam.

"Just don't let him out of your sight," said Sadie.

Meow bowed, mocking Sadie. "Do you think I'd let anyone hurt this wonderful thing?"

Sadie just shook her head.

2

_____

Jonas gathered Sadie into his arms after he heard where Adam had been. "Why didn't Meow answer your messages to him?"

"I have no idea. I guess he was sleeping. He thinks he is Adam's protector and doesn't need to listen to us. I'll be glad when Mom and Dad arrive. Maybe Mom can tell Meow that Adam is our child, not his."

Jonas nodded. He was skeptical that anyone could talk sense into Meow. Jonas rather admired Meow's spunk and intense loyalty. He was sure Meow was the best protector for his son. Sadie was still jealous of Meow's relationship with her mom, clouding her judgment about how attached Meow was to Adam.

"Why don't you take break?" said Jonas. "I can handle the afternoon crowd."

"No, I want to see the Dragon Jubilee."

"Okay, but let Meow keep Adam on his lap."

"Okay, if you say so."

Sadie wasn't happy about the attachment Adam had to Meow. She wondered sometimes if she wasn't being objective, since she still held a grudge against Meow for his relationship with Janet. Sadie knew she needed to let go of it, but it was hard. Growing up with cryptids had altered her perception of normal relationships. She knew that, but she hadn't moved beyond her childhood fear—that she'd lose her mom to the cryptids.

Sadie walked Meow and Adam to the main arena for the Dragon Jubilee. Although this was a celebration of dragons, it was not the main event of the convention. Sadie wasn't sure what the major event was. The cryptids kept the program a secret.

"Granny, Grandpa," screamed Adam. He let go of Sadie's hand and ran to two elderly humans. The humans bent down and hugged the child.

"Mom, Dad, you're here early," said Sadie. She was a bit disappointed. She knew Adam would want to spend the rest of the convention with them. Jonas worried about the jealousy Sadie felt toward her parents' relationship with Adam. He didn't want a scene at the convention.

Adam was on Joseph's shoulders in a flash. Giggling, Adam said, "I'll have the best seat for the jubilee." Janet patted his leg.

Sadie hugged her parents, but they could tell she was miffed with them.

"Sadie, what have we done now?" asked Janet. "We just got here."

"Nothing. You've done nothing. It's just, Adam and Meow…"

Before Sadie could complete her thought, Janet took Sadie in her arms. "Sadie, honey, Adam loves you and Jonas. Why are you so insecure?"

Sadie didn't answer. She turned her back on her mom and motioned them to the VIP box that had been created for Sadie and her family and favorite cryptids. Jonas was already in his seat with Joseph, who had Adam on his lap. Meow was grooming Adam. Cats! Their tongues were wicked. Bessie, Chichi, Sash, Ogua, Willie, Moha, and Spitzy joined Meow in the box. Janet left her seat to hug each of them. Sadie sighed. Her mom was attached to every cryptid that had come into their lives. Sadie knew her mom loved her unconditionally. How many times had Janet worked to keep Sadie safe?

"Come quickly," said Jonas. "Look who's here."

Sadie turned her attention from the cryptids and looked where

Jonas had pointed. "Guiliana, Esme, Aaron!" She ran to embrace the three humans who had shared her early adventures. Esme and Aaron were married now. Aaron had lived as a human lawyer, so he could easily blend into the human culture even as a mansquat.

"Esme," Janet squealed, "when is the baby due?"

Esme patted her tummy. "We don't really know. There has never been a mansquat and human baby. Will it be nine months like humans or eighteen like sasquatches?" Lines of worry were etched on her face.

"I keep telling Esme it'll be fine," said Aaron. "She's just a worrier."

Sadie, her family, the cryptids, and friends settled into their seats just as the dragons began their dance. The dragons did not need costumes. They were all iridescent. The dragons changed color as they completed their segment of the dance. From pink to yellow to red to blue to green—they dazzled the audience as they flew and dove above and below the audience. Their fire rose until the entire amphitheater looked as if the world was on fire. All at once, the fire went out. The audience was on the edge of their seats for the next movement. The crowd was completely silent. When the fire returned, the dragons were circling the amphitheater with only their iridescent wings shining. The audience was in awe. The final action was for each dragon to attend to each member of the audience and fly them around in circles. Sadie could hear Adam laughing as he circled with Draconia, his favorite dragon. Spitzy picked Janet and spun her around the arena. Sadie relaxed, knowing her mom and son were in strong dragon paws. She and Jonas were swept away by Meow, doing somersaults through the air. Sadie thought she'd throw up from the dizzying pace, but Meow saw her turn green and slowed his movements.

Sadie, Jonas, Adam, Janet, and Joseph were placed at the center of the stage. Janet summoned Guiliana, Esme, and Aaron to the stage, explaining their role in the early days of the cryptid movement. The dragons flew above them, illuminating them in a soft light. The crowd was ecstatic. Five minutes of clapping and cheering erupted. Sadie looked overwhelmed. Jonas hugged her after he picked up Adam. Janet, Joseph, and Adam waved to the crowd.

The dragons escorted the celebrities to their box to hear the testimonials. For three hours, Bessie, Nessie, Sash, Spitzy, Chichi, Ogua, Meow, Willie, Moha, and Draconia spoke about the journey the human family had taken over the past few decades. They had created a video of their adventures to show the crowd. Sadie was called on to speak about her encounter with the yowies and caddies. The audience was mesmerized. The glitzy slide show showed how Sadie's DNA had been altered by the caddies. When the show was over, the audience applauded for a solid ten minutes.

The festivities were not over. A huge feast had been prepared under Chichi and Willie's supervision. Adam fell into a food coma from eating too many dodo wings. Jonas had too much dragon beer, which, unlike most people, he felt the effects of. He always had too much. Sadie was helping her parents fix their plates.

Then, all went dark.

When the lights returned, the cryptids were still in the amphitheater. The humans were gone.

3

Meow was caterwauling. Bessie screamed. Chichi was running in circles trying to find where the humans might be. Spitzy, trying to strengthen his fire, muttered, "I'll burn them to a crisp. I'll burn them to a crisp." Moha comforted Willie.

Sash said, "Stay calm." All the sea creatures and dragons stopped. "Dragon guard, assemble."

Sash's security guards assembled quickly and awaited their orders.

"You know the drill. You know your quadrant. Search with your fires on stun so you can neutralize whoever has taken our beloved humans. I'll be in the command center. And remember the telepathic lessons I've been teaching you. I prefer you send bulletins that way, so all of us can hear the news. If you are proficient in telepathy, help those who are struggling."

The dragons began an orderly exit to their quadrants. Sash found Bessie sobbing in Chichi's arms. He motioned for Chichi to move and scooped up Bessie. "Come to the command center with me," Sash told Bessie. "That way, you will be the first to know." Bessie brushed away her tears and let Sash lead her to his office in the command center.

Ogua found Meow frantically grooming. "Meow, you'll lose all your fur."

"I don't know what to do. I don't know what to do without my humans."

Ogua wrapped his front flippers around Meow. "Ouch, watch the spikes!" Ogua readjusted his hold and led Meow to a nest to rest. He poured Meow some milk.

Ogua sighed. "I miss the old days, when all of us would gather at someone's cave and have fun."

"Yes," Meow said, "I'd have Janet on my lap with Adam. Oh, poor Adam. I bet he's scared."

Ogua nodded. "I hope Adam is with Sadie and Jonas. I'd hate to think whoever has them has separated them. You be okay now?"

Meow gave Ogua a great big lick.

"Ugh," said Ogua as he wandered off.

Meow saw the slight smile on his face. "You aren't as tough as your shell, you softie," Meow called after him.

Ogua went into the amphitheater to find out Sash's plan. From what he gathered from the dragons, there was no sign of the humans.

"You there! You turtle! I'm talking to you," said an older woman. Ogua turned to see if the woman meant him.

"Yes, I'm a sea turtle."

"Ogua! It's you," said the woman, and she tried to leap into Ogua's arms. Ogua, thankfully, caught her.

Ogua held her away from him and began to cry. "Alice, Alice..."

"You remember."

"Of course, of course. Why did you leave me?"

"Oggie, I never forgot you. It's just, humans are expected to do certain things in their lives. One is leaving childhood playmates. As I age, I realize I still need to hang on to those childhood memories. When I heard there was a cryptid convention, I had to come. Oh, dear, I missed the dragon dance."

"I'm glad you did," said Ogua. "If you had been here, you would have disappeared with the other humans."

Alice gasped. Ogua led her to a chair and told her about the disappearances. Alice shook her head. She had kept up with the advancements of the cyrtids and had been overjoyed to hear hers was involved in the movement. "How did five humans just disappear?"

Ogua looked down at his flippers. Alice wiped a tear from Ogua's eye and held him until he regained his composure. "Come with me, Alice. I have friends I want you to meet."

"I love your friends. Let's go."

Ogua walked with Alice to Sash's command station. Bessie was overjoyed to see her. "I've heard so much about you."

Sash was glued to his commands center. "Draconia, send me your best guard. I have a human here."

"What?" said Ogua.

"She's in danger. I have no idea who took our human friends, and then you bring me another one."

Alice interjected. "Don't blame Ogua. I would have been here earlier, but I missed the first dragon train. He didn't ask me to come."

"Whatever."

Bessie had never seen Sash so demoralized. "Alice, welcome," said Bessie to deflect from Sash's rudeness. "Don't judge Sash by his first impression. He's only focused on saving his friends."

"I understand."

Bessie took Alice to the small kitchen near Sash's command center and offered her a meal and a drink. "I didn't realize I was so hungry," said Patty. She had never had dodo wings and was smitten.

"Travel does that to you."

"What can I do, Bessie?" asked Alice. "I feel like I'm in the way."

Sash stood at the door of the kitchen. "You may be valuable."

"How?" Bessie and Alice asked at the same time.

"I'm not sure, but stay close," responded Sash.

4

S ash did a roll call of the dragons to assess the situation. Most of the dragons sent their reports using telepathy. Those that couldn't had another dragon send it. None of the dragons had found anything that would indicate where the humans had disappeared to. Sash summoned his sasquatch siblings and cousins, arranging all available dragon trains to transport them to the Himalayas. Sasquatches had amazing tracking abilities and a keen sense of smell. Sash worried that he should have called his family earlier. He hadn't realized the seriousness of the situation.

"What's wrong?" Bessie asked Sash as they waited for the sasquatches to arrive.

"I'm not sure I'm up to this," Sash said.

"Of course, you are."

Sash left the command room. He knew Bessie meant well but couldn't believe he could do it.

"Sash," Bessie followed and yelled, "don't give up hope." She hugged Sash tightly.

Ogua entered the command center. "This is no time to be lovey-dovey." Bessie gave Ogua a hard look. "Oh, I'll leave you alone."

"It's okay, Ogua," Sash said. "She's just giving me some moral support. I'm at a loss as to what I do next."

Ogua scurried from the room.

"What's with him?" Sash asked.

"Who knows? It's Ogua," said Bessie. They had a good laugh.

When Ogua returned, he had Moha, Willie, Chichi, Spitzy, and Meow. "We've been in tougher situations. We have the brain trust together. You know the eight of us can conquer everything. The Band of Eight."

The cryptids all agreed.

Sash said, "I have summoned my sasquatch family. They can smell even faint tracks. The dragons fly and could miss something on the ground. The sasquatches can be the boots on the ground."

The cryptids nodded.

The next day, the sasquatches arrived. Sash's squad was well trained and immediately understood their assignments. The sasquatches formed their units and began a ground search.

"There's nothing to do but wait," said Bessie. "Get some sleep, Sash. You'll be no good to us tired."

Meow gathered Sash in his arms and took him to a nest.

"Let go of me, Meow."

"Sash, just relax on my belly, and you'll be asleep in no time."

"I'll wake up smelling of cat."

"Good. Get rid of the sasquatch smell."

"We do not smell."

"Yes, you do."

The bickering went on until Bessie brought them warm milk. Sash didn't want to drink it at first, but when Meow slurped down his and went for Sash's, Sash gulped the milk in one swallow. Both were snoring when Bessie left the room.

5

When Sash rose from his nap and had showered off the cat smell, he started to analyze the data the sasquatches were sending back. He could not find any patterns, and, so far, the sasquatches hadn't found anything to gather DNA from. He found it hard to be optimistic. When Bessie entered the command station, he tried to be upbeat for her, but she knew he was lying.

"If the sasquatches find nothing, I'm not sure what to do," Sash said. Bessie had no idea how to respond. One by one, the Band of Eight came to the command center.

"What's up?" said Spitzy.

"No news," said Sash.

Willie and Chichi decided to make breakfast. They hoped good food would help them relax and think of a solution. Unfortunately, none of the cryptids had any appetite except Meow, who cleaned everyone's plates with his tongue.

"I need a cat nap. I have cat training to do later," Meow said.

"What on earth are you doing with cats?" exclaimed Ogua. "I don't need any more cat hair in my nest. It's evil glitter." Except for Meow, the cryptids laughed.

"It's not funny. I was reading about string theory."

"You play with yarn, Meow," said Spitzy.

"I know. I was hoping to learn how play with string. I didn't realize it was a physics concept."

Now the cryptids really did laugh. Sash was stomping his feet and shaking the command center. He couldn't catch his breath. Willie had tears coming from her eyes, she laughed so hard. Spitzy spit fire each time he exhaled a laugh.

"Enough," cried Meow. "I do have a mind for science. Why do you think cats always land on their feet? Cats have an innate instinct for physics."

The cryptids regained control of themselves. "Sorry, Meow," Bessie said. "We see you as a pet, not one of us at times. What is string theory?"

Meow explained that it is a theory in physics that says the universe is made of vibrating strings that are smaller than atoms. The strings vibrate, twist, and fold to create the effects we experience as particles, gravity, and more.

"What the heck does that even mean?" said Ogua.

"In string theory, there are ten dimensions. Humans only perceive four dimensions—width, length, height, and time. As I was exploring string theory, I realized that the cats that I was training as support cats would disappear sometimes without a trace. Magically, they would reappear. I started to think that maybe cats could travel between dimensions. I tried to follow one of my cats and saw him disappear. I tried to follow. The wall hit me flat in the face."

"Strange," said Sash.

"Yes. But I've been thinking, if I could send one of my cats to each dimension, they might locate our beloved humans."

The cryptids looked at each other, a bit baffled.

"Why not?" Sash finally said. "If the sasquatches all come home empty handed, then let's give it a try."

Meow bolted out of the room and summoned his cat crew. Sash called after Meow, "It's not for certain. Don't rush."

Meow already had his cats in formation. He had been working with the cats on telepathy and knew it would be the only way to hear the cats' reports from the other dimensions. He ran them through their paces, sending signals to each cat to move seamlessly into the ten dimensions.

Sash was livid. "I said to wait!"

"Don't you think we've lost a lot of time already?"

Sash nodded. This time, Meow was right. Time was of the essence. "Tell your cats to be careful. Something abducted our humans. They did not travel to another dimension by themselves. We don't know what we are dealing with."

Meow saluted Sash and continued to give the cats telepathic messages.

6

While Meow was working with the cats and Sash continued to analyze the sasquatches' findings, Ogua combed through Sadie's research. Sash and Bessie thought looking at Sadie's research was futile. What could it possibly hold that Sadie hadn't published? They let Ogua work. He needed something to do to be useful.

"Eureka!" shouted Ogua. He thundered into the command post. "I know what class of entity might have taken them."

The cryptids assembled, awaiting his results.

"That's my chair," shouted mild-mannered Willie.

"Chill, Willie," said Chichi. "There are enough chairs."

"But I want to sit there."

Bessie hurried to them to settle the dispute.

Ogua was complaining about having to sit near Meow. "He smells," said Ogua.

"Enough with the smells," shouted Sash. "We all smell. After we hear what Ogua has to say, I'm ordering baths for all of us. I know we are all tense. Let's just relax and listen to Ogua."

Ogua had outdone himself. He had charts of the different entities he discovered in Sadie's work. Sadie had left out of her final research the list that she had assembled of myths and legends. Many of these were from indigenous cultures. Feeling that these creatures wouldn't have DNA, Sadie had it in a locked computer file.

"I had to crack open Sadie's locked file. For some reason, I felt it held the key to finding the humans. I believe I'm right." Ogua held up a chart that listed more than a hundred creatures who had appeared over the cultures' history. These creatures were ghosts and goblins, often represented as spirits of the deceased, sometimes with specific characteristics depending on the tribe, and could be either benevolent or malevolent, often appearing in stories as "skinwalkers" or other shape-shifting creatures, with their presence often tied to specific locations like burial grounds or sacred sites; these spirits are often feared and respected, with rituals performed to appease them or protect against their potential harm.

"My guess," said Ogua, "is that skinwalkers infiltrated the jubilee. They could blend in as a dragon or sea creature, even another human. I think there had to be more than one of them to be able to turn off the lights, gather the humans, and then turn the lights back on."

The cryptids were quiet. Could there be shapeshifters? And why would they go after their humans? The cryptids were lost in thought when Meow burst through the door.

"I have a cat in each dimension. They will report to me telepathically." Meow looked around the room at the glum faces. "What happened?"

Sash explained that Ogua thought shapeshifters were responsible for the disappearances. Ogua sat down with a thud. "Then how will we know if it's one of my cats bringing back the humans or if it is a shapeshifter as a cat? Or shapeshifters as our humans?"

Ogua had identified the essential problem—working in dimensions where the cryptids didn't fully understand what was real and unreal.

"Uh, I hate to interrupt, but I might have a solution," said Alice. Alice, Esme, Aaron, and Guiliana came into the command center.

"Oh, dear," said Bessie. "We haven't included you in our plans. How remiss of us. You should be here too."

The sea creatures apologized profusely for leaving them out. Esme said, "We thought you would rather be alone with your kind to mourn your losses."

"Oh, no," said Bessie, "let's let Sash get you up to speed on where we are at."

Sash and Ogua explained string theory and their hypothesis as quickly as they could. The humans asked no questions, something Sash noticed right away. Nor did they ask what string theory was. Usually, Esme, the reporter, peppered them with questions. Aaron usually had legal questions. Guiliana usually offered military help.

"Hey, why don't you humans and Willie go to the kitchen? Willie, fix them something to eat."

"No," said Alice, "we're too worried to eat."

That sealed it for Sash. He couldn't believe Aaron would turn down a meal. The ones they thought were their friends were merely shapeshifters who had changed into them. The bodies were correct, but the shapeshifters couldn't assume the personalities. Sash also wondered if Alice, Aaron, Esme, and Guiliana were in the another dimension too.

"Ah, it's late. We all need to get rest so we can hear the cats' reports in the morning."

"It's not that late, Sash," said Spitzy. Sash gave him a warning look. "You're right." Spitzy yawned. "Let's go to bed."

The cryptids let the shapeshifters leave first. Then he got up and locked the door to the command center.

"I thought we were going to bed," said Bessie.

"Shh, let's wait until they're gone."

"What are you talking about, Sash?"

"They are the shapeshifters."

The cryptids started to talk all at once. Finally, Ogua said, "Let him finish. Explain why you think that, Sash?"

Sash explained that he was watching the humans/shapeshifters carefully as they updated them on the news. The humans they knew would have acted differently.

"I think you're right," said Ogua. "Esme usually wants to know where Meow is right away. She never asked."

"Guiliana looked bored. With her background, she should have contributed what she knew about string theory," said Bessie.

Sash nodded. He stopped the conversation and summoned Meow. Meow bounced in, jubilant that his cats were making progress. "The cats are homing in on the fifth dimension," he said. "There seems to be a strange light and heat coming from it."

"That can wait, Meow," said Sash.

Meow was indignant. "Don't you want them back? What's with you?"

"There's been a development." Sash explained to Meow that the cryptids were certain that Alice, Esme, Aaron, and Guiliana were shapeshifters.

"I... need... milk," Meow cried. Chichi ran off to heat some for him.

"This is no time to be overly dramatic," said Bessie.

"I'm not. If the cats do find our humans and bring them back, the shapeshifters are here posing as our friends. What prevents them from kidnapping the humans again?" Meow said.

"My head hurts," moaned Ogua. "I need milk." Everyone laughed but Meow, who did not find it funny. He took his claw and swung at Ogua.

"Boys, boys, boys," said Bessie. "You are brothers. Remember that."

Meow hung his head. "Sorry."

Ogua glowered at him. No one had realized how soft-hearted Ogua was until this crisis. Spitzy hugged him. All the other cryptids did the same. Ogua said, "Accepted."

Sash interrupted. "I think the shapeshifters are affecting our moods. Trying to divide us. We never quarrel this much."

"How do we get rid of them?" asked Spitzy.

Meow said, "Maybe we can convince them to go search for our humans with one of the cats. Once the cat gets them to a dimension, the cats can push them off the edge. The dimensions are tiny little strings. The cats would enjoy pushing them off. It's like when I push my milk bowl off the table."

Spitzy scoffed. "Whatever, Meow."

"See, we are about to bicker again," said Sash. "I think Meow's plan has some merit. We could ask the four shapeshifters to go with the cats to find the humans. They would take him to a dimension that the humans aren't in. Then push them off."

Meow said that when he gained confirmation from his cats that indeed the humans were in the fifth dimension, he would summon all the cats back except one, who would stay to bring the humans home to them. The rest would lure the shapeshifters to their demise.

"I think each human will need a cat guard," said Ogua.

"Whatever for?" Meow answered.

"Ogua might be right. We don't know how powerful the shapeshifters are. Could one cat keep them all safe?" Ogua said.

"You are doubting my cats' abilities?"

"Hey, knock it off, you two. We need to work together," said Sash. Meow stuck his tongue out a Ogua. Sash stopped Ogua from using his spikes.

Nothing could be done that night, so the cryptids all found their nests and tried to sleep.

7

Even with an extra bowl of warm milk, Meow couldn't sleep, a phenomenon that he never thought would happen. He heard a noise. "Who's there?"

"It's me, Spitzy."

"You can't sleep either?"

"Right. I can't help but think that we need to do something now and not wait until morning. I don't trust those shapeshifters." Meow agreed.

"Do you know if your cats have determined for sure the humans' whereabouts?"

Meow hopped out of the nest to connect to his network of cats. "Eureka! Confirmation that all our humans are in the fifth dimension and doing well. Janet wants to keep one of the cats. She misses me."

"Not now, Meow," said Spitzy.

"Well, yes. I was overcome with emotion for a moment, thinking Janet missed me like I miss her. The cats are awaiting my orders. Should I put the plan in motion?"

"Without consulting Sash?"

"He approved the plan. Let's just do it," said Meow.

"I don't know, Meow. What happens if the plan fails?"

"We try again."

Meow ordered five of the cats to guard the humans. The other five would come to the command center, where Meow would explain that they had to befriend the five shapeshifters and lead them to the first dimension and push them off. The cats were ecstatic; they missed pushing things off the edge.

By morning, five of the cats had arrived. Instead of appearing at Meow's nest, they wandered around the command center kitchen looking for milk. Bessie found them.

"You're back," said Bessie.

"Stating the obvious, aren't we, missy?" hissed one of the cats, aptly named Hissy.

"I see you inherited Meow's sarcasm."

The cat stretched and showed its claws.

"Okay, okay. We love Meow. What are you doing here?"

Hissy explained the plan.

"Wait, was Sash consulted?"

"We only take orders from Meow."

Bessie hurried off to wake Sash and tell him the plan had been implemented without his consent.

"Wait, Meow promised us milk." Bessie stopped and poured five generous portions of milk into their bowls. She left the slurping cats and worried Chichi would be upset the floor was covered in cat spit and milk.

Surprisingly, Sash wasn't upset when Bessie told him what had happened. "Meow was right to move quickly. He did the right thing."

"Okay." Bessie was skeptical. She had always been wary of her brother, Meow. When things went wrong in the sea creature world, usually Meow was to blame.

The cryptids woke up slowly and moved to the command center. Once they heard the rescue operation was underway, they sat in silence awaiting word.

8

Meow kept pacing. He heard from the five cats that were guarding the humans. The cats were on the humans' laps in ready positions. He had yet to hear from those who went to the first dimension.

"Meow, sit still. Explain to us what the fifth dimension is," said Sash, who was getting tired of Meow's pacing. Meow explained in detail along with charts he seemed to whip out of nowhere.

"Those on Earth experience four dimensions—length, width, height, and time. String theory suggestions ten dimensions; subatomic particles and generate electromagnetic fields.

"Physicists Kaluza and Klein believed both forces were generated by the warping of dimensions of space, making electromagnetism a component of gravity. This was important because unifying the fundamental forces could lead to a "theory of everything" (a physics model that combines quantum mechanics with Einstein's relativity)."

"You lost me, Meow," said Sash.

"If Sash can't understand it, none of us will," said Spitzy. He let out a flame of frustration.

Meow went to Spitzy and put his paw on his shoulder. Spitzy leaned into Meow.

"Wait, wait! We were at each other's throats yesterday—now we're civilized again?" Bessie asked. "What's happening?"

"You're right, Bessie," said Ogua. "Do you think the cats have befriended the shapeshifters and are taking them away, allowing us to be ourselves again?"

"I haven't heard," said Meow. "Let me check." Meow zoomed out of the command center and headed to where the shapeshifters were staying.

"Do you think it's dangerous for Meow to get too close to the shapeshifters?" asked Bessie.

"No clue," said Sash. "We just have to wait and see."

In a flash, Meow was back. "The cats are gone, and so are the shapeshifters. I guess they are leading them to the first dimension."

"How will we know the cats successfully knocked them off?"

Meow shrugged. "I guess when the humans return with the cats."

9

All the cryptids gathered in the command center. Some of the dragons were on high alert in case the humans came back and needed to be flown somewhere for medical attention or to avoid the new shapeshifters that might hear about the demise of the other shapeshifters. Sash also kept some of the sasquatches with him. He felt they needed to prepare for the worst.

"What time is it?" asked Ogua.

"Five minutes since you last asked," said Sash.

"Oops. Sorry."

"It's okay, Ogua. We are all feeling the pressure." Sash bopped Ogua's shell affectionately.

Bessie mused that the shapeshifters must be far from them, since they were all civil again. "No bickering today."

Ogua said, "Bessie, brothers and sisters naturally bicker."

"Not like we were. You showed your claws."

Ogua was embarrassed.

"It's okay, Ogua," said Bessie. "We were being influenced. Meow, exactly what are shapeshifters?"

Meow explained that the shapeshifters that had taken their friends were called skinwalkers. The skinwalkers they encountered were tied to the land in the Himalayas somehow. At one time, they were human, but they had done something heinous, possibly even murder, and were doomed to haunt the Earth.

"Yikes," said Willie.

"How do you know this, Meow?" asked Chichi.

"When Ogua cracked Sadie's file, he told me about them. I researched what they were and why they would come here. We must understand the potential danger of interacting with them. The native populations that believed in them, and what's to believe—we know they are real—and who thought to be omniscient, might impart some knowledge to the living which they should not have or, perhaps, might lead them to the land of the dead."

Sash looked thoughtful. "Then there are others?"

Ogua replied, "Yes, there are others. They are tied to tribes or places. The jubilee must have aroused them. Too many creatures in their spot, I guess. We should be okay if we don't stumble into a sacred place again."

"How will be know where they are?" asked Bessie.

"We won't," said Ogua.

"That's why the information was in a secret file in Sadie's research. She must have felt it was too dangerous to explore them," said Sash.

"Right. Also, how do you get DNA from a ghost? She probably felt there wasn't a scientific way to classify them," said Meow.

All the cryptids agreed. Sadie was a stickler for the scientific method. She knew her limits.

"What worries me is that the fifth dimension is small, tiny. Some scientists say its effects can be experienced on Earth, but people don't realize what they are observing," offered Meow. "I believe my cats can see all dimensions. There are some things they won't tell me. Secretive little ones! I had wanted to test my hypothesis. I'm sorry that our friends had to be put in danger for me to have an opportunity."

"It's okay, Meow. My big concern is where Esme, Aaron, Guiliana, and Alice are. I know they weren't here—it was the skinwalkers. But did they have to abduct them to take their shapes? Are they okay?" Bessie asked.

"Good questions," Sash said. "I'll send the fastest dragons to their homes to be sure they are okay. They can surveil the homes and send me a telepathic report."

In no time, the dragons were dispatched. All they had to do now was wait for news of their friends.

10

The dragons quickly reported that Esme, Aaron, and Guiliana were safe. Finding Alice proved difficult, and there was no report. Sash had a dragon stay with Esme and Aaron and another with Guiliana. The dragons also reported that Esme's pregnancy was progressing nicely even with the worries of what might happen since Aaron was a mansquat.

The cryptids were overjoyed to hear their friends were fine and agreed with Sash that a dragon needed to stay with them.

"Why couldn't they find Alice?" asked Ogua. Alice had been his favorite human.

"No report yet."

Sash could see his friends were upset. "Hey, let's see what's on the jubilee schedule. We can wait for the humans and the report on Alice. It will make the time pass faster."

The cryptids reluctantly agreed.

"Dragon ball," said Meow. "I love it."

All the cryptids nodded and filed into the arena.

The arena was crowded, and the game was already underway. The cryptids were rooting for the Firers since Draconia led the team.

He had the biggest dragons on his side. But the Fierce Fires had great skills with the bat.

"Explain the rules to me again," said Ogua.

"Again," cried Sash. "Okay, the team batting must put out the fireball coming at them. If the dragon swings and misses, they are out. If the bat catches on fire, the pitching team is awarded a point. If the dragon swings and puts the fire out because of the wind of bat swing, the batting team gets a point. There are three outs in an inning. First team to ten points wins."

The score was tied at one apiece. Draconia was pitching. He sent a huge fireball at the batter. Ogua said, "The batter will never put that out."

Before anyone could contradict Ogua, the bat caught fire. Another point for Draconia's team. When Draconia's team was up to bat, they put out a fireball. The score was tied again. The score seesawed. In the last inning, Draconia was up to bat. He swung with all his might. The fire went out. The arena exploded into cheers.

Draconia came up to Sash and the others. "Good game, eh?" Draconia had been spending too much time in Canada.

"Yes, it was," said Ogua. "Although, I don't see it's point."

"It doesn't have a point, Ogua. It's just a game," said Draconia. Ogua scowled. Draconia ignored him and asked, "Any word?"

Sash explained that Esme, Aaron, and Guiliana were fine. The dragons were still working on finding Alice. Draconia nodded. "Ah, can I talk to you alone?" Draconia said to Sash.

The rest of the cryptids were going back to the command center. Sash and Draconia stayed behind. "Ogua met Alice a long time ago. Do you think she is still alive?"

"Never gave it a thought, Draconia. I'll run a death notice search when I get back to the command center."

"Good idea. I'm going to shower."

"Draconia, you are getting more humanlike."

"Yeah. Yeah. Yeah. My wife says that all the time." With a wave, Draconia flew toward the showers.

Back at the command center, Sash began his search. He sent a message to Draconia saying Alice had indeed passed away. The two conferred as to whether they should tell Ogua. Draconia told Sash to search to see if Alice had any living children. He felt if Ogua met Alice's living children, he might not mourn as much. Sash began his search.

"What are you searching for?" asked Ogua.

"Nothing important," said Sash as he quickly turned off his screen.

"Why do I get the feeling you're hiding information from me?"

"Nah, I was just checking the weather in Cleveland where our humans live."

Ogua shook his head.

Bessie sent a private message to Sash, knowing something was up. Sash told her Alice was dead. Bessie got a tear in her eye. Sash told her the plan to see if she had living children.

Ogua and Meow went to take a nap. The two had become come close through this terrible ordeal. When Sash was sure they were sound asleep, he began searching for Alice's children. "Eureka," Sash shouted.

"What's up, Sash?" said Bessie.

"Alice has four surviving children. They live all over the United States."

"Who can we get to the quickest?"

"I'm not sure that's the best criteria. Who would be willing to believe that there are sea creatures, dragons, and sasquatches?"

"Who lives closest to the Allegheny River?"

Sash thought for a while. "Patty."

"Then let's try her."

Sash decided Bessie might be a good cryptid to accompany Ogua to Pittsburgh. Now they needed a ruse to tempt Ogua to go.

11

Bessie, who never lied, told Ogua that she and him were to go to Pittsburgh. There was a report that the humans may have appeared there rather than back at the dragon arena. Ogua asked Sash for his fastest dragons to take them there. Sash easily agreed.

"Any news?" Moha asked Sash.

"From Ogua? It's too early."

"No, the other humans."

Sash shook his head. Thirty-six hours had passed since the cats had begun the mission. At first, Sash had been optimistic, especially when their bickering stopped. He thought by now the skinwalkers had been pushed off. If so, why were the cats not bringing the humans back?

Sash woke up Meow, careful not to bother Ogua. "Meow," he whispered, "come with me." Meow hopped out of the nest, stretched, and yawned.

Once back at the command center, Sash told him about the plan to bring an offspring of Alice's back for Ogua. He said he and Bessie wanted her there to ease the pain Ogua would feel when she heard about Alice. Meow nodded.

"I need an update on the cats," Sash said.

"Okay, let me work."

Meow disappeared for over two human hours. Time didn't mean much to cryptids. They marked times in eons and centuries, but they had learned to adapt to human time once they entered businesses with the humans. Sash knew that two human hours was a good deal of time to humans. Meow returned looking crestfallen.

"The cats are with the humans. The humans aren't sure they want to return."

"What?" cried Sash.

"It seems the fifth dimension becomes whatever environment the human sees as ideal. Each of our humans are seeing different things. Sadie saw woods. Jonas saw a blank space. Joseph saw his mansquat home. Janet saw what she believed was the Age of Aquarius, and Adam saw his family together in their home. They are happy there."

Sash slammed his hands down on his computer. He had no idea how to change the humans' minds. Meow rubbed against Sash to calm him.

"Meow, stop it. I'm turning red."

"Well, that will enhance your looks."

"Not now, Meow."

Meow stopped rubbing. "Maybe if one of us goes to the fifth dimension and talks some sense into them."

"That won't work, Meow," said Sash. "We would see an ideal environment and want to stay."

"Right."

"Can your cats just drag them to our dimension?"

"I just told them to lead them. Cats take things literally. I'll give the dragon command." Meow hurried off to begin to communicate to the clowder.

As soon as Meow left, Bessie and Ogua were dropped off at the dragons' lair. They hurried to Sash. "Oh, oh, oh. Thank you, Sash. How can I thank you enough? Oh, Sash, I found my favorite human. She's Patty. She's Alice's daughter. She has so many children, grandchildren, and great-grandchildren I can play with. I said I had to see my other human friends come home safely. Then I'd go live in the

Allegheny River again to be near them. I have a family, Sash." Ogua gathered Sash into his arms and hugged him tightly. Sash was being gored by Ogua's spikes, but he didn't complain. He didn't want to ruin Ogua's moment.

"I'm happy for you, Ogua," said Sash. "Wouldn't it be great to go back to where we used to live before Bessie and I were discovered by Sadie?"

"Yes," said Ogua. "I'm sorry if I'm bragging."

Sash stood up and yelled, "All of the cryptids report to the command center." All of them came running as quickly as they could.

"I know how we get the humans back." Sash explained, "In the fifth dimension, the human or cryptid sees their ideal environment. I bet all of us want to see our former homes before we became involved with the humans." They all nodded. "Then we will go to the fifth dimension and see our homes. We can then lure the humans to our visions. I am sure they will remember our homes and want to come with us. The cats can lead us all home."

"Brilliant," said Spitzy. Moha was in tears anticipating the return of the humans. Bessie was creating earthquakes by jumping up and down.

"Calm down, folks," Sash said. "I'm not a hundred percent sure it will work, but—"

"But we can try," Meow cried.

"Meow, do you have other cats in training?" Sash asked.

Meow hesitated before he answered. "Well, yes. But they are not quite ready for prime time."

"How much more training do they need?"

"I'll run them through the paces right now. I'm hoping only one or two more times will make them available." Meow scurried away to work with his remaining cats.

"Let's hope it works," said Sash with a sigh.

12

The cryptids were all pacing around the command center, anxious to hear what Meow would have to say about the cats. Sash asked Willie and Chichi to make a specular meal for them to have before they left for the fifth dimension. They hurried off to begin preparations. Spitzy kept spitting out fireballs; he did that when he was nervous. Moha was still sobbing, hoping to see her humans and her home again in the fifth dimension. Bessie was trying to calm her. Sash wanted to scream for all of them to get out, because he was just as nervous as they were and didn't want them to see him this way. He refrained.

Meow came back from the cats nearly four hours later. "Good news," said Meow. "When I told the cats the seriousness of the mission, they all took today's training seriously. They are rather young. Teenagers really. They will have to grow up fast."

The cryptids were buoyed by the news. Sash urged everyone to get a good night's sleep. They might be able to begin the mission tomorrow. The next day, however, the cats were in no mood to train. Meow tried to tell them how important this was to them, but, being cats, they were into their yarn and feather toys. Meow took away the toys, but all the cats started caterwauling, which drove the dragons and other cryptids crazy. Meow had no choice but to give them the toys back and wait until the next day to see if they were ready for the mission.

The cryptids were demoralized. Sash suggested they take in more of the jubilee, but no one really felt like participating in the celebration of Sadie and Jonas's accomplishments without them there. Spitzy asked Meow to play fire ball with him. They started a half-hearted game. Chichi was teaching Moha and Willie to knit. Moha was struggling; she only had flippers.

"Where did you learn to knit?" asked Willie.

"Janet taught me," said Chichi. Then she started to cry. The yarn was soaked, and the projects were abandoned.

Everyone was crying or comforting those who were. The strain was affecting all of them. Bessie didn't know what to do to get the cryptids under control. She sent a private message to her mom, Nessie, asking what she could do. Nessie replied she would come to them to try to settle them down. Bessie breathed a sigh of relief. She sent Draconia to get his grandmother.

Nessie arrived late the same day. She was distressed that her children were in such a tizzy. She also expressed deep concern for her children's human friends. Meow was cuddling her on his lap. The other siblings couldn't get to her and were quite angry with Meow, but they stood back. They wanted Meow in a good mood to continue the cat training.

"Meow, honey, I need to tend to my other children," explained Nessie.

"Oh, Mama, I missed you so."

"I know. But so did they?"

Meow reluctantly allowed Nessie to leave his lap. "I need to check on my cat, anyway." Meow, head hanging and tears running down his cheeks, started to leave.

Bessie whispered something to Nessie. "Meow," said Nessie, "come have some milk before you go." Meow bounced into the kitchen, excited that his mom would warm his milk. After making a mess on the kitchen floor—milk and cat spit—he bounced over to where his cats were.

"Where did Meow learn to bounce?" asked Nessie.

Bessie replied, "When Adam was born, he loved *Winnie the Pooh* cartoons. Winnie had a friend, Tigger, a type of a cat. He bounced. Meow had to copy him." Bessie and Nessie had a good laugh and embraced. "I missed you, Mom."

"Daughter, don't tell anyone. You are my favorite dragon—uh, sea creature."

Bessie's eyes were full of tears. The closeness of the two was palpable.

Nessie then visited her children in turn. Willie and Chichi prepared a big midnight snack, and the sea creatures caught Nessie up with all that had happened.

Nessie sighed. "The poor humans." A tear fell on her cheek.

No one wanted to sleep that night. They wanted to spend as much time as they could with their mother. Sash told them they had to get some sleep because they might be transported to the fifth dimension tomorrow. Nessie was concerned.

"No cryptid has ever left this dimension. What if something happens?" Nessie said.

Sash tried to reassure her by telling her that the humans seemed perfectly fine. Nessie countered that the skinwalkers had been human. Maybe humans were safe there, but what about cryptids?

Sash laid his head on the keyboard of the command center computer. He hadn't thought of that. Nessie went to Sash and gathered him in her arms. "Sash, I know you have been working hard to bring the humans back. I didn't mean to denigrate what you are doing."

Sash nodded and hugged Nessie back. "I love you, Nessie. You gave me a great life by sending Bessie to Lake Erie. You are only looking out for your children."

Nessie began to shoo her children to bed. She was tired from her long fight and wanted a nest to sleep in. Meow took her to his, and they cuddle until morning. The rest of the cryptids went to their nests. Sash and Bessie stayed in the command center to monitor any anomalies that might come from the fifth dimension.

"Your mom approves of me," Sash said.

"How do you know?"

"She sent me a message telling me she wished I was a sea creature. I know she meant that as approval of our relationship."

Bessie nodded and hugged Sash around the neck. "Interspecies relationships are frowned upon."

"Why? Why would they be?" Sash said.

Bessie shrugged. She and Sash made a nest from blankets they found around the arena and snuggled until they fell asleep.

In the early morning, Meow gently moved Nessie into the nest and left to work with the cats. The cats were docile, giving Meow hope that the training would go well. Draconia had emptied that arena so Meow would have a quiet space to train them. Nothing much was going on inside. The jubilee was set to end the next day. Meow knew the dragons had planned a big celebration for that day. The dragons were conferring about cancelling the event, since the people being honored were missing. Meow knew the celebration would go on if he could get his beloved humans back.

13

Meow raced into the command center and woke Bessie and Sash. "I think they are ready."

A bit stunned from the rude awakening, Bessie and Sash yawned and asked Meow what he was talking about.

"Today is the day we go to the fifth dimension."

Sash and Bessie inhaled deeply. It was going to happen. Sash told Meow to let the other cryptids sleep so everyone would be fresh for the trip. Meow tried to keep himself calm. "Sash, I get Janet."

"Yes, Sash, you get Janet," Bessie said.

The plan was for Spitzy to rescue Joseph. Sadie would be rescued by Moha. The two of them had become fast friends; Moha organized many of Sadie's note as she worked on her cryptid research. The hope was that Moha could convince Adam to go with Sadie. If not, Ogua was the backup. Adam loved riding on his shell. No one was sure who would be the best to bring Jonas back. Sash volunteered to bring him back, hoping Sash's intelligence would attract him. Janet would be rescued by Meow.

The cryptids were awake early, anxious to see how Meow had done with the cats. They were overjoyed to hear that the mission would happen that day. The ones chosen to go to the fifth dimension were a bit nervous. Bessie wanted to go with Sash, but he refused to let her go. In case there were problems, Bessie would be needed in the command center. Willie and Chichi were relieved they were not chosen. They could lend moral support Bessie. They insisted the travelers have a good breakfast. Who knew when they would eat again?

Meow brought the cats in. Each cryptid would have two cats accompany them. Two cats would be needed to bring the pairs home. The cryptids met their cats. Ogua loved the two assigned to him. They were tortoise shells. Sash wasn't too sure about his. They were rather playful, and he wondered how serious they would be. Spitzy entertained his cats by spitting fireballs that they chased. Sash wanted to trade cats with Spitzy. He felt the playful cats he had would better suit Spitzy's fun. Meow disagreed. Sash's cats were selected to loosen Sash up; he could be so serious sometimes. Moha had the two most beautiful cats the cryptids had ever seen. They were Siamese with gorgeous blue eyes.

Nessie hugged the travelers. She kissed each on the forehead and gave her blessing. The cryptids held on to their cats and disappeared.

"Wow," said Nessie. "They left quickly."

Bessie told Nessie that the cats were fast and stealthy. They sat together in the command center, awaiting word of their siblings/children and the humans. The day dragged. Various dragons came into the command center to see what was happening. They left disappointed, as there hadn't been any word.

"How long do you think it will take?" said Nessie. Bessie rose to make Nessie lotus tea. She knew that would calm her mother.

"I have no idea how time is counted in the fifth dimension," Bessie answered. Nessie nodded and gratefully took the tea from her daughter.

Night came with no word from the cats, the cryptids, or the humans. Nessie urged everyone to try to sleep, but no one was listening to her. No one would sleep until everyone was back on Earth.

Nessie asked the dragons to start a bonfire outside the arena. She wanted everyone to gather, roast marshmallows, and sing dragon songs. She hoped the activities would make the time go faster.

The bonfire was well into its third hour. Everyone seemed to enjoy the camaraderie. As they sung the dragon song for the third time, the earth started to shake, and a great wind arose. The wind was so strong, it put out the bonfire. When the earth and wind settled down, Janet, Adam, Jonas, Sadie, and Joseph appeared in its place. A few seconds later, the cryptids that saved them appeared. The rescue cats roamed the group, begging for milk.

14

The returning humans looked stunned. Sash had Jonas in tow; Moha was hanging on to Sadie, who was visibly agitated. Ogua and his cats escorted Adam home, with Adam riding on his back. Adam started to cry until he saw Sadie and Jonas. Spitzy was dragging Joseph home. Janet was the only one content; Meow was cuddling her.

Bessie carefully approached Sadie. Sadie recognized Bessie, and they hugged. "What happened?" asked Sadie. Bessie said all would be explained soon, once they had adjusted to being back on Earth. Sadie saw Jonas and ran to hug him. Ogua took Adam off his shell and placed him in Jonas's arms. Joseph was babbling away to Spitzy about how cool the mansquat house was that he was in. Janet finally left Meow's embrace to seek out Joseph. Once the humans regained their bearings, Sash explained the happenings since the Dragon Jubilee.

"The fifth dimension?" questioned Jonas. "Physics hasn't yet proven that—"

"I know," said Sash. "But you all have."

The humans explained that they felt abandoned in the fifth dimension. They thought they had been separated by the entities that took them. Sash surmised that was why each of them had their own impressions of what the fifth-dimension space looked like.

"Could you see the skinwalkers who took you?" asked Bessie.

"I didn't," said Jonas. The others agreed.

Sadie looked deep in thought. "Skinwalkers. You broke into my secret research file?"

"We had to, Sadie. We were at a loss as to where you went. When we found the list of ghosts, we realized we weren't working with an evil cryptid."

Sadie gave Sash a hug. "I understand. You see why I didn't study them?"

The group all nodded.

Sadie asked, "Where is Dad?"

Janet was trying to get Joseph to stop chasing the cats. "Your dad wants to go back. He's trying to catch a cat to take him."

Sash wasn't unprepared for this possibility. He knew at least one of the travelers might prefer the fifth dimension. He had found such an overwhelming sense of peace when he entered the dimension. Ignoring his instinct to give into it, he was able to organize the cryptids and cats for the trip home. Sash helped Sadie corral Joseph. With Sadie's help, he led Joseph to a room that Sash had prepared that was blank. He hoped the blank room would reset Joseph's brain.

"How long do you think it will take for Joseph to reset?" asked Sadie.

"No clue," said Sash.

"Are you hungry?" asked Willie.

"Famished," exclaimed Jonas. "How long were we without food and water?"

"I doubt you were," said Sash. "I think you found things in your environment to eat."

"Wow! What an experience," said Sadie. "I wish I could remember more of it."

"I'm glad you don't," said Janet. "I don't want you researching this experience. Think of Adam. He might be traumatized by this. You can't possibly want to unearth something that will harm him."

"Believe me, Mom," said Sadie, "this is an area I am not going to pursue."

Willie and Chichi left to prepare a feast. Sadie then told them what happened to her. "I have no memory of being taken away from the jubilee. I found myself in the woods in the Pacific Northwest looking for yowies and caddies. I remember my time researching there fondly. I guess that's why I immersed myself in that environment."

Jonas felt that he had a blank space, because he always started a new research project with a blank sheet of paper. He said when he started a project, he was motivated and excited. He loved that feeling.

Chichi and Willie called them for the feast they had prepared. Adam was wolfing down dodo legs. Chichi was glad she had made a double batch. She had to send the dragons out dodo hunting to fulfill the demand. Sadie was picking at her food. She said she had no appetite. Janet wouldn't eat either. Willie thought their worry about Joseph's state of mind kept them from eating. Jonas couldn't stop eating. Sash figured he couldn't find food in his blank room. Janet reverted to her hippie college days when she yearned for the Age of Aquarius. Sadie wasn't surprised that Joseph created the mansquat environment. Even though he had lost his mansquat DNA, he fondly remembered his time in the underwater city with Sadie. Adam didn't notice any changes between the fifth dimension and the time on Earth; in his mind, he was still with his parents. She hoped this would spare him any lasting trauma.

Sash had Jonas in tow; Moha was hanging on to Sadie, who was visibly agitated. Janet left the feast to check on Joseph. Joseph was curled into a ball on the floor of the blank room. She approached him carefully and moved her body to cover Joseph. He recognized her and said, "Janet, where am I?"

"On Earth. We were rescued from the fifth dimension and brought back to Earth—to our family and friends. When you came back, you only wished to go back so you could live in your mansquat environment."

"Why would I want to do that?"

"I don't know."

"Janet, I want to be with you, Sadie, and Adam."

Janet hugged Joseph and led him to the feast.

The cryptids and humans applauded when Janet and Joseph came into the arena. Joseph was overwhelmed. "I'm sorry I was so weird when I first arrived," he said.

"Never mind all that," said Bessie. "We are all together now, like in the old days."

Everyone nodded. They were all happy to be together. The feasting and dancing lasted until the wee hours of the morning. They reluctantly went to bed, vowing to be together tomorrow.

15

―――――

"I'm glad we all decided to have breakfast together," said Sash. "We cryptids have something to share with you humans. First, we love you." Janet wiped a tear from her eye.

"Now that cryptids are accepted around the world, the eight of us think the enterprises and advancements will go on indefinitely. Bessie and I would like to go back to Lake Erie. Spitzy, too, would like to return to Buffalo. Meow yearns for the caves near Port Huron. Ogua has found a new family near Pittsburgh. I know Moha is craving her caves near Australia. Willie and Chichi want to be with their sea creatures."

The humans looked surprised.

"I thought you loved living with us," said Janet.

"We do," said Sash, "but we need our homes. Just as you and Joseph returned to Cleveland, we need to go home."

The humans looked at each other and then nodded. "You're right," said Sadie. "We all need our homes. I hope we'll be able to visit you in your native homes."

"Of course," said Bessie. "It's just that our days of working for the humans are over. The other cryptids are in charge and doing a great job. We can help as the need arises. But for now, we want our lives back to the way they were before we met you. Please understand."

Janet was openly crying while Joseph comforted her. Sadie's lips were quivering. Jonas looked bereft. Adam cried, "I want Meow."

Meow gathered Adam in his arms. "I'll be there when you need me. Just call." Adam sobbed quietly.

"They're right," said Sadie. "Their wonderful creatures have done more than their fair share of bringing harmony to Earth. They need their homes just as us humans do."

No one said a word. Eventually, the cryptids and the humans created a circle and joined hands knowing that they had bonds that would never be broken. When the jubilee ended, they all went home —where they belonged.

ABOUT THE AUTHOR

Nadine Nader is a retired professor who lives in Ormond Beach, Florida, with her beloved cats, Sammy and Itzy. She attributes her love of mythical creatures to the song, *Puff the Magic Dragon*, the cartoon series, *Beanie and Cecil*, and the tales of the Loch Ness Monster.

AFTERWORD

Go to hangar1publishing.com to learn more about the Authors and stay up to date with their newest releases.

www.ingramcontent.com/pod-product-compliance
Lightning Source LLC
Chambersburg PA
CBHW061556120626
46550CB00004B/1514